The Words

Dictionary of Musical
Quotations

—

Compiled by Derek Watson

Wordsworth Reference

First published 1991 by W&R Chambers Ltd,
43-45 Annandale Street, Edinburgh.

This edition published 1994 by Wordsworth Editions Ltd,
Cumberland House, Crib Street, Ware, Hertfordshire SG12 9ET.

ISBN 1-85326-327-3

Printed and bound in Denmark by Nørhaven.

The paper in this book is produced from pure wood
pulp, without the use of chlorine or any other substance
harmful to the environment. The energy used in its
production consists almost entirely of hydroelectricity
and heat generated from waste materials, thereby
conserving fossil fuels and contributing little to the
greenhouse effect.

Contents

Introduction

To express music in words is one of life's harder tasks. To convey a
verbal description of its intangible effects, the emotions it arouses, or
the qualities of greatness inherent in this, the most ineffable of arts, is
notoriously difficult. Yet there is a superabundance of prose and
poetry concerned with music, and hence the reason for this selection
of over 2500 items which ranges over four millenia. It is my personal
anthology, and if a reader finds a favourite quotation absent from it,
then in compensation I hope an exploration of the varied hundreds of
writers, musicians and commentators quoted and cited, will afford
new delights and amusements.

I have been guided by the following criteria: in addition to
choosing musical references of literary merit, I include critical
remarks of historic interest, definitions of a witty or illuminating kind,
biographical passages of a telling and concise nature and, importantly,
humorous observations.

I hope the collection will afford a pleasant 'browse', for literature
can be one of the best ladders to furthering and widening musical
appreciation; and I hope, through the comprehensive Indices of
names, works and subjects at the back of the book, it will have value
as a work of reference.

Within each section the order is broadly, but not strictly,
alphabetical: from time to time I begin a subject with one or two
strikingly apt observations; or pause to consider certain topics in a
group, *cf* 'Harmony' section 7: nos 3-8; or place some statements
together for effect, *cf* 'Schumann' section 117: 3-4.

Many colleagues and friends have furnished such a largesse of
ideas for inclusion that I cannot thank them by name, but to Will
Scott and Lyn Pullen who patiently helped to forge the book into its
final shape, my special gratitude.

Derek Watson

List of Topics

DEFINITIONS AND DESCRIPTIONS

Palaeolithic cave paintings of around 40000 years ago give scientific evidence of music-making. But who first sang? Who first played, and on what primeval instrument? Was the music to entertain or for dancing? Did it accompany work, or endeavour to heal and sustain? Here are some opinions on the origins and functions of this sublime art.

1 ORIGINS

1   And Adah bare Jabal: he was the father of such as dwell in tents, and of such as have cattle. And his brother's name was Jubal: he was the father of all such as handle the harp and organ.

Bible, Authorized Version
Genesis, Ch 4, vv 20–1

2   The single harmony produced by all the heavenly bodies singing and dancing together springs from one source and ends by achieving one purpose, and rightly bestowed the name not of 'disordered' but of 'ordered universe' upon the whole.

Aristotle (384–322 BC)
Metaphysics

> 3   When Music, Heav'nly Maid, was young,
> While yet in early Greece she sung,
> The Passions oft, to hear her Shell,
> Throng'd around her magic cell.
>
> William Collins (1721–59)
> *The Passions, an Ode for Music*, 1746

> 4   *Water* and *Air* he for the *Tenor* chose,
> *Earth* made the *Base*, the *Treble Flame* arose,
> To th'active *Moon* a quick brisk stroke he gave,
> To *Saturn's string* a touch more soft and grave.
> The motions *Strait*, and *Round*, and *Swift*, and *Slow*,
> And *Short* and *Long*, were mixt and woven so,
> Did in such artful *Figures* smoothly fall,
> As made this decent measur'd *Dance* for *All*.
> And this is *Musick*.
>
> Abraham Cowley (1618–67)
> *Davideis*, 1656

5   The formation of scales and of the web of harmony is a product of artistic invention, and is in no way given by the natural structure or by the natural behaviour of our hearing, as used to be generally maintained hitherto.

Hermann von Helmholtz (1821–94)
Theory of Sound, 1862

6   [I] know no more of Stave or Crotchet
Than did the primitive Peruvians,
Or those old ante-queer-Diluvians
That lived in the unwash'd world with Tubal,
Before that dirty Blacksmith Jubal,
By stroke on anvil, or by summ'at,
Found out, to his great surprise, the gammet.

Charles Lamb (1775–1834)
To William Ayrton

7   But hark, what music? . . .
The music of the spheres . . .
Most heavenly music!
It nips me into listening, and thick slumber
Hangs upon mine eyes.
(Pericles)

William Shakespeare (1564–1616)
Pericles, 1607–8, Act V, Sc I

8   Preposterous ass, that never read so far
To know the cause why music was ordained!
Was it not to refresh the mind of man,
After his studies or his usual pain?
(Lucentio)

William Shakespeare (1564–1616)
The Taming of the Shrew, 1592, Act III, Sc I

9   Music! soft charm of heav'n and earth,
Whence didst thou borrow thy auspicious birth?
Or art thou of eternal date,
Sire to thyself, thyself as old as fate?

Edmund Smith (1672–1710)
Ode in Praise of Music

10   The oldest, truest, most beautiful organ of music, the origin to which alone our music owes its being, is the human voice.

Richard Wagner (1813–83)
Opera and Drama, 1851

2 DEFINITIONS

See also 13 Philosophy

1   Music is the art of sounds in the movement of time.

Anonymous
Quoted in Ferruccio Busoni (1866–1924), *The Essence of Music,* June 1923

2   Mathematics is music for the mind; music is mathematics for the soul.

Anonymous
Quoted in Shapiro, *An Encyclopedia of Quotations about Music,* 1978

> 3   Music, the greatest good that mortals know,
> And all of heaven we have below.
>
> Joseph Addison (1672–1719)
> *A Song for St Cecilia's Day*

4   The exaltation of the mind derived from things eternal bursting forth in sound.

St Thomas Aquinas (1225–74)
Summa Theologiae, 1266–73

5   It is not easy to determine the nature of music, or why anyone should have a knowledge of it.

Aristotle (384–322 BC)
Politics

6   Music is the best means we have of digesting time.

W.H. Auden (1907–73)
Quoted in Craft, *Stravinsky: Chronicle of a Friendship,* 1972

7   An agreeable harmony for the honour of God and the permissible delights of the soul.

Johann Sebastian Bach (1685–1750)

8   Tone is light in another shape . . . In music instruments perform the functions of the colours employed in painting.

Honoré de Balzac (1799–1850)
Gambara, 1839

9   Music fathoms the sky.

Charles Baudelaire (1821–67)
Quoted in Shapiro, *An Encyclopedia of Quotations about Music,* 1978

10   Good music is that which penetrates the ear with facility and quits the memory with difficulty.

Thomas Beecham (1879–1961)
BBC broadcast, 17 November 1953

11   Music is an innocent luxury, unnecessary, indeed, to our existence, but a great improvement and gratification of the sense of hearing. It consists, at present, of MELODY, TIME, CONSONANCE, and DISSONANCE.

Charles Burney (1726–1814)
A General History of Music, 1776–89

12   Music is well said to be the speech of angels.

Thomas Carlyle (1795–1881)
The Opera, 1852

13   For I shall enter in a large sea of the praise of Musicke, and call to rehearsall how much it hath alwaies beene renowned among them of olde time, and counted a holy matter: and how it hath beene the opinion of most wise Philosophers, that the worlde is made of musike, and the heavens in their moving make a melodie, and our soule is framed after the verie same sort and therefore lifteth up it selfe, and (as it were) reviveth the vertues and force of it selfe with Musicke . . .

Baldassare Castiglione (1478–1529)
The Booke of the Courtyer, 1528, trans Hoby, 1561

14   Look out! Be on your guard because alone of all the arts, music moves all around you.

Jean Cocteau (1889–1963)
Cock and Harlequin, 1918

15   Music is the art of thinking with sounds.

Jules Combarieu (1859–1916)
Quoted in Dent, *Mozart's Operas*, 1913

16   Music might be defined as a system of proportions in the service of a spiritual impulse.

George Crumb (1929–   )
Quoted in Shapiro, *An Encyclopedia of Quotations about Music*, 1978

17   Music is another planet.

Alphonse Daudet (1840–97)
Quoted in Mencken, *Dictionary of Quotations*, 1942

18   Music is the arithmetic of sounds as optics is the geometry of light.

Claude Debussy (1862–1918)
Quoted in *The Penguin Dictionary of Modern Quotations*, 1980

19   Music is the eye of the ear.

Thomas Draxe (d 1618)
Bibliotheca, 1616

20   Music is the only noise for which one is obliged to pay.

Alexandre Dumas (1802–70)
Attributed

21   My idea is that there is music in the air, music all around us, the world is full of it and you simply take as much as you require.

Edward Elgar (1857–1934)
Quoted in Buckley, *Sir Edward Elgar*, 1904

22   Music is the poor man's Parnassus.

Ralph Waldo Emerson (1803–82)
Letters and Social Aims, 1876, 'Poetry and Imagination'

23   Music is nothing else but wild sounds civilized into time and tune.

Thomas Fuller DD (1608–61)
Worthies of England: Musicians, 1662

24   Music means itself.

Eduard Hanslick (1825–1904)
The Beautiful in Music, 1854

25   Music is a strange thing. I would almost say it is a miracle. For it stands halfway between thought and phenomenon, between spirit and matter, a sort of nebulous mediator, like and unlike each of the things it mediates – spirit that requires manifestation in time, and matter that can do without space.

Heinrich Heine (1797–1856)
Letters on the French Stage, 1837
Quoted in Graf, *Composer and Critic*, 1947

26   Where words leave off, music begins.

Heinrich Heine (1797–1856)
Quoted by Tchaikovsky in a letter to Nadezhda von Meck, 1878

27   Music is the most expensive of all noises.

Josef Hofmann (1876–1957)
Attributed

28   Geometry in time.

Arthur Honegger (1892–1955)
I am a Composer, 1951

29   Music is that which cannot be said but upon which it is impossible to be silent.

Victor Hugo (1802–85)
Attributed

30   Music is the vapour of art. It is to poetry what reverie is to thought, what fluid is to liquid, what the ocean of clouds is to the ocean of waves.

Victor Hugo (1802–85)
Les Rayons et les ombres, 1840

31   Music is an ocean, but the repertory . . . is hardly even a lake; it is a pond.

Aldous Huxley (1894–1963)
Quoted in *Time*, December 1957

32   Music is one of the ways God has of beating in on man.

Charles Ives (1874–1954)
Epitaph for David Twichell, 1924

33   Music is a language by whose means messages are elaborated, that such messages can be understood by the many, but sent out only by the few, and that it alone among all the languages unites the contradictory character of being at once intelligible and untranslatable – these facts make the creator of music a being like the gods, and make music itself the supreme mystery of human knowledge.

Claude Levi-Strauss (1908–   )
Mythologiques I: Le cru et le cuit, 1964

34   Music is the human treatment of sounds.

Jean-Michel Jarre (1948–   )
Interview, 1978

35   Music, I say, is a pattern of the everlasting life of heaven, because in heaven as in music, is perfect freedom and perfect pleasure.

Charles Kingsley (1819–75)
From a Christmas sermon

36   Music is the moonlight in the gloomy night of life.

Jean Paul (Johann Paul Richter) (1763–1825)
Titan, 1800–3

37   O Music! Reverberation from a distant world of harmony! Sigh of the angel within us! When the word is speechless, and the embrace, and the eye, and tear; when our dumb hearts lie lonely behind the ironwork of our breasts–then it is Thou alone through whom they call to one another in their dungeons and through whom, in their desert habitation, they unite their distant sighs!

Jean Paul (1763–1825)
Quoted in Liszt, *Essay on Berlioz*, 1855

38   It is the only sensual pleasure without vice.

Dr Samuel Johnson (1709–84)
Hill (ed), *Johnsonian Miscellanies*, 1897, II

39   Music is a secret and unconscious mathematical problem of the soul.

Gottfried Wilhelm von Leibniz (1646–1716)
The Monadology, 1714

40   Music is the universal language of mankind.

Hendry Wadsworth Longfellow (1807–82)
Outre-Mer

41   Music has always seemed to me personally a magic marriage between theology and the so diverting mathematic.
(Leverkühn)

Thomas Mann (1875–1955)
Doctor Faustus, 1947, trans Lowe-Porter

42   Music is art. Muzak the science.

Muzak Corporation, slogan

43   Music is life, and, like it, inextinguishable.

Carl Nielsen (1865–1931)
Motto of his Symphony No 4, 1916

44   Music is the universal language of mankind.

Christopher North (1785–1854)
Noctes Ambrosianae, 1822–35

45   And grant that a man read all the books of music that ever were wrote, I shall not allow that music is or can be understood out of them, no more than the taste of meats out of cookish receipt books.

Roger North (1653–1734)
The Musicall Gramarian, 1728

46   Music is not a science any more than poetry is. It is a sublime instinct, like genius of all kinds.

Ouida (pseudonym of Marie Louise de la Ramée) (1839–1908)
Quoted in Shapiro, *An Encyclopedia of Quotations about Music,* 1978

47   Music: That one of the fine arts which is concerned with the combination of sounds with a view to beauty of form and the expression of emotion.

Oxford English Dictionary, 3rd ed, 1944

48   [Music] The only universal tongue.

Samuel Rogers (1763–1855)
Italy, 1822–8

49   Music is a kind of harmonious language.

Gioachino Rossini (1792–1868)
Quoted in Zanolini, *Biografia di Gioachino Rossini,* 1875

50   Music is what unifies.

Seu-Ma-Tsen (145–87 BC)
Quoted in Stravinsky, *Poetics of Music,* 1947

51   If I were to begin life again, I would devote it to music. It is the only cheap and unpunished rapture on earth.

Sydney Smith (1771–1845)
Letter to the Countess of Carlisle, 1844

52   Music is the crystallization of sound.

Henry David Thoreau (1817–62)
Journal, 1841

53   Music is made up of a large number of individual sounds, and is either a single melody or a part song.

Johannes Tinctoris (*c* 1435–1511)
Dictionary of Musical Terms, c 1475

54   Music is that skill consisting of performance in singing and playing, and it is threefold, namely harmonic, organal, and rhythmical. Harmonic music is that which is performed by the human voice. Organal music is that which is made by instruments which produce sound by wind. Rhythmical music is that which is made by instruments which render the sound by touch.

Johannes Tinctoris (*c* 1435–1511)
Ibid

55   Music's a rum go!
Ralph Vaughan Williams (1872–1958)
Attributed

56   Music . . . is the outward and audible signification of inward and spiritual realities.
Peter Warlock (Philip Heseltine) (1894–1930)
The Sackbut, 1920

57   Music is natural law as related to the sense of hearing.
Anton von Webern (1883–1945)
The Path to the New Music, pub 1960, trans Black

3   THE PURPOSE OF MUSIC

1   The function of music is to release us from the tyranny of conscious thought.
Thomas Beecham (1879–1961)
Quoted in Atkins and Newman, *Beecham Stories*, 1978

2   Einstein said that 'the most beautiful experience we can have is the mysterious'. Then why do so many of us try to explain the beauty of music, thus apparently depriving it of its mystery?
Leonard Bernstein (1918–90)
The Unanswered Question, 1976

3   Music is a pastime, a relaxation from more serious occupations.
Alexander Borodin (1833–87)
Letter to V. A. Krylov, 1867

4   Among other things proper to recreate man and give him pleasure, music is either the first or one of the principal, and we must think it is a gift of God deputed to that purpose.
Jean Calvin (1509–64)
The Geneva Psalter, 1543

5   So long as the human spirit thrives on this planet, music in some living form will accompany and sustain it and give it expressive meaning.
Aaron Copland (1900–90)
Music as an Aspect of the Human Spirit, radio broadcast, 1954

6 Music is the medicine of a troubled mind.

Walter Haddon (1516–72)
Lucubrationes Poemata 'Musica', 1567

7 You can't mess with people's heads, that's for sure. But that's what music's all about, messing with people's heads.

Jimi Hendrix (1942–70)
Quoted in Shapiro, *An Encyclopedia of Quotations about Music*, 1978

8 Is it not a prime function of the composer to influence, and indeed educate, habits of listening?

Hans Werner Henze (1926–   )
Music and Politics, 1982, 'German Music in the 1940s and 1950s'

9 Music is a science that would have us laugh and sing and dance.

Guillaume de Machaut (*c* 1300–77)
Quoted in Shapiro, *An Encyclopedia of Quotations about Music*, 1978

10 Music . . . is made particularly and principally to charm the spirit and the ear, and to enable us to pass our lives with a little sweetness amidst all the bitterness that we encounter here.

Marin Mersenne (1588–1648)
Harmonie universelle, 1636

11 How valuable a thing music is, and how useful for checking the mad impulses of the mind.

Richard Mulcaster (*c* 1530–1611)
For the Music of Thomas Tallis and William Byrd, 1575

12 Music hath two ends, first to please the sense, and that is done by the pure dulcor of harmony . . . and secondly to move the affections or excite passion. And that is done with measures of time joined with the former. And it must be granted that pure impulse artificially acted and continued hath great power to excite men to act but not to think . . . The melody is only to add to the diversion.

Roger North (1653–1734)
The Musicall Gramarian, 1728

13 Music is the nearest at hand, the most orderly, the most delicate, and the most perfect, of all bodily pleasures; it is also the only one which is equally helpful to all the ages of man.

John Ruskin (1819–1900)
Music in Greek Education

14   For changing peoples' manners and altering their customs there is nothing better than music.
Shu Ching (sixth century BC)
Quoted in Shapiro, *An Encyclopedia of Quotations about Music,* 1978

15   Music hath caught a higher pace than any virtue that I know. It is the arch-reformer; it hastens the sun to its setting; it invites him to his rising; it is the sweetest reproach, a measured satire.
Henry David Thomas
Journal, 1842

16   The purpose of music is to draw toward a total exaltation in which the individual mingles, losing his consciousness in a truth immediate.
Iannis Xenakis (1922–   )
In *The New York Times,* 21 April 1976

4   SILENCE

1   The tense silence between two movements – in itself music, in this environment – leaves wider scope for divination than the more determinate, but therefore less elastic, sound.
Ferruccio Busoni (1866–1924)
Entwurf einer neuen Aesthetik der Tonkunst, 1907

2   Try as we may to make a silence, we cannot.
John Cage, (1912–   )
Silence, 1961, 'Experimental Music', 1957

> 3   No voice; but oh! the silence sank like
>   music on my heart.
>   Samuel Taylor Coleridge (1772–1834)
>   *The Rime of the Ancient Mariner,* 1798, Pt VI

4   [*Of Pelleas et Mélisande:*] Quite spontaneously I have used silence as a means of expression (don't laugh). It is perhaps the only means of bringing into relief the emotional value of a phrase.
Claude Debussy (1862–1918)
Letter to Chausson, 1893

5   Elected Silence, sing to me
     and beat upon my whorlèd ear,
     Pipe me to pastures still and be
     The music that I care to hear.
     Gerald Manley Hopkins (1844–89)
     The Habit of Perfection, 1866

6   The rests . . . are just as important as the notes. Often these are far more expressive and appealing to the imagination. For this reason one could wish that many modern composers would confine themselves to rests–but perhaps that is too much to ask.
Carl Nielsen (1865–1931)
Living Music, 1953, 'Musical Problems', trans Spink

7   There's no music in a 'rest', Katie, that I know of: but there's the making of music in it. And people are always missing that part of the life-melody.
John Ruskin (1819–1900)
Ethics of the Dust, 1866, Lecture IV, 'The Crystal Orders'

8   The notes I handle no better than many pianists. But the pauses between the notes–ah, that is where the art resides.
Artur Schnabel (1882–1951)
Quoted in *Chicago Daily News*, 1958

9   Rests always sound well!
Arnold Schoenberg (1874–1951)
Quoted in Reich, *Schoenberg*, 1971

10   It is the little rift within the lute,
     That by and by will make the music mute,
     And ever widening slowly silence all.
     Alfred, Lord Tennyson (1809–92)
     Merlin and Vivien, 1857

11   Whereto serve ears if that there be no sound?
Thomas, Lord Vaux (1510–56)

12   The music in my heart I bore,
     Long after it was heard no more.
     William Wordsworth (1770–1850)
     The Solitary Reaper, 1807

5 RHYTHM

1   In the beginning there was rhythm
Hans von Bülow (1830–94)

2   'I know I have to beat time when I learn music.'
'Ah! that accounts for it,' said the Hatter. 'He won't stand beating.'
Lewis Carroll (1832–98)
Alice in Wonderland, 1865

3   I got rhythm,
I got music.
Ira Gershwin (1896–1983)
Song from *Girl Crazy*, 1930

4   Fascinating Rhythm.
Ira Gershwin (1896–1983)
Song title, 1924

5   Rhythm, the primitive and predominating element of all Art.
Vincent d'Indy (1851–1931)
Cours de composition musicale, I, 1903

6   All God's Chillun got Rhythm.
Gus Kahn (1886–1941)
Song title, 1937

7   Music begins to atrophy when it departs too far from the dance; . . .
poetry begins to atrophy when it gets too far from music.
Ezra Pound (1885–1972)
ABC of Reading, 1934, 'Warming'

8   Of all the elements united in the performance of music, rhythm is
the one most natural to us, as it is equally natural to all animals
Jean-Philippe Rameau (1683–1764)
Le Nouveau Système de musique théoretique, 1726

9   Music do I hear.
Ha, ha; keep time! How sour sweet music is
When time is broke and no proportion kept.
So is it in the music of men's lives.
(Richard II)
William Shakespeare (1564–1616)
Richard II, 1595, Act V, Sc V

10   The most exciting rhythms seem unexpected and complex, the most beautiful melodies simple and inevitable.

W. H. Auden (1907–73)
The Dyer's Hand, 1962, 'Notes on Music and Opera'

6   MELODY

1   Melody is the mirthful maistrace.

Anonymous
Cockelbie's Sow, fifteenth century

2   What felicity it is to hear a tune again which *has* made one happy!

Jane Austen (1775–1817)
Emma, 1815

3   Composers should write tunes the chauffeurs and errand boys can whistle.

Thomas Beecham (1879–1961)
Quoted in *The York Times*, 9 March 1961

> 4   The song is ended
>   But the melody lingers on.
>
> Irving Berlin (1888–1989)
> Song from *Ziegfeld Follies*, 1927

5   A Pretty Girl is Like a Melody.

Irving Berlin (1888–1989)
Song title, 1919

6   By MELODY is implied a series of sounds more fixed, and generally more lengthened, than those of common speech; arranged with grace, and, with respect to TIME, of proportional lengths, such as the mind can easily measure, and the voice express.

Charles Burney (1726–1814)
A General History of Music, 1776–89

7   A melody is not merely something you can hum.

Aaron Copland (1900–90)
Quoted in *The York Times*, 1949

8   Intonation, i.e., the 'melody' of speech, is the foundation of music.
Sergei Eisenstein (1898–1948)
Notes of a Film Director, 1946

9   Melody is the main thing: harmony is useful only to charm the ear.
Joseph Haydn (1732–1809)
Quoted in Landowska, *Landowska on Music*, 1969

10   I have sought above all a melodic line, which should be ample, generous, free-flowing, and not the laboured juxtaposition of little fragments which jar on one another.
Arthur Honegger (1892–1955)
I am a Composer, 1951

11   Melody alone never grows old.
Vincent d'Indy (1851–1931)
Attributed

12   Three things belong to composing, first of all melody; then again melody; then finally, for the third time, melody.
Salomon Jadassohn (1831–1902)
Book of Instrumentation, 1889

13   The art of dramatic writing is to compose a melodic curve which will, as if by magic, reveal immediately a human being in one definite phase of his existence.
Leoš Janáček (1854–1928)
Last Year, This Year, 1905

14   Fair melody! kind Siren! I've no choice;
     I must be thy sad servant evermore;
     I cannot choose but kneel here and adore.
   John Keats (1795–1821)
   Endymion, 1818, IV

15   The highest activities of consciousness have their origins in physical occurrences of the brain, just as the loveliest melodies are not too sublime to be expressed by notes.
W. Somerset Maugham (1874–1965)
A Writer's Notebook, 1949

16   Melody is a form of remembrance ... It must have a quality of inevitability in our ears.
Gian-Carlo Menotti (1911–   )
Time, 1 May 1950

17   Melody is the very essence of music. When I think of a good melodist I think of a fine race-horse. A contrapuntist is only a post-horse.
Wolfgang Amadeus Mozart (1756–91)
Letter to Michael Kelly, 1786

18   I have never doubted the importance of melody. I like melody very much, and I consider it the most important element in music, and I labour many years on the improvement of its quality in my compositions . . . It sometimes happens that the composer works over his melody and corrects it for so long that, without noticing it, he makes it extremely complicated and loses its simplicity. In the process of work, I fell into this trap.
Sergei Prokofiev (1891–1953)
Letter to the Soviet Composers' Union, 1948

19   . . . the pianist would play to them – for their two selves – the little phrase by Vinteuil which was, so to speak, the national anthem of their love. He would begin with the sustained tremolos of the violin part which for several bars were heard alone, filling the whole foreground; until suddenly they seemed to draw aside, and – as in those interiors by Pieter de Hooch which are deepened by the narrow frame of a half-opened door, in the far distance, of a different colour, velvety with the radiance of some intervening light – the little phrase appeared, dancing, pastoral, interpolated, episodic, belonging to another world. It rippled past, simple and immortal, scattering on every side the beauties of its grace, with the same ineffable smile . . .
Marcel Proust (1871–1922)
Du côté de chez Swann, 1913, trans Scott-Moncrieff and Kilmartin

20   Happy tune? Is there such a thing? If so, I never heard it.
Franz Schubert (1797–1828)
Attributed

21   The most perfect melodic shapes are found in Mozart; he has the lightness of touch which is the true objective . . . Listen to the remarkable expansion of a Mozart melody, to Cherubino's 'Voi che sapete', for instance. You think it is coming to an end, but it goes farther, ever farther.
Richard Strauss (1864–1949)
To the critic M. Marschalk, 1918, quoted in Trenner, *R. Strauss, Dokumente*, 1954

22   Sweetest melodies
Are those by distance made more sweet.
William Wordsworth (1770–1850)
Personal Talk, 1807

23   One ought not to sing in churches anything except plainsong in unison.

Gabriel Fauré (1845–1924)
Le Monde musical, 1904

24   [Of plainsong:] I see no mystery in it; just dullness.

Frederick Delius (1862–1934)
Quoted in Fenby, *Delius as I knew him*, 1936

7   HARMONY

1   Hark! hear you not a heavenly harmony?
Is't Jove, think you, that plays upon the
   spheres?
Heavens! is not this a heavenly melody,
Where Jove himself a part in music bears?

Thomas Bateson (d 1630)
Madrigal

2   The Spartans were indignant at Timotheus the Milesian, because by complicating music he had harmed the minds of the boys whom he had taken as pupils and had turned them from the modesty of virtue, and because he had perverted harmony, which he found modest, into the chromatic genius, which is more effeminate.

Boethius (Anicius Manlius Severinus, *c* 480–525)
De Institutione Musica

3   Seated one day at the organ,
I was weary and ill at ease,
And my fingers wandered idly
Over the noisy keys;
I know not what I was playing,
Or what I was dreaming then,
But I struck one chord of music,
Like the sound of a great Amen.

Adelaide Ann Proctor (1825–64)
The Lost Chord, 1858, set famously by Arthur Sullivan

4 I have sought but I seek it vainly,
That one lost chord divine,
Which came from the soul of the Organ,
And enter'd into mine.
It may be that Death's bright Angel
Will speak in that chord again,
It may be that only in heaven
I shall hear that grand Amen.

Ibid

5 It should be 'The Lost Progression', for the young lady was mistaken in supposing she had ever heard any single chord 'like the sound of a great Amen'. Unless we are to suppose that she had already found the chord of C major for the final syllable of the word and was seeking the chord for the first syllable . . . Fancy being in the room with her while she was strumming about and hunting after her chord! Fancy being in heaven with her when she had found it!

Samuel Butler (1835–1902)
Note-Books, pub 1912

6 Sullivan committed an unpardonable blasphemy against the art of music when he set Adelaide Proctor's poem about the Lost Chord . . . That which trains the imagination is good; that which starves or dulls the imagination is bad. Sitting at the keyboard and fumbling for lost chords is bad for the imagination.

Donald Francis Tovey (1875–1940)
The Training of the Musical Imagination, 1936

7 [On *The Lost Chord*:] We may thankfully hope that that chord is now lost for ever.

Donald Francis Tovey (1875–1940)
Musical Articles for the Encyclopaedia Brittanica, 1944

8 What we need are more songs like *The Lost Chord*. There is something of the stature and grandeur of Beethoven about it.

Clara Butt (1873–1936)
Attributed

9   So it was Monday, and Aunt Jane . . . had the tea party at which you
played *Poissons d'Or*. And when it (the goldfish) was finished Mrs Lucas
gave a great sigh, and said, 'Don't those inverted fifths make you wince,
Miss Bracely?' . . . What she meant, I suppose, was consecutive fifths:
you can't invert a fifth. So I said (I really meant it as a joke): 'Of course
there is that, but you must forgive Debussy for the sake of that wonderful
passage of submerged tenths!' And she took it quite gravely, and shook
her head, and said she was afraid she was a purist.

E. F. Benson (1867–1940)
Queen Lucia, 1920

10   If man is the tonic and God the dominant, the Devil is certainly the
sub-dominant and woman the relative minor.

Samuel Butler (1835–1902)
Note-Books, pub 1912

11   And after shewede he hym the nyne
             speres,
       And after that the melodye herde he
       That cometh of thilke speres thryes thre,
       That welle is of musik and melodye
       In this world here, and cause of armonye.

Geoffrey Chaucer (*c* 1345–1400)
The Parlement of Foules, 1369–87

12   Plato defines melody to consist of harmony, number and words:
harmony naked of itself, words the ornament of harmony, number the
common friend and uniter of them both.

John Dowland (1563–1626)
The First Booke of Songes, 1597

13   From harmony, from heavenly harmony
       This universal frame began:
           When Nature underneath a heap
       Of jarring atoms lay,
           And could not heave her head,
       The tuneful voice was heard from high:
           'Arise, ye more than dead.'
       Then cold, and hot, and moist, and dry,
           In order to their stations leap,
       And Music's power obey.

John Dryden (1631–1700)
A Song for St Cecilia's Day, 1687

14 From harmony to harmony
    Through all the compass of the notes it ran,
    The diapason closing full in Man.
    John Dryden (1631–1700)
    Ibid

15 The mere concord of octaves was a delight to Maggie, and she would often take up a book of studies rather than any melody, that she might taste more keenly by abstraction the more primitive sensation of intervals.
George Eliot (1819–80)
The Mill on the Floss, 1860

16 Many have held the soul to be
    Nearly allied to harmony.
    Matthew Green (1696–1737)
    The Spleen, 1737

17 The key and its body of chords is not the natural basis of tonal activity. What Nature provides is the intervals. The juxtaposition of intervals, as of chords, which are the extensions of intervals, *gives rise to the key*. We are no longer the prisoners of the key.
Paul Hindemith (1895–1963)
The Craft of Musical Composition, 1937

18 All concord's born of contraries.
Ben Jonson (1572–1637)
Cynthia's Revels, 1601, Act V, Sc II

19 Do you know that our soul is composed of harmony?
Leonardo da Vinci (1452–1519)
Notebooks

20 The melting voice through mazes
        running,
    Untwisting all the chains that tie
    The hidden soul of harmony.
    John Milton (1608–74)
    L'Allegro, 1632

21 It will be a great absurdity to use a sad harmony to a merry matter, or a merry harmony to a sad, lamentable or tragical ditty.
Thomas Morley (*c* 1557–1602)
A Plaine and Easie Introduction of Practicall Musicke, 1597

22   Harmony alone can stir the emotions. It is the one source from which melody directly emanates, and draws its power.
Jean-Philippe Rameau (1683–1764)
Observations sur notre instinct pour la musique, 1734

23   He who does not take a thorough pleasure in a simple chord progression, well constructed, beautiful in its arrangement, does not love music; he who does not prefer the first 'Prelude' in the *Well-Tempered Clavier* played without nuances as the composer wrote it for the instrument, to the same prelude embellished with a passionate melody, does not love music; he who does not prefer a folk tune of a lovely character, or a Gregorian chant without any accompaniment to a series of dissonant and pretentious chords does not love music.
Camille Saint-Saëns (1835–1921)
École buissonnière, 1913

24   'Tis no matter how it be in tune, so it make noise enough.
(Jaques)
William Shakespeare (1564–1616)
As You Like It, 1599, Act IV, Sc II

25   How irksome is this music to my heart!
     When such strings jar, what hope of harmony?
     (Henry)
     William Shakespeare (1564–1616)
     Henry VI Pt II, 1590–1, Act II, Sc I

26   If there is nothing new to be found in melody then we must seek novelty in harmony.
Georg Philipp Telemann (1681–1767)
Letter to C. H. Graun about Rameau, 1751–2

27   Harmony is a certain pleasantness caused by an agreeable sound.
Johannes Tinctoris (*c* 1435–1511)
Dictionary of Musical Terms, *c* 1475

28   Dust as we are, the immortal spirit
         grows
     Like harmony in music; there is a dark
     Inscrutable workmanship that reconciles
     Discordant elements, makes them cling
         together
     In one society.
     William Wordsworth (1770–1850)
     The Prelude, 1805, I

8 TONALITY

1 'Getting into the key of C sharp', he said, 'is like an unprotected female travelling on the Metropolitan Railway, and finding herself at Shepherd's Bush, without quite knowing where she wants to go to. How is she ever to get safe back to Clapham Junction?'

Samuel Butler (1835–1902)
The Way of All Flesh, 1903

2 Atonality has its uses, but only in relation to tonality. The moment it is elevated into an exclusive principle it loses all meaning and *raison d'être*. Its very name is negative – it is like talking of 'absence of cats' as if it were a positive conception.

Cecil Gray (1895–1951)
Pauline Gray (ed), *Notebooks*, 1989

3 Music, as long as it exists, will always take its departure from the major triad and return to it. The musician cannot escape it any more than the painter his primary colours or the architect his three dimensions.

Paul Hindemith (1895–1963)
The Craft of Musical Composition, 1937

4 Tonality is a natural force, like gravity.

Paul Hindemith (1895–1963)
Ibid

5 We can no longer tolerate this fetishism of tonality, which has been a burden on entire generations of musicians.

Arthur Honegger (1892–1955)
I am a Composer, 1951

6 Atonality is against nature. There is a centre to everything that exists. The planets have the sun, the moon, the earth ... All music with a centre is tonal. Music without a centre is fine for a moment or two, but it soon sounds all the same.

Alan Hovhaness (1911–)
Quoted in Ewen, *American Composers*, 1982

7 I am also guilty of atonality, which is often related to formalism, although I must confess with happiness that I began to yearn for tonal music long ago.

Sergei Prokofiev (1891–1953)
Letter to the Soviet Composers' Union, 1948

8   Or like a Beethovian semitonal modulation
       to a wildly remote key,
    As in the Allegretto where that happens with
       a sudden jump of seven sharps,
    And feels like the sunrise gilding the peak of the
       Dent Blanche,
    While the Arolla valley is still in cloud.
Hugh MacDiarmid (1892–1978)
The Kind of Poetry I Want, 1943

9   Tonality is the perspective of harmony.
Donald Francis Tovey (1875–1940)
BBC Radio talk, 1937

---

9 DISCORD

See also 25 'Modern' Music

---

1   Dissonances are generally played more loudly and consonances more softly, because the former stimulate and exacerbate the emotions, while the latter calm them.
Carl Philipp Emanuel Bach (1714–88)
Essay, 1753

2   [Discord] occasions a momentary distress to the ear, which remains unsatisfied, and even uneasy, till it hears something better ... the ear must be satisfied at last.
Charles Burney (1726–1814)
Present State of Music in France and Italy, 1771

3   I am convinced that provided the ear be at length made amends, there are few dissonances too strong for it.
Charles Burney (1726–1814)
Ibid

4   DISSONANCE ... is the DOLCE PICCANTE of Music, and operates on the ear as a poignant sauce on the palate: it is a zest, without which the auditory sense would be as much cloyed as the appetite, if it had nothing to feed on but sweets.
Charles Burney (1726–1814)
A General History of Music, 1776–89

5   Discords make the sweetest airs,
    And curses are a sort of prayers.

Samuel Butler (1618–80)
Hudibras, 1678

6   Disharmony, to paraphrase Bergson's statement about disorder, is simply a harmony to which many are unaccustomed.

John Cage (1912–   )
Silence, 1961, 'Experimental Music', 1957

7   No sound is dissonant which tells of life.

Samuel Taylor Coleridge (1772–1834)
This Lime-Tree Bower my Prison, 1797

8   [Of discords:]
    Le régal de l'ouïe.
    A feast for the ear.

Claude Debussy (1862–1918)
Quoted in *La Revue musicale*, 1926

9   The fairest harmony springs from discord.

Heraclitus (*c* 540–480 BC)
Quoted in Aristotle, *Nicomachean Ethics*

10   *Concordia discors.*
     Harmony in discord.

Horace (Quintus Horatius Flaccus, 65–8 BC)
Epistles, I, xii

11   Unfortunately, musical history is full to overflowing with unresolved dissonances.

Franz Liszt (1811–86)
Attributed

12   How doth music amaze us when of sound discords she maketh the sweetest harmony? And who can show us the reason why two basins, bowls, brass pots, or the like, of the same bigness, the one being full, the other empty, shall stricken be a just diapason in sound one to the other?

Henry Peacham (*c* 1576–*c* 1643)
The Compleat Gentleman, 1622

13   Medicine, to produce health, must know disease; music, to produce harmony, must know discord.

Plutarch (*c* AD 46–120)

14 All discord, harmony not understood.
Alexander Pope (1688–1744)
Essay On Man, 1732–4

15 Dissonances are only the more remote consonances.
Arnold Schoenberg (1874–1951)
Quoted in Machlis, *Introduction to Contemporary Music*, 1963

16 What distinguishes dissonances from consonances is not a greater or lesser degree of beauty, but a greater or lesser degree of comprehensibility.
Arnold Schoenberg (1874–1951)
Style and Idea, 1950

17   Melodious discord, heavenly tune harsh-
        sounding,
        Ear's deep-sweet music, and heart's deep-sore
        wounding.
        William Shakespeare (1564–1616)
        Venus and Adonis, 1592–4

18   Take but degree away, untune that
        string,
        And hark what discord follows; each thing
        melts,
        In mere oppugnancy.
        (Ulysses)
        William Shakespeare (1564–1616)
        Troilus and Cressida, 1601–2, Act I, Sc III

19 The technical history of modern harmony is a history of the growth of toleration by the human ear of chords that at first sounded discordant and senseless to the main body of contemporary professional musicians.
George Bernard Shaw (1856–1950)
The Reminiscences of a Quinquagenarian, an improvised speech, 6 December 1910

20 Discord oft in musick makes the sweeter lay.
Edmund Spenser (1552–99)
The Faerie Queene, 1590

21 A dissonance is a combination of different sounds that by nature is displeasing to the ears.
Johannes Tinctoris (*c* 1435–1511)
Dictionary of Musical Terms, *c* 1475

22   [Of Milhaud's dissonances:] The worst of it is that you get used to
them!
Charles-Marie Widor (1844–1937)
Quoted in Machlis, *Introduction to Contemporary Music,* 1963 (Widor taught Milhaud)

10   MUSIC IN NATURE

1   That's the wise thrush; he sings each
        song twice over,
     Lest you think he never could recapture
     The first fine careless rapture!

     Robert Browning (1812–89)
     Home Thoughts from Abroad, 1842–5

2   There's music in the sighing of a reed;
     There's music in the gushing of a rill;
     There's music in all things, if men had ears:
     Their earth is but an echo of the spheres.

     George Gordon, Lord Byron (1788–1824)
     Don Juan, 1819–24, Canto 15

3   See deep enough, and you see musically; the heart of nature being
everywhere music, if you can only reach it.
Thomas Carlyle (1795–1881)
On Heroes, Hero-Worship and the Heroic in History, 1841

4   And hear the pleasant cuckoo, loud and long –
     The simple bird that thinks two notes a song.

     W.H. Davies (1871–1940)
     April's Charms

5   Crave the tuneful nightingale to help you
        with her lay,
     The ousel and the throstlecock, chief music
        of our May.

     Michael Drayton (1562–1631)
     Shepherd's Garland, eclogue iii

6   I have heard the mermaids singing, each
        to each;
    I do not think that they will sing to me.
    T.S. Eliot (1888–1965)
    The Love Song of J. Alfred Prufrock, 1917

7   The silver Swan, who living had no
        Note,
    When death approached unlocked her silent
        throat,
    Leaning her breast against the reedy shore,
    Thus sung her first and last and sung no
        more.
    Farewell all joys, O death come close mine
        eyes,
    More Geese than Swans now live, more fools
        than wise.
    Anonymous
    From Orlando Gibbons (1583–1625), *First Set of Madrigals*, 1612

8   The Dolphins—the sweet conceipters of Music.
Robert Greene (*c* 1558–92)
Menaphon, 1587

9   The hills are alive with the sound of music.
    Oscar Hammerstein II (1895–1960)
    Song from *The Sound of Music*, 1959

10   There is no music in nature, neither melody or harmony. Music is
the creation of man.
H.R. Haweis (1838–1901)
Music and Morals, 1871

11   Where are the songs of Spring? Ay,
        where are they?
    Think not of them, thou hast thy music too.
    John Keats (1795–1821)
    To Autumn, 1819

12   Where the nightingale doth sing
    Not a senseless, tranced thing.
    But divine melodious truth.
    John Keats (1795–1821)
    Ode, 1819

13   Thou wast not born for death, immortal
        Bird!
     No hungry generations tread thee down;
     The voice I hear this passing night was heard
     In ancient days by emperor and clown:
     Perhaps the self-same song that found a path
     Through the sad heart of Ruth, when, sick for
        home,
     She stood in tears amid the alien corn;
     The same that oft-times hath
     Charm'd magic casements, opening on the foam
     Of perilous seas, in faery lands forlorn.

John Keats (1795–1821)
Ode to a Nightingale, 1819

14   Now more than ever seems it rich to die,
        To cease upon the midnight with no pain,
        While thou art pouring forth thy soul abroad
        In such an ecstasy!
        Still wouldst thou sing, and I have ears in
        vain –
        To thy high requiem become a sod.

John Keats (1795–1821)
Ibid

15   I hear the wind among the trees
        Playing the celestial symphonies;
        I see the branches downward bent,
        Like keys of some great instrument.

Henry Wadsworth Longfellow (1807–82)
A Day of Sunshine

16   We probably derive all our basic rhymes and themes from Nature,
which offers them to us, pregnant with meaning in every animal noise.

Gustav Mahler (1860–1911)
Quoted in Bauer-Lechner, *Recollections of Gustav Mahler*, 1980

17   I have seen dawn and sunset on moors and
        windy hills
        Coming in solemn beauty like slow old tunes
        of Spain.

John Masefield (1878–1967)
Beauty

18   Among the artistic hierarchy, birds are probably the greatest musicians to inhabit our planet.

Olivier Messiaen (1908–)
Quoted in Johnson, *Messiaen*, 1975

19   Sweet bird, that shunn'st the noise of
        folly,
     Most musical, most melancholy!

John Milton (1608–74)
Il Penseroso, 1632

20   The dolphin, a creature fond not only of man but of the musical art, is charmed by harmonious melody, and especially the sound of the hydraulus [hydraulic organ].

Pliny the Elder (Gaius Plinius Secundus, AD 23–79)
Natural History

21   The crow doth sing as sweetly as the
        lark,
     When neither is attended: and I think,
     The nightingale, if she should sing by day,
     When every goose is cackling, would be
        thought
     No better a musician than the wren.
     (Portia)

William Shakespeare (1564–1616)
The Merchant of Venice, 1596–8, Act V, Sc I

22   It is the lark that sings so out of
        tune,
     Straining harsh discords and unpleasing
        sharps.
     (Juliet)

William Shakespeare (1564–1616)
Romeo and Juliet, 1595–6, Act III, Sc V

23   [The thunder,]
     That deep and dreadful organ pipe.
     (Alonso)

William Shakespeare (1564–1616)
The Tempest, 1613, Act III, Sc III

24   Hail to thee, blithe Spirit!
        Bird thou never wert,
        That from Heaven, or near it,
        Pourest thy full heart
        In profuse strains of unpremeditated art.
        Percy Bysshe Shelley (1792–1822)
        To a Skylark, 1819

25   And singing still dost soar, and soaring ever singest.
        Percy Bysshe Shelley (1792–1822)
        Ibid

26   Deer walk upon our mountains, and the
            quail
        Whistle about us their spontaneous cries.
        Wallace Stevens (1879–1955)
        Sunday Morning

27   The God of Music dwelleth out of doors.
Edith M. Thomas
Music

28   Perhaps in our joy of musical rhythm, there is expressed something
of the primal joy of procreation . . . The domain of rhythm extends from
the spiritual to the carnal.
Bruno Walter (1876–1962)
Of Music and Music-making, 1957

29   Most owls seems to hoot exactly in B flat according to several
pitch-pipes used in the tuning of harpsichords, and strictly at concert
pitch.
Gilbert White (1720–93)
Journal, 4 December 1770
The Natural History and Antiquities of Selbourne, 1789

11 MYTHOLOGY

1   Come, woeful Orpheus, with thy charming
     lyre
   And tune thy voice unto thy skilful wire.
   Some strange chromatic notes do you devise
   That best with mournful accents sympathise.
   Of sourest sharps and uncouth flats make
     choice
   And I'll thereto compassionate my voice.

Anonymous
Byrd, *Psalmes, Songs and Sonnets*, 1611

2   When Orpheus strikes the trembling
     lyre,
    The streams stand still, the stones admire;
      The list'ning savages advance,
    The wolf and lamb around him trip,
    The bears in awkward measures leap,
      And tigers mingle in the dance;
    The moving woods attended as he played,
    And Rhodope was left without a shade.

Joseph Addison (1672–1719)
A Song for St Cecilia's Day

3   'This is the way,' laughed the great
     god Pan
   (Laughed while he sat by the river),
   'The only way since gods began
   To make sweet music, they could not succeed.'
   Then, dropping his mouth to a hole in the
     reed,
   He blew in power by the river.

Elizabeth Barrett Browning (1806–61)
A Musical Instrument

4 'The name of those fabulous animals (pagan, I regret to say) who used to sing in the water, has quite escaped me.' Mr George Chuzzlewit suggested 'Swans.' 'No,' said Mr Pecksniff. 'Not swans. Very like swans, too. Thank you.' The nephew . . . propounded 'Oysters.' 'No,' said Mr Pecksniff . . . 'nor oysters. But by no means unlike oysters; a very excellent idea; thank you my dear sir, very much. Wait. Sirens! Dear me! Sirens, of course.'

Charles Dickens (1812–70)
Martin Chuzzlewit, 1843–4, Ch 4

5 Musical as is Apollo's lute.

John Milton (1608–74)
Comus, 1634

> 6 Drive far off the bar'brous dissonance
>   Of Bacchus and his revellers.
>
>   John Milton (1608–74)
>   *Paradise Lost*, 1667, VII

> 7 Or bid the soul of Orpheus sing
>   Such notes as, warbled to the string,
>   Drew iron tears down Pluto's cheek.
>
>   John Milton (1608–74)
>   *Il Penseroso*, 1632

> 8 He that but once too nearly hears
>   The music of forfended spheres
>   Is thenceforth lonely, and for all
>   His days as one who treads the Wall
>   Of China, and, on this hand, sees
>   Cities and their civilities
>   And, on the other, lions.
>
>   Coventry Patmore (1823–96)
>   *The Victories of Love*, Bk I ii, from *Mrs Graham*

9 For Orpheus' lute was strung with
     poets' sinews:
  Whose golden touch could soften steel and
     stones,
  Make tigers tame and huge leviathans
  Forsake unsounded deeps to dance on sands . . .
  (Proteus)

William Shakespeare (1564–1616)
The Two Gentlemen of Verona, 1592–3, Act III, Sc II

10   Wilt thou have music? hark! Apollo
        plays
    And twenty caged nightingales do sing.
    (Lord)

William Shakespeare (1564–1616)
The Taming of the Shrew, 1592, Induction, Sc II

11   ... as sweet and musical
    As bright Apollo's lute, strung with his
        hair.
    (Biron)

William Shakespeare (1564–1616)
Love's Labour's Lost, 1590–4, Act IV, Sc III

12   Since once I sat upon a promontory,
    And heard a mermaid on a dolphin's back
    Uttering such dulcet and harmonious breath,
    That the rude sea grew civil at her song,
    And certain stars shot madly from their
        spheres,
    To hear the sea-maid's music.
    (Oberon)

William Shakespeare (1564–1616)
A Midsummer Night's Dream, 1595, Act II, Sc I

13   The words of Mercury are harsh after the songs of Apollo.
(Armado)

William Shakespeare (1564–1616)
Love's Labour's Lost, 1590–4, Act V, Sc II

14   Orpheus with his lute made trees
    And the mountain-tops that freeze,
    Bow themselves when he did sing:
    To his music plants and flowers
    Ever sprung; as sun and showers
    There had made a lasting spring.
    Everything that heard him play,
    Even the billows of the sea,
    Hang their heads, and lay by.

William Shakespeare (1564–1616)
Henry VIII, 1613, Act III, Sc I

15   Triton blowing loud his wreathed horn.

Edmund Spenser (1552–99)
Colin Clout's Home Again, 1595

12   THE EFFECTS OF MUSIC

1   Music,
   Music for a while
   Shall all your cares beguile.

John Dryden (1631–1700) and Nathaniel Lee (*c* 1649–92)
Oedipus, 1692, set to music by Purcell

2   Music can noble hints impart
   Engender fury, kindle love;
   With unsuspected eloquence can move,
   And manage all the man with secret art.

Joseph Addison (1672–1719)

3   To some people music is like food; to others like medicine; to others like a fan.

The Arabian Night's Entertainments, c 1450

4   Music exalts each joy, allays each
    grief,
   Expels diseases, softens every pain,
   Subdues the rage of passion and the plague.

John Armstrong MD (1709–79)
The Art of Preserving Health, 1744

5   Generally music feedeth that disposition of the spirits which it findeth.

Francis Bacon (1561–1626)
Sylva Sylvarum, 1627

6   Is there a heart that music cannot
    melt?
   Alas! how is that rugged heart forlorn!

James Beattie (1735–1803)
The Minstrel, 1771

7   'Dumb keyboards' have been invented; practice on them for a while in order to see that they are worthless. Dumb people cannot teach us to speak.

Robert Schumann (1810–56)
Wolff (ed), *On Music and Musicians,* 1946

8 Nothing is better than music; when it takes us out of time, it has done more for us than we have the right to hope for.
Nadia Boulanger (1887–1979)
Le Monde musical, 1919

9 Theophrastus right well prophesied, that diseases were either procured by music, or mitigated.
Robert Burton (1577–1640)
Anatomy of Melancholy, 1621

10 Many times the sound of a trumpet on a sudden, bells ringing, a carman's whistle, a boy singing some ballad tune early in the street, alters, revives, recreates a restless patient that cannot sleep in the night, etc.
Robert Burton (1577–1640)
Ibid

11 No mirth without music.
Robert Burton (1577–1640)
Ibid

12 [Music] cures all irksomeness and heaviness of the soul. Labouring men that sing to their work can tell as much, and so can soldiers when they go to fight, whom terror of death cannot so much affright as the sound of trumpet, drum, fife, and suchlike music animates.
Robert Burton (1577–1640)
Ibid

13 Who is there that, in logical words, can express the effect music has on us? A kind of inarticulate unfathomable speech, which leads us to the edge of the Infinite and lets us for moments gaze into that.
Thomas Carlyle (1795–1881)
On Heroes, Hero-Worship, and the Heroic in History, 1841

14 Music doth extenuate fears, furies, appeaseth cruelty, abateth heaviness, and to such as are wakeful it causeth quiet rest; it cures all irksomeness and heaviness of soul.
Cassiodorus (*c* 485 – *c* 580)

15 I believe music . . . together with many other vanities is meet for women, and peradventure for some also that have the likeness of men, but not for them that be men indeed; who ought not with such delicacies to womanish their minds.
(Lord Gaspar)
Baldassare Castiglione (1478–1529)
The Booke of the Courtyer, 1528, trans Hoby, 1561

16   I cannot sing the old songs
I sang long years ago,
For heart and voice would fail me,
And foolish tears would flow.
Claribel, born Charlotte A. Barnard (1830–69)
Fireside Thoughts

17   It is by the odes that the man is aroused. It is by the rules of propriety that the character is established. It is from music that the finish is received.
Confucius (551–478 BC)
On Music

18   When music and courtesy are better understood and appreciated, there will be no war.
Confucius (551–478BC)
Ibid

19   Music hath charms to soothe a savage
breast,
To soften rocks, or bend a knotted oak.
William Congreve (1670–1729)
The Mourning Bride, 1697

20   Music alone with sudden charms can bind
The wand'ring sense, and calm the troubled
mind.
William Congreve (1670–1729)
Hymn to Harmony

21   Most people use music as a couch . . . But serious music was never meant to be used as a soporific.
Aaron Copland (1900–90)
The New York Times, 1949

22   Music, to a nice ear, is a hazardous amusement, as long attention to it is very fatiguing.
William Cullen (1710–90)
First Lines of the Practice of Physic, 1778–84

23   Timotheus, to his breathing Flute,
And sounding Lyre,
Could swell the Soul to rage, or kindle soft
Desire.
John Dryden (1631–1700)
Alexander's Feast, 1697

24   Where gripinge grefes the hart would
        wounde
    And dolefulle dumps the mynde oppresse,
    There musicke with her silver sound
    With spede is wont to send redresse.

Richard Edwards (1524–66)
Paradyse of Dainty Devises, pub 1576

25 Music–makes a people's disposition more gentle; e.g.
'The Marseillaise'.

Gustave Flaubert (1821–80)
Dictionary of Received Ideas, pub 1913

26 [Of Beethoven's Symphony No 5:] All sorts and conditions are
satisfied by it.

E.M. Forster (1879–1970)
Howard's End, 1910

27 Much music marreth men's manners.

Galen (*c* AD 130–201)
Quoted in Ascham, *Toxophilus*, 1545

28   Music has charms, we all may find,
    Ingratiate deeply with the mind.
    When art does sound's high power advance,
    To music's pipe the passions dance;
    Motions unwill'd its powers have shown,
    Tarantulated by a tune.

Matthew Green (1696–1737)
The Spleen, 1737

29 Music is a safe kind of high.

Jimi Hendrix (1942–1970)
Quoted in Green, *The Book of Rock Quotes*, 1982

30 Music helps not the toothache.

George Herbert (1593–1633)
Jacula Prudentum, 1640

31   The mellow touch of music most doth
        wound
    The soul, when it doth rather sigh than
        sound.

Robert Herrick (1591–1674)
Soft Music, 1648

32   The reactions music evokes are not feelings, but they are the images, memories of feelings.

Paul Hindemith (1895–1963)
A Composer's World, 1952

33   *O laborum*
              Dulce lenimen medicumque.
              O sweet and healing balm of troubles.
              Horace (Quintus Horatius Flaccus, 65–8 BC)
              Odes, 1, 32

34   Polly was finding the song more and more interesting because she thought she was beginning to see a connection between the music and the things that were happening. When a line of dark firs sprang up on a ridge about a hundred yards away, she felt that they were connected with a series of deep prolonged notes which the Lion had sung a second before. And when he burst into a rapid series of lighter notes she was not surprised to see primroses suddenly appearing in every direction . . .

C.S. Lewis (1898–1963)
The Magician's Nephew, 1955

35   Music does not lie to the feelings.

Franz Liszt (1811–86)
Berlioz and his 'Harold' Symphony, 1855

36   Music is one of the greatest gifts that God has given us: it is divine and therefore Satan is its enemy. For with its aid many dire temptations are overcome; the devil does not stay where music is.

Martin Luther (1483–1546)
In Praise of Music

37   The sweetness and delightfulness of music has a natural power to lessify melancholy passions.

Increase Mather (1639–1723)
Remarkable Providences, 1684

38   Music is a beautiful opiate, if you don't take it too seriously.

Henry Miller (1891–1980)
The Air-Conditioned Nightmare, 1945

39 All their music [in Utopia], both that they play upon instruments, and that they sing with man's voice, doth so resemble and expresses natural affections; the sound and tune is so applied and made agreeable to the thing; that whether it be a prayer, or else a ditty of gladness, of patience, of trouble, of mourning, or of anger, the fashion of the melody doth so represent the meaning of the thing, that it doth wonderfully move, stir, pierce and enflame the hearers' minds.

Thomas More (1478–1535)
Utopia, 1516, trans Robynson, 1551

40 Music's the cordial of a troubled
        breast,
      The softest remedy that grief can find;
      The gentle spell that charms our care to rest
      And calms the ruffled passions of the mind.
      Music does all our joys refine,
      And gives the relish to our wine.

    John Oldham (1653–83)
    An Ode on St Cecilia's Day, 1683

41 *Enervant animos citharae, lotosque, lyraeque.*
    Lutes, flutes and lyres enervate the mind.

Ovid (43 BC–AD 17)
Remedia Amoris

42 [Music] is an enemy to melancholy and dejection of the mind, which St Chrysostom truly called the Devil's bath; yea, a curer of some diseases – in Apulia in Italy and thereabouts it is most certain that those who are stung with the tarantula are cured only by music.

Henry Peacham (1576?–1643?)
The Compleat Gentleman, 1622

43 Music is a science peculiarly productive of a pleasure that no state of life, public or private, secular or sacred; no difference of age or season; no temper of mind or condition of health exempt from present anguish; nor, lastly, distinction of quality, renders either improper, untimely, or unentertaining.

Samuel Pepys (1633–1703)
Letter to the Master of University College, Oxford, 1700

44 The law ... ought to employ your music ... in order to lead hardened criminals to repentance. No one could resist it ... and the day is not far distant, in these times of humanitarian ideas, when similar psychological methods will be used to soften the hearts of the vicious.

Pope Pius IX (1792–1878)
After hearing Liszt play in 1862, quoted in Wohl, *Franz Liszt*, trans 1887

45 Music has charms alone for peaceful
     minds.
     Alexander Pope (1688–1744)
     Sappho to Phaon, 1712

46 And learn, my sons, the wondrous power
     of Noise,
     To move, to raise, to ravish ev'ry heart.
     Alexander Pope (1688–1744)
     The Dunciad, 1728, II

47 Music's force can tame the furious
     beast:
     Can make the wolf or foaming boar restrain
     His rage; the lion drop his crested mane
     Attentive to the song.
     Matthew Prior (1664–1721)
     Solomon, or the Vanity of Human Wishes, 1718

48 Music is an intellectual or sensual pleasure, according to the
temperament of him who hears it.
Thomas de Quincey (1785–1859)
Confessions of an English Opium Eater, 1822

49 In sweet music is such art,
     Killing care and grief of heart
     Fall asleep, or hearing die.
     William Shakespeare (1564–1616)
     Henry VIII, 1613, Act III, Sc I

50 Though music oft hath such a charm
     To make bad good, and good provoke to harm.
     (Duke Vincentio)
     William Shakespeare (1564–1616)
     Measure for Measure, 1604–5, Act IV, Sc I

51 This music mads me. Let it sound no more,
     For though it have holp madmen to their wits,
     In me it seems it will make wise men mad.
     (Richard)
     William Shakespeare (1564–1616)
     Richard II, 1595, Act V, Sc V

52 A lamentable tune is the sweetest music to a woeful mind.
Philip Sidney (1554–86)
Arcadia, 1590, II

53   When a singer at a prison concert sang 'Home, Sweet Home', the inmates were so deeply moved that seven of them escaped the same night, and were re-arrested in their respective homes the next day.
From a musical journal, 1885, quoted by Slonimsky, *A Thing or Two about Music*, 1948

54   The sound of the flute will cure epilepsy and sciatic gout.
Theophrastus (*c* 372–286 BC)

55   When I hear music, I fear no danger. I am invulnerable. I see no foe. I am related to the earliest times, and to the latest.
Henry David Thoreau (1817–62)
Journal, 1857

56   I can fancy a man who had led a perfectly commonplace life, hearing by chance some curious piece of music, and suddenly discovering that his soul, without his being conscious of it, had passed through terrible experiences, and known fearful joys, or wild romantic loves, or great renunciations.
Oscar Wilde (1854–1900)
The Critic as Artist, 1891

13 PHILOSOPHY

See also 2 Definitions

1   To those who are not tone-deaf the argument that music vaguely of the period *must* express that period is unsound. Unsound because we are not listening with the ears of that period. I hold that Richard Strauss gives to modern ears a better notion of the daughter of Clytemnestra and Agamemnon than any concatenation of conch, ram's horn, harp, pipe, lute, theorbo, shawm, sackbut, psaltery, tabor and cymbals that Euripides could have heard.
James Agate (1877–1947)
The Later Ego, 1948

2   I cannot conceive of music that expresses absolutely nothing.
Béla Bartók (1881–1945)
Quoted by Machlis, *Introduction to Contemporary Music*, 1963

3   Music is a part of us, and either ennobles or degrades our behaviour.
Boethius (Anicius Manlius Severinus, *c* 480–525)
De Institutione Musica

4   Sure there is music even in the beauty, and the silent note which
Cupid strikes, far sweeter than the sound of an instrument. For there is a
magic wherever there is a harmony, order or proportion; and thus far we
maintain the music of the spheres: for those well-ordered motions, and
regular paces, though they give no sound unto the ear, yet to the
understanding they strike a note most full of harmony.

Thomas Browne (1605–84)
Religio Medici, 1643

5   Music is a roaring-meg against melancholy, to rear and revive the
languishing soul; affecting not only the ears, but the very arteries, the
vital and animal spirits, it erects the mind and makes it nimble.

Robert Burton (1577–1640)
Anatomy of Melancholy, 1621

6   Many men are melancholy by hearing music, but it is pleasing
melancholy that it causeth; and therefore, to such as are discontent, in
woe, fear, sorrow, or dejected, it is a most present remedy.

Robert Burton (1577–1640)
Ibid

7   There can be no mischief sure where there is music.

Miguel de Cervantes (1547–1616)
Don Quixote, 1605

8   Nothing is more odious than music without hidden meaning.

Frédéric Chopin (1810–49)
Quoted in *Le Courrier musical*, 1910

9   Though the entertainments of music are very engaging; though they
make a great discovery of the soul; and show it capable of strange
diversities of pleasure: yet to have our passion lie at the mercy of a little
minstrelsy; to be fiddled out of our reason and sobriety; to have our
courage depend upon a drum, or our devotions upon an organ, is a sign
we are not as great as we might be.

Jeremy Collier (1650–1726)
An Essay of Music, 1702

10   Indeed Musick, when rightly ordered, cannot be prefer'd too
much. For it recreates and exalts the Mind at the same time. It composes
the Passions, affords a strong Pleasure, and excites a Nobleness of
thought.

Jeremy Collier (1650–1726)
Ibid

11 Virtue is the strong stem of man's nature, and music is the blossoming of virtue.

Confucius (551–479 BC)

12 Music produces a kind of pleasure which human nature cannot do without.

Confucius (551–479 BC)
Book of Rites

13 If a man lacks the virtues proper to humanity, what has he to do with music?

Confucius (551–479 BC)
Analects

14 The whole problem can be stated quite simply by asking, 'Is there a meaning to music?' My answer would be, 'Yes.' And 'Can you state in so many words what the meaning is?' My answer to that would be 'No.'

Aaron Copland (1900–90)
What to Listen for in Music, 1939

15 The greatest moments of the human spirit may be deduced from the greatest moments in music.

Aaron Copland (1900–90)
Music as an Aspect of the Human Spirit, radio broadcast, 1954

16 Musical modes are nowhere altered without changes in the most important laws of the state.

Damon of Athens (fl fourth century BC)

17 Human song is generally admitted to be the basis or origin of instrumental music. As neither the enjoyment nor the capacity of producing musical notes are faculties of the least use to man in reference to his daily habits of life, they must be ranked among the most mysterious with which he is endowed.

Charles Darwin (1809–82)
The Descent of Man, 1871

18 The music of the ancients was more moving than ours, not because they were more learned, but because they were less.

René Descartes (1596–1650)
Letter to Mersenne

19 Music takes us out of the actual and whispers to us dim secrets that startle our wonder as to who we are, and for what, whence, and whereto.

Ralph Waldo Emerson (1803–82)

20   Music was invented to deceive and delude mankind.
Ephorus (fourth century BC)
History, Preface

21   Architecture in general is frozen music.
Friedrich von Schelling (1775–1854)
Philosophie der Kunst, 1809

22   A distinguished philosopher spoke of architecture as *frozen* music, and his assertion caused many to shake their heads. We believe this really beautiful idea could not be better reintroduced than by calling architecture *silent* music.
Johann Wolfgang von Goethe (1749–1832)
Conversations with Eckermann, 1837

23   Music is something innate and internal, which needs little nourishment from without, and no experience drawn from life.
Johann Wolfgang von Goethe (1749–1832)
Letter, 1831

24   Music can be translated only by music. Just so far as it suggests worded thought, it falls short of its highest office.
Oliver Wendell Holmes (1809–94)
Over the Teacups

25   The laws of morals and the laws of art are the same.
Zoltán Kodály (1882–1967)
Address to the Budapest Academy of Music, 1953

26   It is obvious that things which can appear only objectively to perception can in no way furnish connecting points to music; the poorest of apprentice landscape painters could give with a few chalk strokes a much more faithful picture than a musician operating with all the resources of the best orchestra. But if these same things are subjected to dreaming, to contemplation, to emotional uplift, have they not a peculiar kinship with music, and should not music be able to translate them into its mysterious language?
Franz Liszt (1811–86)
Robert Schumann's Piano Compositions, 1837

27   Music quickens time, she quickens us to the finest enjoyment of time.
Thomas Mann (1875–1955)
The Magic Mountain, 1924, trans Lowe-Porter

28   Without music, life would be a mistake.
Friedrich Nietzsche (1844–1900)
Götzendämmerung, 1889

29   All art constantly aspires towards the condition of music, because, in its ideal, consummate moments, the end is not distinct from the means, the form from the matter, the subject from the expression; and to it therefore, to the condition of its perfect moments, all the arts may be supposed constantly to tend and aspire.
Walter Pater (1839–94)
Studies in the History of the Renaissance, 1873, 'The School of Giorgione'

30   The business of music should in some measure lead to the love of the beautiful.
Plato (*c* 428–*c* 348 BC)
The Republic

31   We shall never become musicians unless we understand the ideals of temperance, fortitude, liberality and magnificence.
Plato (*c* 428–*c* 348 BC)
Ibid

32   The man who has music in his soul will be most in love with the loveliest.
Plato (*c* 428–*c* 348 BC)
Ibid

33   The life of man in every part has need of harmony and rhythm.
Plato (*c* 428–*c* 348 BC)
Laws

34   Music is a moral law. It gives a soul to the universe, wings to the mind, flight to the imagination, a charm to sadness, gaiety and life to everything. It is the essence of order, and leads to all that is good, just and beautiful, of which it is the invisible, but nevertheless dazzling, passionate, and eternal form.
Plato (*c* 428–*c* 348 BC)

35   There is geometry in the humming of the strings. There is music in the spacings of the spheres.
Pythagoras (sixth century BC)
Quoted in Aristotle, *Metaphysics*

36   All one's life is a music, if one touches the notes rightly, and in time.
John Ruskin (1819–1900)

37   Music is a means of giving form to our inner feelings without attaching them to events or objects in the world.

George Santayana (1863–1952)
Little Essays, 1920

38   Art is the cry of distress uttered by those who experience at first hand the fate of mankind. Who are not reconciled to it, but come to grips with it. Who do not apathetically wait upon the motor called 'hidden forces', but hurl themselves in among the moving wheels, to understand how it all works. Who do not turn their eyes away to shield themselves from emotions, but open them wide, so as to tackle what must be tackled. Who do, however often close their eyes, in order to perceive things incommunicable by the senses, to envision within themselves the process that only seems to be in the world outside. The world revolves within: what bursts out is merely the echo – the work of art!

Arnold Schoenberg (1874–1951)
Quoted in Reich, *Schoenberg,* 1971

39   Music is the occult metaphysical exercise of a soul not knowing that it philosophizes.

Arthur Schopenhauer (1788–1860)
Quoted in Shapiro, *An Encyclopedia of Quotations about Music,* 1978

40   Music never expresses the phenomenon, but only the inner nature, the in-itself of all phenomena, the will itself.

Arthur Schopenhauer (1788–1860))
The World as Will and Idea, 1818

41   Music stands quite alone. It is cut off from all the other arts . . . It does not express a particular and definite joy, sorrow, anguish, horror, delight or mood of peace, but joy, sorrow, anguish, horror, delight, peace of mind *themselves,* in the abstract, in their essential nature, without accessories, and therefore without their customary motives. Yet it enables us to grasp and share them fully in this quintessence.

Arthur Schopenhauer (1788–1860)
Ibid

42   Music will express any emotion, base or lofty, she is absolutely unmoral . . .

George Bernard Shaw (1856–1950)
Music in London, 1890–4

43   One and the same thing can at the same time be good, bad, and indifferent, for example, music is good to the melancholy, bad to those who mourn, and neither good nor bad to the deaf.
Baruch Spinoza (1632–77)
Ethics, 1677

44   Those things that act through the ears are said to make a noise, discord, or harmony, and this last has caused men to lose their heads to such a degree that they have believed God himself is delighted with it.
Baruch Spinoza (1632–77)
Ibid

45   Music revives the recollections it would appease.
Madame de Staël, born Anne Louise Germaine Necker (1766–1817)
Corinne, 1807

46   The entire pleasure of music consists in creating illusions, and common-sense rationality is the greatest enemy of musical appreciation.
Stendhal (1783–1842)
Life of Rossini, 1824

47   Just as my fingers on these keys
Make music, so the selfsame sounds
On my spirit make a music, too.

Music is feeling, then, not sound.
Wallace Stevens (1879–1955)
Peter Quince at the Clavier

48   Music is the sound of universal laws promulgated.
Henry David Thoreau (1817–62)

14 TALKING ABOUT MUSIC

1 'What is that you are saying, Fitzwilliam? What are you talking of? What are you telling Miss Bennett? Let me hear what it is.' 'We are speaking of music, madam,' he said, when no longer able to avoid a reply. 'Of music! Then pray speak aloud. It is of all subjects my delight. I must have my share in the conversation, if you are speaking of music. There are few people in England, I suppose, who have more true enjoyment of music than myself, or a better natural taste. If I had ever learned, I should have been a great proficient . . .'
Jane Austen (1775–1817)
Pride and Prejudice, 1813

2 If the music doesn't say it, how can words *say* it for the music?
John Coltrane (1926–67)
Quoted in Hentoff, *Jazz is*, 1978

3 I detest politicking, the struggle for or against something in music; music reaches people of its own accord, when it wants to. It cannot be imposed, can hardly be explained, cannot be propagated.
Hans Werner Henze (1926–)
Music and Politics, 1982, 'Wavering and Positionless', 1957

4 The hardests of all the arts to speak of is music, because music has no meaning to speak of.
Ned Rorem (1923–)
Music from Inside Out, 1967

5 There is nothing more difficult than talking about music.
Camille Saint-Saëns (1835–1921)
Quoted in Harding, *Saint-Saëns*, 1965

6 Verbal communciation about music is impossible except among musicians.
Virgil Thomson (1896–1989)
The State of Music, 1939

15 POETIC REFLECTIONS

1   Let a florid music praise,
The flute and the trumpet,
Beauty's conquest of your face . . .
W.H. Auden (1907–73)
Twelve Songs, 1936, III

2   Music touches places beyond our
    touching
deeper than the personal . . .
Keith Bosley (1937–)
Romantic Piano Concerto

3   Browning formed the exception to the rule that poets and literary men care less for music than painters, in whom love of our art seems almost invariably to be inborn . . . Thackeray and Dickens had a certain liking for music, but Tennyson listened to it with great indifference, and his loud talk while I was playing some superlatively fine work has now and then *agacé* my nerves.
Charles Hallé (1819–95)
Kennedy (ed), *Autobiography*, 1972

4   Who hears music, feels his solitude
Peopled at once.
Robert Browning (1812–89)
Balaustian's Adventure, 1871

5   'Brave Galuppi! that was music! good
    alike at grave and gay!
I can always leave off talking when I hear a
    master play.'
Robert Browning (1812–89)
A Toccata of Galuppi's, 1855

6   Such sweet
Soft notes as yet musician's cunning
Never gave the enraptured air.
Robert Browning (1812–89)
The Pied Piper of Hamelin, 1845

7   There is no truer truth obtainable
By Man than comes of music.
Robert Browning (1812–89)
Parleyings with Certain People: 'Charles Avison', 1887

8   For music (which is earnest óf a heaven
    Seeing we know emotions strange by it,
    Not else to be revealed,) is like a voice,
    A low voice calling fancy, as a friend,
    To the green woods in the gay summer time.
    Robert Browning (1812–89)
    Pauline, 1833

9   And today's music manufacture, – Brahms,
    Wagner, Dvořák, Liszt, – to where – trumpets,
        shawms
    Show yourself joyful!
    Robert Browning (1812–89)
    Parleyings with Certain People: Charles Avison, 1887

    10   Her voice, the music of the spheres,
         So loud, it deafens mortals' ears;
         As wise philosophers have thought,
         And that's the cause we hear it not.
         Samuel Butler (1612–80)
         Hudibras, 1664

    11   The angels all were singing out of
             tune,
         And hoarse with having little else to do.
         George Gordon, Lord Byron (1788–1824)
         The Vision of Judgement, 1822

12   Her fingers witched the chords they
         passed along,
     And her lips seemed to kiss the soul in song.
     Thomas Campbell (1777–1844)
     Theodric, 1824

    13   When to her lute Corinna sings,
         Her voice revives the leaden strings,
         And both in highest notes appear,
         As any challeng'd echo clear.

         But when she doth of mourning speak,
         Ev'n with her sighs the strings do break.
         Thomas Campion (1567–1620)
         A Book of Airs, 1610–12

14   A damsel with a dulcimer
       In a vision once I saw:
       It was an Abyssinian maid,
       And on her dulcimer she play'd,
       Singing of Mount Abora.
       Could I revive within me,
       Her symphony and song,
       To such a deep delight t'would win me,
       That with music loud and long,
       I would build that dome in air,
       That sunny dome, those caves of ice,
       And all who heard should see them there,
       And all should cry, Beware! Beware!

Samuel Taylor Coleridge (1772–1834)
In Xanadu did Kubla Khan . . ., 1816

15 An ear for music is very different from a taste for music. I have no ear whatever; I could not sing an air to save my life; but I have the intensest delight in music, and can detect good from bad.

Samuel Taylor Coleridge (1772–1834)
Table Talk, 1830

16 Good music never tires me, nor sends me to sleep. I feel physically refreshed and strengthened by it, as Milton says he did.

Samuel Taylor Coleridge (1772–1834)
Table Talk, 1835

17   O Music, sphere-descended maid,
       Friend of pleasure, wisdom's aid.

William Collins (1721–59)
The Passions, an Ode for Music, 1747

18   There is in souls a sympathy with
       sounds,
       And, as the mind is pitch'd, the ear is
       pleas'd
       With melting airs, or martial brisk, or
       grave:
       Some chord in unison with what we hear
       Is touch'd within us, and the heart replies.

William Cowper (1731–1800)
The Task, 1785, VI

19 Thence, as sweet music to the ear comes
        sliding
    Through the piped organ, comes into my mind
    The vision of thy life and times betiding.
    Dante (1265–1321)
    Paradiso, Canto xvii, trans Dorothy L. Sayers, 1962

20 Can doleful notes to measured accents
        set
    Express unmeasured griefs which time forget?
    No, let chromatic tunes, harsh without
        ground,
    Be sullen music for a tuneless heart.
    John Danyel (or Daniel)
    Song, 1606

21 Who loves not music and the heavenly
        muse,
    That man God hates.
    John Dowland (1563–1626)
    Commendatory poem to William Leighton's *Teares or Lamentations of
    a Sorrowfull Soule*, 1614

22 What passion cannot Music raise and
        quell?
    John Dryden (1631–1700)
    A Song for St Cecilia's Day, 1687

23 Music sweeps by me as a messenger
    Carrying a message that is not for me.
    George Eliot (1819–80)
    The Spanish Gypsy, 1868, III

24 Music as well consists
    In th'ear, as in the playing.
    John Ford (*c* 1586–*c* 1640)
    'Tis Pity She's a Whore, 1633

25 O Music
    In your depths we deposit our hearts and
        souls.
    Thou hast taught us to see with our ears
    And hear with our hearts.
    Kahlil Gibran (1883–1931)
    The Prophet, 1923

26   His chiefest recreation was music, in which heavenly art he was a most excellent master, and did himself compose many divine hymns and anthems, which he set and sung to his lute or viol; and though he was a lover of retiredness, yet his love of music was such, that he went usually twice every week, on certain appointed days to the cathedral church in Salisbury . . . to enjoy his heaven upon earth . . .

Izaak Walton (1593–1683)
Life of George Herbert, 1670

27   [Of music:]
      Sweetest of sweets, I thank you! when
         displeasure
      Did through my body wound my mind,
      You took me hence, and in your house of
         pleasure
      A dainty lodging me assigned.

      George Herbert (1593–1633)

28   Now I in you without a body move,
      Rising and falling with your wings;
      We both together sweetly live and love,
      Yet say sometimes, 'God help poor kings!'

      George Herbert (1593–1633)

29   Begin to charm, and as thou strok'st
         mine ears
      With thy enchantment, melt me into tears.
      Then let thy active hand scud o'er thy lyre:
      And make my spirits frantic with the fire.
      That done, sink down into a silv'ry strain,
      And make me smooth as balm and oil again.

      Robert Herrick (1591–1674)
      To Music, 1648

30   Even on my jolie Lute, by night,
      And trim'ling trible string,
      I shall with all my minde and might,
      Thy glorie gladlie sing.

      Alexander Hume (*c* 1557–1609)
      Hymnes or Sacred Songs, 1599

31   For not the notes alone, or new-found
        air,
     Or structure of elaborate harmonies,
     With steps that to the waiting treble climb,
     Suffice a true-touched ear. To that will
        come
     Out of the very vagueness of the joy
     A shaping and a sense of things beyond us,
     Great things and voices great . . .
     Leigh Hunt (1784–1859)
     A Thought on Music, 1815

32   Fled is that music:–Do I wake or
        sleep?
        John Keats (1795–1821)
        Ode to a Nightingale, 1819

33   Heard melodies are sweet, but those
        unheard
     Are sweeter; therefore, ye soft pipes, play
        on;
     Not to the sensual ear, but, more endear'd,
     Pipe to the spirit ditties of no tone . . .
     John Keats (1795–1821)
     Ode on a Grecian Urn, 1820

34   But many days have past since last my
        heart
     Was warm'd luxuriously by divine Mozart,
     By Arne delighted, or by Handel madden'd
     Or by the song of Erin pierced and sadden'd.
     John Keats (1795–1821)
     Epistle to Charles Cowden Clarke, 1816

35   Let me have music dying, and I seek
     No more delight.
        John Keats (1795–1821)
        Endymion, 1818

36   The music, yearning like a God in pain.
John Keats (1795–1821)
The Eve of St Agnes, 1819

37   Some cry up Haydn, some Mozart,
Just as the whim bites. For my part,
I do not care a farthing candle
For either of them nor for Handel.
Cannot a man live free and easy,
Without admiring Pergolesi?
Or thro' the world with comfort go,
That never heard of Doctor Blow?

Charles Lamb (1775–1834)
Free Thoughts on Several Eminent Composers, 1830

38   The devil, with his foot so cloven,
For aught I care may take Beethoven;
And, if the bargain does not suit,
I'll throw him Weber in to boot.

Charles Lamb (1775–1834)
Ibid

39   Milton almost requires a solemn service of music to be played before you enter upon him.

Charles Lamb (1775–1834)
Essays of Elia, 1833

40   The measured malice of music.

Charles Lamb (1775–1834)
Essays of Elia, 1820–3

41   There's sure no passion in the human
soul,
But finds its food in music.

George Lillo (1693–1739)
Fatal Curiosity, 1736

42   And the night shall be filled with
music,
And the cares that infest the day,
Shall fold their tents, like the Arabs,
And as silently steal away.

Henry Wadsworth Longfellow (1807–82)
The Day Is Done

43   The best texbook for teaching composition is . . . Walter de la Mare's *Peacock Pie*.

Gustav Holst (1874–1934)
Quoted in Imogen Holst, *Holst*, 1974

44 Sweep thy faint strings, Musician,
With thy long lean hand;
Downward the starry tapers burn,
Sinks soft the waning sand;
The old hound whimpers, couched in sleep,
The embers smoulder low;
Across the walls the shadows
Come and go.

Sweep softly thy strings, Musician,
The minutes mount to hours;
Frost on the windless casement weaves
A labyrinth of flowers;
Ghosts linger in the darkening air,
Hearken at the open door;
Music hath called them, dreaming,
Home once more.

Walter de la Mare (1873–1956)
The Song of the Shadows; Peacock Pie, 1913

45 Then music, the mosaic of the air,
Did of all these a solemn noise prepare:
With which she gained the empire of the ear,
Including all between the earth and sphere.

Andrew Marvell (1621–78)
Music's Empire

46 Such sweet compulsion doth in music lie.

John Milton (1608–74)
Arcades, 1633

47 Thus sang the uncouth swain to th' oaks
and rills,
While the still morn went out with sandals
gray;
He touch'd the tender stops of various
quills,
With eager thought warbling his Doric lay.

John Milton (1608–74)
Lycidas, 1637

48 Ring out ye crystal spheres,
Once bless our human ears
(If ye have power to touch our senses so)
And let your silver chime
Move in melodious time;
And let the base of heav'n's deep organ blow,
And with your ninefold harmony
Make up full consort to th' angelic symphony.

John Milton (1608–74)
On the Morning of Christ's Nativity

49 And music, too–dear music! that can
    touch
Beyond all else the soul that loves it much–
Now heard far off, so far as but to seem
Like the faint, exquisite music of a dream.

Thomas Moore (1779–1852)
Lalla Rookh, The Veiled Prophet of Khorassan, 1817

50 It is in music, perhaps, that the soul most nearly attains the great
end for which, when inspired by the poetic sentiment, it struggles–the
creation of supernal beauty.

Edgar Allen Poe (1809–49)
The Poetic Principle, 1850

51 Descend ye Nine! descend and sing;
The breathing instruments inspire,
Wake into voice each silent string,
And sweep the sounding lyre!

Alexander Pope (1688–1744)
Ode on St Cecilia's Day, c 1708

52 By music, minds an equal temper know,
Nor swell too high, nor sink too low.
If in the breast tumultuous joys arise,
Music her soft, assuasive voice applies;
Or, when the soul is press'd with cares,
Exalts her in enlivening airs.

Alexander Pope (1688–1744)
Ibid

53   Music, the fiercest grief can charm,
     And fate's severest rage disarm:
     Music can soften pain to ease.
     And make despair and madness please
     Our joys below it can improve,
     And antedate the bliss above.

Alexander Pope (1688–1744)
Ibid

54   Music resembles poetry; in each
Are nameless graces which no methods teach,
And which a master-hand alone can reach.

Alexander Pope (1688–1744)
An Essay on Criticism, 1711

55   With horns and trumpets now to madness
        swell,
        Now sink in sorrows with a tolling bell.

Alexander Pope (1688–1744)
The Dunciad, 1728

56   Hark! the numbers, soft and clear,
     Gently steal upon the ear;
     Now louder, and yet louder rise,
     And fill with spreading sounds the skies;
     Exulting in triumph now swell the bold notes,
     In broken air, trembling, the wild music
        floats;
     Till, by degrees, remote and small,
     The strains decay,
     And melt away
     In a dying, dying fall.

Alexander Pope (1688–1744)
Ode on St Cecilia's Day, c 1708

57   It suffered poets, critics, chat
     And will no doubt survive Darmstadt . . .

Peter Porter (1929–   )
Three Poems for Music

58   The truth is Dr Dulcamara's got
The Times Music Critic's job; the *rustici*
Are cooking on Sicilian gas, Venetian
   composers
Are setting Goethe to gongs and spiels and
   phones,
Teutons still come south to add a little
Cantilena to their klangschönheit
(Not to mention the boys of Naples), and
   those apostles,
The Twelve Notes, are at work on their Acts
To beautify our arrogance.
Peter Porter (1929–)
Poems Ancient and Modern, 1964, 'Homage to Gaetano Donizetti'

59 Music: breathing of statues.
Perhaps: stillness of pictures. You speech, where
speeches end. You time, vertically poised on the courses of vanishing
hearts.

Feelings for what? Oh, you transformation of feelings into
. . . audible landscape!
You stranger: Music.
Rainer Maria Rilke (1875–1926)
An die Musik ('To Music'), trans Leishman

60   You gracious Art, how often in gloomy
   hours,
When Life's tumultuous round ensnared me,
You have kindled warm love in my heart,
And carried me into a better world!
Franz von Schober (1796–1882)
An die Musik ('To Music') (lyrics set famously by his friend Schubert)

61   How sweet the moonlight sleeps upon
   this bank!
Here we will sit and let the sounds of music
Creep in our ears; soft stillness and the
   night
Become the touches of sweet harmony.
(Lorenzo)
William Shakespeare (1564–1616)
The Merchant of Venice, 1596–8, Act V, Sc I

62   There's not the smallest orb which thou
           beholds't
      But in his motion like an angel sings,
      Still quiring to the young-eyed cherubins;
      Such harmony is in immortal souls;
      But, whilst this muddy vesture of decay
      Doth grossly close it in, we cannot hear it.

      William Shakespeare (1564–1616)
      Ibid

63   For do but note a wild and wanton herd
      Or race of youthful and unhandled colts
      Fetching mad bounds, bellowing and neighing
           loud,
      Which is the hot condition of their blood –
      If they but hear perchance a trumpet sound,
      Or any air of music touch their ears,
      You shall perceive them make a mutual stand,
      Their savage eyes turned to a modest gaze
      By the sweet power of music. Therefore the
           poet
      Did feign that Orpheus drew trees, stones and
           floods,
      Since naught so stockish, hard and full of
           rage
      But more for the time doth change his nature.
      The man that hath no music in himself,
      Nor is not moved by concord of sweet sounds,
      Is fit for treasons, stratagems, and spoils;
      The motions of his spirit are dull as night,
      And his affections dark as Erebus:
      Let no such man be trusted.
      (Lorenzo)

      William Shakespeare (1564–1616)
      Ibid

64   Whom God loveth not, they love not music.

Thomas Morley (*c* 1558–1602)
Madrigals to Five Voyces, 1598

65   The skies, the fountains, every region
      near
      Seemed all one musical cry! I never heard
      So musical a discord, such sweet thunder.
      (Hippolyta)
      William Shakespeare (1564–1616)
      A Midsummer Night's Dream, 1595, Act IV, Sc I

66   Let music sound while he doth make his
      choice;
      Then, if he lose, he makes a swan-like end,
      Fading in music . . . He may win;
      And what is music then? The music is
      Even as the flourish when true subjects bow
      To a new-crowned monarch; such it is
      As are those dulcet sounds in break of day
      That creep into the dreaming bridegroom's ear
      And summon him to marriage.
      (Portia)
      William Shakespeare (1564–1616)
      The Merchant of Venice, 1596–8, Act III, Sc I

67   Be not afeard: the isle is full of
      noises,
      Sounds and sweet airs, that give delight, and
      hurt not.
      Sometimes a thousand twangling instruments
      Will hum about mine ears, and sometime voices
      That, if I then had waked after a long sleep,
      Will make me sleep again; and then, in
      dreaming,
      The clouds methought would open and show
      riches
      Ready to drop upon me, that when I waked
      I cried to dream again.
      (Caliban)
      William Shakespeare (1564–1616)
      The Tempest, 1613, Act III, Sc II

68   This music crept by me upon the waters,
      Allaying both their fury and my passion
      With its sweet air.
      (Ferdinand)
      William Shakespeare (1564–1616)
      Ibid, Act I, Sc II

69   Music to hear, why hear'st thou music
          sadly?
     Sweets with sweets war not, joy delights in
          joy:
     Why lov'st thou that which thou receiv'st not
          gladly,
     Or else receiv'st with pleasure thine annoy?
     If the true concord of well-tuned sounds,
     By unions married, do offend thine ear,
     They do but sweetly chide thee.
     William Shakespeare (1564–1616)
     Sonnet VIII

70   It always seems to me that the right sphere for Shelley's genius was
the sphere of music, not of poetry.
Matthew Arnold (1822–88)
Maurice de Guerin, 1865, note

          71   Music, when soft voices die,
               Vibrates in the memory.
               Percy Bysshe Shelley (1792–1822)
               To–, pub 1824

     72   We–are we not formed, as notes of
               music are,
          For one another, though dissimilar?
          Percy Bysshe Shelley (1792–1822)
          Epipsychidion, 1821

     73   Sounds overflow the listener's brain,
          So sweet, that joy is almost pain.
          Percy Bysshe Shelley (1792–1822)
          Prometheus Unbound, 1820, II ii

74   Just accord all music makes.
Philip Sidney (1554–86)
To the Tune of a Spanish Song

          75   Eftsoons they heard a most melodious
                    sound,
               Of all that mote delight a dainty ear.
               Edmund Spenser (1552?–1599)
               The Faerie Queene, 1589, II

76   Is the sun yet cast out of heaven?
     Is the song yet cast out of man?
     Life that had song for its leaven
     To quicken the blood that ran.

     Algernon Charles Swinburne (1837–1909)
     The Last Oracle

77   There is sweet music here that softer
        falls
     Than petals from blown roses on the grass,
     Or night-dews on still waters between walls
     Of shadowy granite, in a gleaming pass;
     Music that gentlier on the spirit lies,
     Than tired eyelids upon tir'd eyes;
     Music that brings sweet sleep down from the
     blissful skies.

     Alfred, Lord Tennyson (1809–92)
     The Lotus-Eaters, 1833

78   Oh I'm a martyr to music.
(Mrs Organ Morgan)

Dylan Thomas (1914–53)
Under Milk Wood, 1954

79   *Les sanglots longs*
     Des violons
     De l'automne
     Blessent mon coeur
     D'une langueur
     Monotone.
     The long sobbings of the violins of autumn
     wound my heart with monotonous langour.

     Paul Verlaine (1844–96)
     Chanson de l'automne

80   *De la musique avant toute chose . . . De la musique encore et toujours!*
     Music before everything else . . . Music again and forever!

Paul Verlaine (1844–96)
Art poétique, 1874

81   All music is what awakes from you when you are reminded by the instruments,
It is not the violins and the cornets, it is not the oboe nor the beating drum, nor the score of the baritone singer singing his sweet romanza, nor that of the men's chorus, nor that of the women's chorus.
It is nearer and farther than they.

Walt Whitman (1819–91)
A Song for Occupations, 1891–2

82   A quality
Which music sometimes has, being the Art
Which is most nigh to tears and memory.

Oscar Wilde (1854–1900)
The Burden of Itys, 1881

83   Her ivory hands on the ivory keys
Strayed in a fitful fantasy,
Like the silver gleam when the poplar trees
Rustle their pale leaves listlessly.

Oscar Wilde (1854–1900)
In the Gold Room: A Harmony, 1881

84   Hearing often-times
The still, sad music of humanity.

William Wordsworth (1770–1850)
Lines composed a few miles above Tintern Abbey, 1798

84   How thankful we ought to feel that Wordsworth was only a poet and not a musician. Fancy a symphony by Wordsworth! Fancy having to sit it out! And fancy what it would have been if he had written fugues!

Samuel Butler (1835–1902)
Note-Books, pub 1912

86   At the grey round of the hill
Music of a lost kingdom
Runs . . .

W.B. Yeats (1865–1939)
Four Plays for Dancers

16 FROM THE NURSERY

1 The formation of the musical ear depends on early impressions. Infants who are placed within the constant hearing of musical sounds, soon learn to appreciate them, and nurses have the merit of giving the first lessons in melody; for we learn from the lives of eminent composers, that their early fondness for the art may be traced to the ditties of the nursery.

William Gardiner (1770–1853)
The Music of Nature, 1832

2 Little Boy Blue, come blow your horn,
The sheep's in the meadow.
The cow's in the corn.

Nursery rhyme, *c* 1750

3 Little Tommy Tucker
Sings for his supper;
What shall we give him?
White bread and butter.

Anonymous
Tommy Thumb's Pretty Song Book, c 1744

4 Ride a cock-horse to Banbury Cross,
To see a fine lady upon a white horse,
Rings on her fingers and bells on her toes,
And she shall have music wherever she goes.

Nursery rhyme

5 Sing a song of sixpence, a pocket full of rye.
Four and twenty blackbirds baked in a pie.

Nursery rhyme

6 Tom, Tom, the piper's son,
He learned to play when he was young,
But all the tune that he could play
Was 'Over the hills and far away'.

Nursery rhyme, *c* 1650

FORMS AND STYLES

We can find old wine in new vessels and new wine in old. As Konstantin concludes in Chekhov's *The Seagull,* it may not be a question of old or new forms, but rather of writing without thinking of forms at all: a free flowing from the heart.

---

17 STRUCTURES

---

1 I am more and more convinced that music, by its very nature, is something that cannot be poured into a tight and traditional form. It is made up of colours and rhythms.

Claude Debussy (1862–1918)
Letter to J. Durand, 3 September 1907

2 Our composers have run all their concertos into little else than tedious divisions.

Charles Avison (1709–70)
An Essay on Musical Expression, 1752

> 3 Long ago concertos were conversations:
> later they were more of a controversy
> in the course of which the Romantic hero·
> seizes the laurels.
>
> Keith Bosley (1937–)
> *Romantic Piano Concerto*

4 Why on earth didn't I know that one could write a violincello concerto like this? If I had only known, I would have witten one long ago!

Johannes Brahms (1833–97)
After reading the score of Dvořák's cello concerto, quoted in Robertson, *Dvořák,* 1964

5 One can't define form in so many words, but if I was asked I should say that it was nothing more than imparting spiritual unity to one's thought.

Frederick Delius (1862–1934)
Quoted in Fenby, *Delius as I knew him,* 1936

6   Form is something created through a thousand years of exertions by the most outstanding masters, and yet no disciple can ever be too eager to appropriate it. It would be a foolish conceit of badly misunderstood originality if everyone searched and groped around in his own way for something which is already perfected.

Johann Peter Eckermann (1792–1854)
Contributions to Poetry, quoted by Brahms in his commonplace book

7   The overture ought to apprise the spectators of the nature of the action that is to be represented and to form, so to speak, its argument.

Christoph Willibald von Gluck (1714–87)
Dedication to *Alceste*, 1769

8   The sonata was said by a German critic to be intended by the earliest writers to show in the first movement what they could do, in the second what they could feel, and in the last how glad they were to have finished.

Philip H. Goepp
Symphonies and their Meaning, 1897

9   The sonata is an essentially dramatic art form, combining the emotional range and vivid presentation of a full-sized stage drama with the terseness of a short story.

Donald Francis Tovey (1875–1940)
Broadcast talk, 1937

10   How can inspired form in music be scientifically differentiated from empty form?

Eduard Hanslick (1825–1904)
Quoted in Gal, *Johannes Brahms*, 1961

11   To write music is to raise a ladder without a wall to lean it against. There is no scaffolding: the building under construction is held in balance only by the miracle of a kind of internal logic, an innate sense of proportion.

Arthur Honegger (1892–1955)
I am a Composer, 1951

12   One yearns unspeakably for a composer who gives out his pair of honest themes, and then develops them unashamed, and then hangs a brisk coda to them, and then shuts up.

H.L. Mencken (1880–1956)
Huneker in Motley, 1914

13 Masterworks can't be taken apart like watchworks; what happens within them is what happens, that is all; not what a musicologist tells us happens. Meditation more than analysis will take us towards the heart of music, but to reach that heart is paradoxically to kill it.

Ned Rorem (1923–)
The Later Diaries, 1983

14 What gives Sebastian Bach and Mozart a place apart is that these two great expressive composers never sacrificed form to expression. As high as their expression may soar, their musical form remains supreme and all-sufficient.

Camille Saint-Saëns (1835–1921)
Letter, 1907

15 Music is now so foolish that I am amazed. Everything that is wrong is permitted, and no attention is paid to what the old generation wrote as compostion.

Samuel Scheidt (1587–1654)
Quoted in Shapiro, *An Encyclopedia of Quotations about Music*, 1978

16 You cannot expect the Form before the Idea,
For they will come into being together.
(Aron)

Arnold Schoenberg (1874–1951)
Moses und Aron, II

17 In music there is no form without logic, there is no logic without unity.

Arnold Schoenberg (1874–1951)

18 How rich in content and full of significance the language of music is, we see from the repetitions, as well as the *Da capo*, the like of which would be unbearable in works composed in a language of words, but in music are very appropriate and beneficial, for, in order to comprehend it fully, we must hear it twice.

Arthur Schopenhauer (1788–1860)
The World as Will and Idea, 1818

19 Only when the form grows clear to you, will the spirit become so too.

Robert Schumann (1810–56)
Letter to Clara Wieck, 1840

20   With me, the form of each composition is the outcome of the subject.
Bedřich Smetana (1824–84)
Quoted in Cardus, *The Delights of Music,* 1966

21   Rhapsodies . . . are not a very difficult formula, if one can think up enough tunes.
Virgil Thomson (1896–1989)
Modern Music, 1935

22   Form is the balance between tension and relaxation.
Ernst Toch (1887–1964)
Quoted in Machlis, *Introduction to Contemporary Music,* 1963

23   It shows what can still be done with the old forms by somebody who knows how to handle them.
Richard Wagner (1813–83)
On the *Handel Variations* by Brahms

18   SYMPHONY

1   I am not made for the symphony; I need the theatre, I can do nothing without it.
Georges Bizet (1838–75)
Quoted in Dean, *Bizet,* 1975

2   My symphony is long and not exactly amiable.
Johannes Brahms, (1833–97)
On his First Symphony, letter to Carl Reinecke

3   A great symphony is like a man-made Mississippi down which we irresistably flow from the instant of our leave-taking to a long foreseen destination.
Aaron Copland (1900–90)
Quoted in Machlis, *Introduction to Contemporary Music,* 1963

4   Now, it's Sibelius, and when they're tired of him, they'll boost up Mahler and Bruckner.
Frederick Delius (1862–1934)
Quoted in Fenby, *Delius as I knew him,* 1936

5   I frequently compare a symphony or a sonata with a novel in which the themes are the characters. After we have made their acquaintance, we follow their evolution, the unfolding of their psychology. Their individual features linger with us as if present. Some of these characters arouse feelings of sympathy, other repel us. They are set off against one another or they join hands; they make love; they marry or they fight.

Arthur Honegger (1892–1955)
I am a Composer, 1951

6   A symphony must be like the world, it must embrace everything.

Gustav Mahler (1860–1911)
Remark to Sibelius, Helsinki, 1907

7   Only life suffered can transform a symphony from a collection of notes into a message of humanity.

Dimitri Mitropoulos (1896–1960)
February 1954

8   After the symphonies of Beethoven, it was certain that the poetry that lies too deep for words does not lie too deep for music, and that the vicissitudes of the soul, from the roughest form to the loftiest aspiration, can make symphonies without the aid of dance tunes.

George Bernard Shaw (1856–1950)
The Perfect Wagnerite, 1898

9   A symphony is a stage play with the parts written for instruments instead of for actors.

Colin Wilson (1931–   )
Brandy of the Damned, 1964

19   FUGUE

1   *Brander:* For the Amen, a fugue,
               A fugue, a chorale:
               Let's improvise a masterly piece!

   Mephistopheles (to Faust):

               Listen well to this, doctor: we'll see
               Bestiality, naked and unashamed!

Hector Berlioz (1803–69)
The Damnation of Faust, 1846

2   [Counterpoint] is the art of producing a mass of harmony, in which the notes of all the chords are formed by good melodic lines. Of course this ultimately begs the question, because the stern logician then asks us what harmony is. And the only possible answer to that, is that it is, ultimately, good counterpoint.

Donald Francis Tovey (1875–1940)
BBC broadcast talk, 1937

3   Fugue is a texture the rules of which do not suffice to determine the shape of the composition as a whole. Schemes such as that laid down in Cherubini's treatise, which legislate for the shape, are pedagogic fictions.

Donald Francis Tovey (1875–1940)
Musical Articles for the Encyclopaedia Britannica, 1944

> 4   So your fugue broadens and thickens,
>   Greatens and deepens and lengthens,
>   Till one exclaims–'But where's the music,
>   the dickens?'
>
>   Robert Browning (1812–89)
>   *Master Hughes of Saxe-Gotha*, 1855

5   Counterpoint isn't genius, only a means to an end. And it's given me plenty of trouble.

Anton Bruckner, (1824–96)
Letter to Franz Beyer, 1893

6   Counterpoint can be the nastiest thing in music.

Claude Debussy (1862–1918)
Letter to Vasnier, 1885

7   There is an old saying that fugues are the type of music in which the voices come in one by one while the audience goes out one by one, but there is no statistical evidence to support this; audiences have been known to leave in droves.

Antony Hopkins (1921–   )
Downbeat Music Guide, 1977

> 8   His volant touch
>   Instinct through all proportions low and high
>   Fled and pursued transverse the resonant
>   fugue . . .
>
>   John Milton (1608–74)
>   *Paradise Lost*, pub 1667, XI

9   A three-voice fugue . . . resembles a family of identical triplets in perfect agreement, or a madman talking to himself.
Ned Rorem (1923–)
Pure Contraption, 1974

10   There has been demonstration of the universal truth by fugue, and it may be that more wisdom is to be found in that than in the religions and religious books of all the world together.
Sacheverell Sitwell (1897–1988)
Orpheus and His Lyre

---

20   STYLES

---

1   [Of Baroque music:] Muzak for the intelligentsia.
Anonymous, *c* 1970

2   Classic means standard, accepted, long familiar, in the repertory. To me it used to mean: as opposed to Romantic: form before meaning as opposed to meaning before form. It grows from inside out, while Romantic grows from outside in.
Ned Rorem (1923–)
The Later Diaries, 1983

3   I've learnt what 'classical' means. It means something that sings and dances through sheer joy of existence. And if the *Parthenon* is the only building in the world that does so, then there is only one classical building in the world.
Gustav Holst (1874–1934)
Letter to Vaughan Williams, Salonica, March 1919

4   It might not be too dangerous . . . to liken all art of all ages to a 'classic' inhalation after which comes a romantic exhalation, then again the classic inhalation, ad infinitum . . . Art cannot hold its breath too long without dying.
George Antheil (1900–59)
Bad Boy of Music, 1945

5   But all the world understands my language.

Joseph Haydn (1732–1809)
Reply to Mozart, who had tried to dissuade him from visiting England in 1790, citing his ignorance of the language

6   The old romanticism is dead; long live the new!

Arnold Schoenberg (1874–1951)
Quoted in Machlis, *Introduction to Contemporary Music*, 1963

21   PROGRAMME MUSIC

1   There is no such thing as Abstract music; there is good music and bad music. If it is good, it means something; and then it is Programme Music.

Richard Strauss (1864–1949)
Quoted in Shapiro, *An Encyclopedia of Quotations about Music*, 1978

2   I consider that music, by its very nature, is essentially powerless to *express* anything at all, whether a feeling, an attitude of mind, a psychological mood, a phenomenon of nature, etc . . . *Expression* has never been an inherent property of music. That is by no means the purpose of its existence. If, as is nearly always the case, music appears to express something, this is only an illusion, and not a reality.

Igor Stravinsky (1882–1971)
Chroniques de ma vie, 1935

3   Almost the only thing music can represent unambiguously is the cuckoo – and that it can't differentiate from a cuckoo-clock.

Brigid Brophy (1929–   )
A Literary Person's Guide to Opera, 1965

4   Music is, before everything, the language of spiritual generalizations. The more it attempts to communicate concrete facts, the more it sacrifices of its innermost character.

Bernard van Dieren (1884–1936)
Down Among the Dead Men, 1935

5   There never was a more imbecile notion than the twentieth-century cult of Pure Music, for the simple reason that although in one sense all music must be programme music, since it is concerned with human emotions, in another sense music, in so far as it *is* music, can never be anything but pure.

W.H. Mellers (1914–)
The Textual Criticism of Music, 1939

6   If descriptive music is a mistake, let it be: the mistake usually lies in the description only, not in the music.

Sidney Lanier (1842–81)
The Physics of Music, 1875

7   The programme or title in itself contain a germ of feeling or movement, but never a crude description of concrete events.

Carl Nielsen (1865–1931)
Quoted in Simpson, *Carl Nielsen,* 1952

8   The painter turns a poem into a painting: the musician sets a picture to music.

Robert Schumann (1810–56)
Aphorisms, c 1833

9   I always say, 'First of all let me hear that you have made beautiful music; after that I will like your programme too.'

Robert Schumann (1810–56)
Quoted in *Neue Zeitschrift,* 1843

10   Music must progress until it can depict even a teaspoon.

Richard Strauss (1864–1949)
Quoted by Ernest Newman, 1910

22   NATIONALISM

1   Racial consciousness is absolutely necessary in music, even though nationalism is not.

Ernest Bloch (1880–1959)
In *c* 1912, quoted in Ewen, *American Composers,* 1982

2 ... in order to create an indigenous music of universal significance, three conditions are imperative. First, the composer must be part of a nation that has a profile of its own – that is the most important; second, the composer must have in his background some sense of· musical culture and, if possible, a basis in folk or popular art; and third, a superstructure of organized musical activities must exist – to some extent at least – at the service of the native composer.

Aaron Copland (1900–90)
Music and Imagination, 1952

3 The future music of this country [America] must be founded on what are called the Negro melodies.

Antonin Dvořák (1841–1904)
Interview in the *New York Herald*

4 In the Negro melodies of Anmerica I find all that is needed for a great and noble school of music.

Antonin Dvořák (1841–1904)
Interview in the *New York Herald*

5 English music is white and evades everything.

Edward Elgar (1857–1934)
Attributed

6 I want everything to be national: above all, the subject – and the music likewise – so much so that my dear compatriots will feel they are at home, and so that abroad I shall not be considered a braggart or a crow who seeks to deck himself in borrowed plumes.

Mikhail Glinka (1804–57)
Letter, 1832

7 I am searching, with a noble, sensitive and natural melody, and with a form of declamation exactly in accord with the prosody of each language and the character of each people, to establish the means of producing a music belonging to all nations, and to obliterate the ridiculous distinction of national musics.

Christoph Willibald von Gluck (1714–87)
Letter to d'Auvergne, published in *Le Mercure de France,* 1773

8 These people have no ear, either for rhythm or music, and their unnatural passion for piano playing and singing is thus all the more repulsive. Nothing on earth is more terrible than English music, save English painting.

Heinrich Heine (1797–1850)
Lutetia, 1840–3

9   Wagner is Wagner whether writing of Cornwall or Nuremberg. Elgar is Elgar whether writing of Poland or of the Severn Valley. Gounod showed his nationality most clearly in a German subject, Bizet in a Spanish one.

Gustav Holst (1874–1934)
Letter to the *Musical Herald*, 1915

10   Please, no national music! To the devil with all this 'folksiness'! Here I am in Wales . . . and a harper sits in the vestibule of every inn and never stops playing so-called folk-melodies, that is, infamous, common, faked stuff.

Felix Mendelssohn (1809–47)
Letter to Zelter, 1829

11   You will find sobriety and dolour in French music just as in German or Russian. But the French have a keener sense of proportion. We realize that sombreness and good humour are not mutually exclusive. Our composers, too, write profound music, but when they do, it is leavened with that lightness of spirit without which life would be unendurable.

Francis Poulenc (1899–1963)
Quoted in Gelatt, *The Saturday Review of Literature*, 1950

12   African music is primarily rhythmic and physical; Asian is primarily melodic and spiritual; and European music is primarily harmonic and polyphonic, emotional and intellectual. The sum of the physical, the spiritual, the emotional and intellectual, is the whole being of an individual's life. So the sum of world music is the complete music of mankind.

Ronald Stevenson (1928–   )
Western Music, 1971

13   The art of music above all other arts is the expression of the soul of a nation.

Ralph Vaughan Williams (1872–1958)
Quoted in Headington, *The Bodley Head History of Western Music*, 1974

14   I think there is no work of art which represents the spirit of a nation more surely than *Die Meistersinger* of Richard Wagner. Here is no plaything with local colour, but the raising to its highest power all that is best in the national consciousness of his own country. This is universal art in truth, universal because it is so intensely national.

Ralph Vaughan Williams (1872–1958)
National Music, 1932

15   Whereas the Greek work of art expressed the spirit of a splendid nation, the work of art of the future is intended to express the spirit of free people irrespective of all national boundaries; the national element in it must be no more than an ornament, an added individual charm, and not a confining boundary.

Richard Wagner (1813–84)
Art and Revolution, 1849

23   NATIONAL CHARACTERISTICS AND CONTRASTS

1   It is easier to understand a nation by listening to its music than by learning its language.

Anonymous
Quoted in Mencken, *Dictionary of Quotations,* 1942

2   If artists in the North and those in the South have different tendencies, then let them be *different!* They should all preserve the *characteristics proper to their respective nations,* as Wagner so well expressed it. Happy you, to be still the sons of Bach! And we? We too, the sons of Palestrina, once had a great school – of our own! Now it has become bastardized and is in danger of collapsing! If only we could turn back again?!

Giuseppe Verdi (1813–1901)
Letter to Hans von Bülow, 14 April 1892

3   The Germans, who make doctrines out of everything, deal with music learnedly; the Italians, being voluptuous, seek in it lively though fleeting sensations; the French, more vain than perceptive, manage to speak wittily of it; and the English pay for it without meddling.

Stendhal (1783–1842)
Raison, Folie

4   The best way of playing the clavier or any other instrument is that which succeeds in skilfully combining what is neat and brilliant in the French state with what is ingratiating in the Italian way of singing. For this the Germans are particularly well adapted as long as they remain unprejudiced.

Carl Philipp Emanuel Bach (1714–88)
Essay, 1753

5 The Chinese scale, take it which way we will, is certainly very Scottish.

Charles Burney (1726–1814)
In 1789, quoted in Headington, *The Bodley Head History of Western Music*, 1974

6 The Italian style and the French style have for long divided the Republic of Music in France. For my part, I have always valued those works which have merit, without regard for their composer or country of origin.

François Couperin (1668–1733)
Les Goûts réunis, 1724

7 Diverse nations have diverse fashions, and differ in habits, diet, studies, speech and song. Hence it is that the English do carol; the French sing; the Spaniards weep; the Italians, which dwell about the coasts of Ianua, caper with their voices; the others bark; but the Germans (which I am ashamed to utter) do howl like wolves.

John Dowland (1563–1626) trans:
Andreas Ornithoparcus His Micrologus, 1609

8 English music is literary, while American music is painterly.

Morton Feldman (1926–)
Lecture, 29 April 1966

> 9 There was an age, (its memory will
>   last!)
>   Before Italian airs debauched our taste.
>
> Elijah Fenton (1683–1730)
> *An epistle to Mr Southerne, from Kent, January 28, 1710–11*

10 In the opinion of many, Scotland not only equalled Ireland her teacher in music, but has prevailed over and surpassed her, so that they look to Scotland as the fountain of this art.

Giraldus Cambrensis (1146?–1220?)
Topographia Hibernica, c 1185

11 [On Irish music:] The only thing to which I find that this people apply a commendable industry is playing upon musical instruments; in which they are incomparably more skilful than any other nation I have ever seen.

Giraldus Cambrensis (1146?–1220?)
Ibid

12   What the English like is something they can beat time to, something that hits them straight on the drum of the ear.
George Frideric Handel (1685–1759)
Quoted in Schmid, *C.W. von Gluck*, 1854

13   According to Schumann, the world's music is like a great fugue in which the various nations sound alternatively.
Zoltán Kodály (1882–1967)
Address, 1956

14   The Italians exalt music; the French enliven it; the Germans strive after it; and the English pay for it well. The Italians serve music; the French make it into a companion; the Germans anatomize it, and the English compel it to serve them.
Johann Mattheson (1681–1764)
Das Neu-eröffnete Orchester, 1713

15   One must acknowledge that the accents of passion are very often lacking in French airs, because our songs are content to tickle the ear with ornamentation without concerning themselves with the excitation of passion in their listeners.
Marin Mersenne (1588–1648)
Harmonie universelle, 1636

16   If only the accursed French language were not so villainous with *musique*! – It is a misery – even German is divine beside it. And when it comes to the singers and songstresses – they ought never to be called that – for they do not sing, but shriek, howl, and that full-throatedly, through nose and gullet.
Wolfgang Amadeus Mozart (1756–91)
Letter, 1778

17   And show that music may have as good a
        fate
     In Albion's Glen as Umbria's green retreat,
     And with Corelli's soft Italian song,
     Mix 'Cowdenknowes' and 'Winter nights are long'.
     Allan Ramsay (1685?–1758)
     To the Music Club, 1721
     [Albion=Scotland]

18   I believe that I have demonstrated that there is neither rhythm nor
melody in French music . . . that French singing is endless squawking,
unbearable to the unbiased ear . . . And so I deduce that the French
have no music and cannot have any music – and if they ever have, more's
the pity for them.

Jean-Jacques Rousseau (1712–78)
Lettre sur la musique française, 1753

19   It is the accent of languages that determines the melody of each
nation.

Jean-Jacques Rousseau (1712–78)
Dictionnaire de musique, 1767

20   Our music differs from German music. Their symphonies can live
in halls; their chamber music can live in the home. Our music, I say,
resides principally in the theatre.

Giuseppe Verdi (1813–1901)
Letter to Piroli, 1883

21   Much English music has the insipid flavour of the BBC Variety
Orchestra playing an arrangement of a nursery tune.

Colin Wilson (1931–   )
Brandy of the Damned, 1964

24 SERIALISM

See also 115 Schoenberg

1   I do not compose principles, but music.

Arnold Schoenberg (1874–1951)
Quoted in MacDonald, *Schoenberg,* 1976

2   The twelve-toners behave as if music should be seen and not heard.

Ned Rorem (1923–   )
Paris Diary, 1966

3   To find the composer of the *Gurrelieder* fathering such theories is as
disconcerting as to discover Einstein telling fortunes in Bond Street.

Donald Francis Tovey (1875–1940)
Musical Articles for the Encyclopaedia Britannica, 1944

4   The introduction of my method of composing with twelve notes does not facilitate composing; on the contrary, it makes it more difficult.

Arnold Schoenberg (1874–1951)
Style and Idea, 1950, trans Newlin

5   There is little probability that the twelve-note scale will ever produce anything more than morbid or entirely cerebral growths. It might deal successfully with neuroses of various kinds, but I cannot imagine it associated with any healthy and happy concept such as young love or the coming of spring.

Arnold Bax (1883–1953)
Music and Letters, 1951

6   Twelve-note technique . . . does not allow me to work swiftly.

Alban Berg (1885–1935)
Letter to Schoenberg, 1930

7   With it [twelve-note music], music moved out of the world of Newton and into the world of Einstein. The tonal idea was based on a universe defined by gravity and attraction. The serial idea is based on a universe that finds itself in perpetual expansion.

Pierre Boulez (1925–   )
Quoted in Peyser, *Boulez*, 1976

8   [Of twelve-note music:] I can see it taking no part in the music-lover's music-making.

Benjamin Britten (1913–76)
Quoted in Headington, *Britten*, 1981

9   Dodecaphony's mechanistic heresy.

Hans Werner Henze (1926–   )
Music and Politics, 1982, 'German Music in the 1940s and 1950s'

10   To limit oneself to home-made tonal systems of this sort seems to me a more doctrinaire proceeding than to follow the strictest diatonic rules of the most dried-up old academic.

Paul Hindemith (1895–1963)
The Craft of Musical Composition, 1937

11   To my knowledge I am the only composer of my generation who has thoroughly and consistently practiced what is called 'serialism', and I have been blamed (a) for doing it all, (b) for doing it too late, and (c) for still being at it.

Ernst Krenek (1900–   )
Horizons Circled, 1974

12 The twelve-tone school tried to revive the spirit of the old forms, while neo-classicism presented replicas of their façades with interesting cracks added.
Ernst Krenek (1900–)
Ibid

13 Serial music is doomed to the same fate as all previous music: at birth it already harboured the seeds of its own dissolution.
György Ligeti (1923–)

14 Once, in the course of a long conversation with Schoenberg, I told him of my opinion that the twelve-note method had been over-publicized and in the process itself as well as in the controversy which resulted, had become greatly distorted in the minds of many people; and that this had led to strained and artificial attitudes towards the music itself. He replied, somewhat glumly, 'Yes, you are right, and I have to admit that it's partly my fault.' After a pause he recovered his animation and added, 'But it's still more the fault of some of my disciples.'
Roger Sessions (1896–)
Quoted in MacDonald, *Schoenberg*, 1976

25 'MODERN' MUSIC

See also 9 Discord

1 If we look around in modern music we will find that we have a terrible deal of mind and astonishingly few ideas.
August Wilhelm Ambros (1816–76)
Culturhistorische Bilder aus dem Musikleben der Gegenwart, 1860

2 Wee also have Sound-houses, where wee practise and demonstrate all Sounds, and their Generation. Wee have harmonies which you have not, of Quarter Sounds, and lesser Slides of Sounds. Diverse instruments of Musick likewise to you unknowne, some sweeter than you have; together with Bells and Rings that are dainty and sweet. Wee represent Small Sounds as well as Great and Deepe; likewise Great Sounds, Extenuate and Sharpe; wee make diverse Tremblings and Warblings of Sounds, which in their Originalle are Entire. Wee represent and imitate all Articulate Sounds and Letters and the Voices and Notes of Beasts and Birds. Wee have certain Helps, which sett to the Eare doe further the Hearing greatly . . . Wee also have means to convey Sounds in Trunks and Pipes, in strange Lines, and Distances.
Francis Bacon (1561–1626)
The New Atlantis, 1626

3   I have never been able to go along with all this accoustic research, this technological and electronic hunt for new sounds, which is undertaken in the new laboratories. I do not have the impression that any useful advances have come to light.
Hans Werner Henze (1926–)
Music and Politics, 1982, 'German Music in the 1940s and 1950s'

4   [Of modern music:] Three farts and a raspberry, orchestrated.
John Barbirolli (1899–1970)
Quoted in Kennedy, *Barbirolli, Conductor Laureate*, 1971

5   Art demands of us that we shall not stand still.
Ludwig van Beethoven (1770–1827)
Quoted in Scott, *Beethoven*, 1934

6   Music was chaste and modest so long as it was played on simpler instruments, but since it has come to be played in a variety of manners and confusedly, it has lost the mode of gravity and virtue and fallen almost to baseness.
Boethius (Anicius Manlius Severinus, *c* 485–524)
De Consolatione Philosophiae

7   We look for new sonorities, new intervals, new forms. Where it will lead, I don't know. I don't want to know. It would be like knowing the date of my death.
Pierre Boulez (1925–)

8   If this word 'music' is sacred and reserved for eighteenth- and nineteenth-century instruments, we can substitute a more meaningful term: organization of sound.
John Cage (1912–)
Silence, 1961, 'The Future of Music: Credo', 1937

9   I believe that the use of noise to make music will continue and increase until we reach a music produced through the aid of electrical instruments
John Cage (1912–)
Ibid

10   The resources of sonority are still largely unexplored.
Charles Gounod (1818–93)
Letter to Saint-Saëns

11   The public doesn't want new music; the main thing that it demands of a composer is that he be dead.

Arthur Honegger (1892–1955)
I am a Composer, 1951

12   Music was originally discreet, seemly, simple, masculine, and of good morals. Have not the moderns rendered it lascivious beyond measure?

Jacob of Liège (*c* 1425)

13   Modern music is as dangerous as cocaine.

Pietro Mascagni (1863–1945)
Interview, Berlin, December 1927

14   In poetry there are two giants: coarse Homer and refined Shakespeare. In music there are two giants: the thinker Beethoven, and the super-thinker Berlioz. When around the four we gather all their generals and aides-de-camp, we have a pleasant company; but what has this company of subalterns achieved? Skipping and dancing along in the paths marked out by the giants – but to dare to 'go very far ahead', this is terrifying!

Modest Mussorgsky (1839–81)
Letter to V.V. Stasov, 1872

15   What we know as modern music is the noise made by deluded speculators picking through the slagpile.

Henry Pleasants (1910–   )
The Agony of Modern Music, 1955

16   [Of the late quartets of Beethoven:] The polluted source from which have sprung the evil musicians of modern Germany, the Liszts, Wagners, Schumanns, not to mention Mendelssohn in certain equivocal details of his style.

Pierre Scudo (1806–64)
In 1862, quoted in Dean, *Bizet*, 1975

17   The key to the understanding of contemporary music lies in repeated hearing: one must hear it till it sounds familiar.

Roger Sessions (1896–   )
The Musical Experience, 1950

18   To me, working with electronic music is composing with living sounds . . . I think of musical space as open rather than bounded.

Edgar Varèse (1883–1965)
Quoted in Schuller, *Perspectives of New Music*, 1965

CREATION

The imaginative faculty that finds out musical tunes, gives them form, further development and variation, is motivated either by the innermost depths or by crass commercialism. The roots of creation can be quietly hinted at in plain words, or revealed in flights of sublime reflection.

26 CREATIVITY

1   Let us now praise famous men, and our fathers that begat us . . . Such as found out musical tunes, and recited verses in writing: Rich men furnished with ability, living peaceably in their habitations.

Apocrypha
Ecclesiasticus, Ch 44, vv 1–5

2   The men on the heights, with clean brains and full hearts, are worthy of our admiration whether they ask us to laugh with them, or meditate with them and share their melancholy.

Bernard van Dieren (1884–1936)
Down Amoung the Dead Men, 1935

3   There are composers who write difficult music with ease, and others who write a facile music with difficulty.

Georges Auric (1899–1983)
Quoted in Honneger, *I am a Composer*, 1951

4   There is no real creating without hard work. That which you would call invention–that is to say, a thought, an idea–is simply an inspiration for which I am not responsible, which is no merit of mine. It is a present, a gift, which I ought even to despise until I have made it my own by dint of hard work.

Johannes Brahms (1833–97)
Quoted in Gal, *Johannes Brahms*, 1961

5   Transcription occupies an important place in the literature of the piano, and looked at from the right point of view, every important piece is the reduction of a big thought to a practical instrument.

Ferruccio Busoni (1866–1924)
Letter to his wife, 1913

6   All great artists are innovators.

Pablo Casals (1876–1973)
Lloyd Webber (ed), *Song of the Birds*, 1985

7   Let us not forget that the greatest composers were also the greatest thieves. They stole from everyone and everywhere.

Pablo Casals (1876–1973)
Ibid

8   Ah, it's a pretty trade we're in! I'm writing piano pieces for four hands. Why do I do it? you ask. How in hell should I know, my poor d'Estaleuse! It's stupidity, of course – my publisher won't even take them. One will be too long – never too short, you'll observe; another too difficult – never too easy; and none of them *practical*!

Emmanuel Chabrier (1841–94)
Letter, 1884

9   The sense of musical delight, with the power of producing it, is a gift of the imagination.

Samuel Taylor Coleridge (1772–1834)
Quoted in Shapiro, *An Encyclopedia of Quotations about Music*, 1978

10   There is only one real happiness in life, and that is the happiness of creating.

Frederick Delius (1862–1934)
Quoted in Fenby, *Delius as I knew him*, 1936

11   Composed it on the spot – Mars by day, Apollo by night – bang the fieldpiece, twang the lyre.

Charles Dickens (1812–70)
Pickwick Papers, 1836

12   I should like to see every man tinkering with every other man's art; what kaleidoscopic multitudinous results we should see!

Percy Grainger (1882–1961)
From *Grainger Journal*, Vol IV, No 1, October 1981, letter to the Scottish music critic D.C. Parker, 23 August 1916

13   There are only twelve notes. You must treat them carefully.
Paul Hindemith (1895–1963)

14   The musician – that is, he who develops music to clear, distinct consciousness – is everywhere surrounded by melody and harmony. It is not an empty simile and not an allegory when musicians say that colours, scents, and beams appear to them as tones, and that musicians are aware of their intermingling as in a wonderful concert.
E.T.A. Hoffman (1776–1822)
Kreisleriana, 1814

15   Never compose anything unless the not composing of it becomes a positive nuisance to you.
Gustav Holst (1874–1934)
Letter to W.G. Whittaker, 1921

16   There are *too many* composers whose names begin with B. Bach, Beethoven, Brahms – Bax, Bliss, BRITTEN, Bantock, Bartók, Bush, Busch – and others I don't at the moment recall.
John Ireland (1879–1962)
Letter to Geoffrey Bush, 1942

17   Composers must not be characterized. We must not take Beethoven and Mozart and stick a pin through each one like so many bugs and butterflies in a glass case, and say this one Beethoven belongs to the class of the big beetles *(Coleopters gigans)* and Mozart to the class of butterflies(–!). If we do, the composers will become as dry and dusty as an entomologist's collection.
Sidney Lanier (1842–81)
Notes and Fragments

18   The good composer is slowly discovered; the bad composer is slowly found out.
Ernest Newman (1868–1959)
Attributed

19   To produce music is also in a sense to produce children.
Friedrich Nietzsche (1844–1900)
The Will to Power, 1888

20   We are the music makers,
We are the dreamers of dreams,
Wandering by lone sea-breakers,
And sitting by desolate streams; –
World-losers and world-forsakers,
On whom the pale moon gleams;
We are the movers and shakers
Of the world for ever, it seems.

Arthur O'Shaughnessy (1844–81)
Ode, 1974

21   The divine inspiration of music, poetry, and painting do not arrive at perfection by degrees, like the other sciences, but by starts, and like flashes of lightning, one here, another there, appear in various lands, then suddenly vanish.

Pierre de Ronsard (1524–85)
Dedication to *Livre des mélanges*, 1560

22   Nothing primes inspiration more than necessity, whether it be the presence of a copyist waiting for your work or the prodding of an impresario tearing his hair. In my time, all the impresarios in Italy were bald at thirty.

I composed the overture to *Otello* in a little room in the Barbaja palace wherein the baldest and fiercest of directors had forcibly locked me with a lone plate of spaghetti and the threat that I would not be allowed to leave the room alive until I had written the last note.

I wrote the overture to *La Gazza Ladra* the day of its opening in the theatre itself, where I was imprisoned by the director and under the surveillance of four stagehands who were instructed to throw my original text through the window, page by page, to the copyists waiting below to transcribe it. In default of pages, they were ordered to throw me out of the window bodily.

I did better with *The Barber*. I did not compose an overture, but selected for it one which was meant for a semi-serious opera called *Elisabetta*. The public was completely satisfied.

I composed the overture to *Comte Ory* while fishing, with my feet in the water, and in the company of Signor Agnado who talked of Spanish finance. The overture for *William Tell* was composed under more or less similar circumstances. And as for *Mosé*, I did not write one.

Gioachino Rossini (1792–1868)
To an unknown correspondent

23   The composer reveals the innermost being of the world and expresses the deepest wisdom in a language which his own reason does not understand; like a somnambulist, who tells things of which he has no clear knowledge in his waking state. This is the reason why, in a composer more than in any other artist, man and artist are quite separate and distinct.

Arthur Schopenhauer (1788–1860)
The World as Will and Idea, 1818

24   The fact is there are no rules, and there never were any rules, and there never will be any rules of musical composition except rules of thumb, and thumbs vary in length, like ears.

George Bernard Shaw (1856–1950)
Music in London, 1890–4

25   [On being asked how he composed:] Sitting down.

Píotr Ilyich Tchaikovsky (1840–93)
Attributed

26   The unconscious is the womb of all musical creation; all master-pieces are born there.

Alan Walker (1930–   )
An Anatomy of Musical Criticism, 1968

---

27   COMPOSERS ON MUSIC

---

1   I have always believed that I need a circumference of silence. As to what happens when I compose, I really haven't the faintest idea.

Samuel Barber (1910–81)
Quoted in Ewen, *American Composers,* 1982

2   In maintaining that the question of the origin of a theme is completely unimportant from the artist's point of view, Stravinsky is right. The question of origins can only be interesting from the point of view of musical documentation.

Béla Bartók (1881–1945)
Melos, 1920

3   Beethoven can write music, thank God – but he can do nothing else on earth.

Ludwig van Beethoven (1770–1827)
Letter to Ferdinand Ries, 20 December 1822

4   I am not in the habit of altering my compositions once they are finished. I have never done this, for I hold firmly that the slightest change alters the character of the composition.
Ludwig van Beethoven (1770–1827)
Letter, 1813

5   Instrumentation is, in music, the exact equivalent of colour in painting.
Hector Berlioz (1803–69)
A travers chants, 1862

6   In art . . . as in letters, what makes success is talent, and not ideas . . . The public understands the idea *later*. To achieve this *later*, the artist's talent must manifest itself in an agreeable form and so ease the road for the public, not repel it from the outset. Thus Auber, who had so much talent and few ideas, was almost always understood, while Berlioz, who had genius but no talent at all, was almost never understood.
Georges Bizet (1838–75)
Letter, 1871

7   To the devil with all those who have seen in our sublime art nothing but an innocent tickling of the ear.
Georges Bizet (1838–75)
Letter to A. Marmontel, 1857

8   Words created divergencies between beings, because their precise meanings put an opinion around the idea. Music only retains the highest and purest substance of the idea, since it has the privilege of expressing all, whilst excluding nothing.
Nadia Boulanger (1887–1979)
In 1920, quoted in Kendall, *The Tender Tyrant: Nadia Boulanger*, 1976

9   I do not easily think in words, because words are not my medium . . . I also have a very real dread of becoming one of those artists who *talk*. I believe so strongly that it is dangerous for artists to *talk*.
Benjamin Britten (1913–76)
Speech of acceptance of an Honorary Doctorate at Hull University, 1962

10   Music was born free, and to win freedom is its destiny.
Ferruccio Busoni (1866–1924)
Sketch of a New Aesthetic of Music, trans 1911

11   I prophesy that in music melody will triumph over all other compositional techniques: universal polyphony as the end-product of melodic writing, the mother of harmony, and bearer of the idea.
Ferruccio Busoni (1866–1924)
Conclusion to his edition of *The Well-Tempered Clavier*, 1915

12   New Music, new listening. Not an attempt to understand something that is being said, for, if something were being said, the sounds would be given in the shapes of words. Just an attention to the activity of sounds.
John Cage (1912–   )
Silence, 1961

13   A composer knows his work as a woodsman knows a path he has traced and retraced, while a listener is confronted by the same work as one is in the woods by a plant he has never seen before.
John Cage (1912–   )
Ibid, 'Experimental Music', 1957

14   And what is the purpose of writing music? . . . simply a way to wake up to the very life we're living, which is so excellent once one gets one's mind and one's desires out of its way and lets it act of its own accord.
John Cage (1912–   )
Ibid

15   It is better to make a piece of music than to perform one, better to perform one than to listen to one, better to listen to one than to misuse it as a means of distraction, entertainment, or acquisition of 'culture'.
John Cage (1912–   )
Ibid

16   Music is in a continual state of becoming.
Aaron Copland (1900–90)
Music and Imagination, 1952

17   It is a revelation, a thing to be reverenced. Performances of a great musical work are for us what the rites and festivals of religion were to the ancients – an initiation into the mysteries of the human soul.
Frederick Delius (1862–1934)
Letter to Philip Heseltine, 27 May 1917

18   Only this much is certain, that as no mother bears children to see them blown to rags or choked in poison gas, so no composer plans his works for the monstrous fate of falling into the conventional concert programme, to hang there like a dead soldier's body on barbed wire.
Bernard van Dieren (1884–1936)
Down among the Dead Men, 1935

19   All the worst things happen in the best works, and the worst music appears to be streaked all through with the most luscious bits.
Bernard van Dieren (1884–1936)
Ibid

20   Is it not in music, and in music alone that the secret of music must be sought?
Paul Dukas (1865–1935)
Attributed

21   I have a mistress. Lovers have come and gone, but only my mistress stays. She is beautiful and gentle. . . She is a swinger. She has grace. To hear her speak, you can't believe your ears. She is ten thousand years old. She is as modern as tomorrow, a brand-new woman every day, and as endless as time mathematics. Living with her is a labyrinth of ramifications. I look forward to her every gesture.
   Music is my mistress, and she plays second fiddle to none.
Duke Ellington (1899—1974)
Music Is My Mistress, 1973

22   If you are going to have a big foot in the future, you've got to have a big foot in the past.
Lukas Foss (1922–   )
Quoted in Ewen, *American Composers*, 1982

23   Composing is like making love to the future.
Lukas Foss (1922–   )
New York Post, 18 October 1975

24   Not many composers have ideas. Far more of them know how to use strange instruments which do not require ideas.
George Gershwin (1898–1937)
The Composer in the Machine Age, 1930

25   It is proportion that beautifies everything, this whole Universe consists of it, and Musicke is measured by it.
Orlando Gibbons (1583–1625)
First Set of Madrigals, 1612

26   There is no musical rule that I have not willingly sacrificed to dramatic effect.
Christoph Willibald von Gluck (1714–87)
Alceste, 1767, Preface

27   Salvation Army Booth objected to the devil having all the good tunes. I object to jazz and vaudeville having all the best instruments!

Percy Grainger (1882–1961)
Spoon River, 1930, Preface

28   The greatest music is begotten through the unison of pure fantasy and mathematics.

Cecil Gray (1891–1951)
Notebooks, 1989, Pauline Gray (ed)

29   Woe to the artist enslaved by rules who does not dare yield to the flight of his genius. There must be deviations from the rules in order to express almost anything. One must know how to describe the same man who leaves by the door and the madman who jumps out the window. . . However, only the man who is familiar with the rules may sometimes violate them, for he alone can know that, in certain cases, the rule is not enough.

André Ernest Grétry (1741–1813)

30   I am sure my music has a taste of codfish in it.

Edvard Grieg (1843–1907)
Speech, 1903

31   Musical ideas pursue me to the point of torture. I cannot get rid of them, they stand before me like a wall. If it is an *allegro* that pursues me, my pulse beats faster, I cannot sleep; if an *adagio*, I find my pulse beating slowly. My imagination plays upon me as if I were a keyboard.

Joseph Haydn (1732–1809)
In old age, quoted in Dies, *Biographische Nachrichten über Joseph Haydn*, 1810

32   There is no such thing as an unmusical person.

Hans Werner Henze (1926–   )
Music and Politics, 1982, 'Does Music have to be Political?', 1969

33   Each new piece is the first you have ever written.

Hans Werner Henze (1926–   )
Ibid, 'Music as a Means of Resistance', 1963

34   Music . . . is as far from being abstract as is a language, a death, a love. The mere fact that it is endlessly invented, wrested from the material, that through it something is snatched from fleeting time as it rushes by, that something is preserved, that in the concretization of time a longing is expressed and fulfilled – all this prohibits the use of the word 'abstract'.

Hans Werner Henze (1926–   )
Ibid, 'Signs', 1955

35   My profession . . . consists of bringing truths nearer to the point where they explode.

Hans Werner Henze (1926–   )
Ibid, 'German Music in the 1940s and 1950s'

36   A true musician believes only what he hears.

Paul Hindemith (1895–1963)
The Craft of Musical Composition, 1937

37   Is not music the mysterious language of a distant realm of spirits, whose lovely sounds re-echo in our soul and awaken a higher, because more intensive, life? All the passions, arrayed in shining and resplendent armour, vie with each other, and ultimately merge in an indescribable longing that fills our breasts. This is the heavenly effect of instrumental music.

E.T.A. Hoffmann (1776–1822)
The Poet and the Composer, 1816

38   When I'm composing, I feel just like a mathematician.

Gustav Holst (1874–1934)
Quoted in Imogen Holst, *Holst*, 1974

39   The modern composer is a madman who persists in manufacturing an article which nobody wants.

Arthur Honegger (1892–1955)
I am a Composer, 1951

40   Composing is not a profession. It is a mania – a harmless madness.

Arthur Honegger (1892–1955)
Ibid

41   The composer, as in old China, joins Heaven and Earth with threads of sounds.

Alan Hovhaness (1911–   )
Quoted in Shapiro, *An Encyclopedia of Quotations about Music*, 1978

42   I have sat through an Italian opera, till, for sheer pain, and inexplicable anguish, I have rushed out into the noisiest places of the crowded streets, to solace myself with sounds which I was not obliged to follow, and get rid of the distracting torment of endless, fruitless, barren attention!

Charles Lamb (1775–1834)
Essays of Elia, 1820–3, 'A Chapter on Ears'

43   Mine was the kind of piece in which nobody knew what was going on – including the composer, the conductor and the critics. Consequently I got pretty good notices.
Oscar Levant (1906–72)
A Smattering of Ignorance, 1940

44   I don't like my music, but what is my opinion against that of millions of others.
Frederick Loewe (1901–   )
Attributed

45   Tradition is *Schlamperei*.
Gustav Mahler (1860–1911)
Attributed

46   We do not compose – we are composed.
Gustav Mahler (1860–1911)
Attributed

47   What is best in music is not to be found in the notes.
Gustav Mahler (1860–1911)
Attributed

48   There is so much talk about music and yet so little is said. For my part, I believe that words do not suffice for such a purpose, and if I found they did suffice I would finally have nothing more to do with music. People often complain that music is too ambiguous, that what they should be thinking as they hear it is unclear, whereas everyone understands words. With me it is exactly the reverse, and not only with regard to an entire speech, but also with individual words. These too, seem to me so ambiguous, so vague, so easily misunderstood in comparison to genuine music which fills the soul with a thousand things better than words.
Felix Mendelssohn (1809–47)
Letter to Marc-André Souchay, 1842

49   I have no aesthetic rules, or philosophy, or theories. I love to write music. I always do it with pleasure, otherwise I just do not write it.
Darius Milhaud (1892–1974)
Quoted in Copland, *Darius Milhaud*, 1947

50   Nevertheless, the passions, whether violent or not, should never be so expressed as to reach the point of causing disgust; and music, even in situations of the greatest horror, should never be painful to the ear but should flatter and charm it, and thereby always remain music.
Wolfgang Amadeus Mozart (1756–91)
Letter to his father, 1781

51   [Of his *Sinfonia semplice:*] Each instrument is like a person who sleeps, whom I have to wake to life.

Carl Nielsen (1865–1931)
Quoted in Simpson, *Carl Nielsen*, 1952

52   It is the duty of the composer, like the poet, the sculptor or the painter, to serve his fellow men, to beautify human life and point the way to a radiant future. Such is the immutable code of art as I see it.

Sergei Prokofiev (1891–1953)
Quoted in Samuel, *Prokofiev*, trans 1971

53   Music is yet in its nonage, a forward child which gives hope of what he may be hereafter in England when the masters of it shall find more encouragement. It is now learning Italian, which is its best master, and studying a little of the French air, to give it somewhat more of gaiety and fashion.

Henry Purcell (1659–95)

54   While composing music is not the time to recall the rules which might hold our genius in bondage. We must have recourse to the rules only when our genius and our ear seem to deny what we are seeking.

Jean Philippe Rameau (1683–1764)
Le Nouveau Système de musique théorique, 1726

55   In music the ear obeys only nature. It takes account of neither measure nor range. Instinct alone leads it.

Jean Philippe Rameau (1683–1764)
Observations sur notre instinct pour la musique, 1734

56   The composer who stumbles in taking a step forward is worth more attention than the composer who shows us how easily he can step backwards.

Ernest Reyer (1823–1909)
In 1872, quoted in Dean, *Bizet*, 1975

57   If music could be translated into human speech, it would no longer need to exist.

Ned Rorem (1923–)
Music from Inside Out, 1967

58   Composition is notation of distortion of what composers think they've heard before. Masterpieces are marvellous misquotations.

Ned Rorem (1923–)
Paris Diary, 1966

59   To see itself through, music must have idea or magic. The best has both. Music with neither dies young, though sometimes rich.

Ned Rorem (1923–   )
Pure Contraption, 1974

60   It is *conscious* plagiarism that demonstrates invention: we are so taken with what someone else did that we set out to do likewise. Yet prospects of shameful exposure are such that we disguise to a point of opposition; then the song becomes ours. No one suspects. It's *unconscious* stealing that's dangerous.

Ned Rorem (1923–   )
Paris Diary, 1966

61   Music is a sublime art precisely because, unable to imitate reality, it rises above ordinary nature into an ideal world, and with celestial harmony moves the earthly passions.

Giaochino Rossini (1792–1868)
Quoted in Zanolini, *Biografia di Gioachino Rossini*, 1875

62   The language of music is common to all generations and nations; it is understood by everybody, since it is understood with the heart.

Giaochino Rossini (1792–1868)
Ibid

63   Delight must be the basis and aim of this art. Simple melody–clear rhythm!

Giaochino Rossini (1792–1868)
Letter, 1868

64   Music that does not surge is not great music.

Carl Ruggles (1876–1971)
Quoted in Wilson, *Brandy of the Damned*, 1964

65   When I don't like a piece of music, I make a point of listening to it more closely.

Florent Schmitt (1870–1958)
Attributed

66   The belief in technique as the only means of salvation must be suppressed, the striving toward truth furthered.

Arnold Schoenberg (1874–1951)
Problems of Art Instruction, 1911

67   If it is art it is not for all, and if it is for all it is not art.

Arnold Schoenberg (1874–1951)
Attributed

68   Emotion is specific, individual, and conscious; music goes deeper than this, to the energies which animate our psychic life, and out of these creates a pattern which has an existence, laws, and human significance of its own. It reproduces for us the most intimate essence, the tempo and the energy, of our spiritual being; our tranquillity and our restlessness, our animation and our discouragement, our vitality and our weakness — all, in fact, of the fine shades of dynamic variation of our inner life. It reproduces these far more directly and more specifically than is possible through any other medium of human communication.

Roger Sessions (1896–1985)
The Composer and his Message, 1941

69   What I'd like best of all, time and again, would be to set myself to music.

Richard Strauss (1864–1949)
Letter to Hugo von Hoffmannsthal, 12 July 1927

70   What is an inspiration? In general, a musical inspiration is known as a motive, a melody with which I am suddenly 'inspired', unbidden by the intelligence, particularly in the morning immediately on awakening, or in a dream — Sachs in the *Meistersinger*: 'Glaubt mir, des Menschen wahrster Wahn wird ihm im Träume aufgetan.' Did my imagination work independently at night, without my consciousness, without being bound to recollection (Plato)? . . . When at night I am stuck at a certain point in my composition . . . I shut the piano on my sketchbook, go to bed, and when I wake up in the morning, the continuation is there. By means of which mental or physical process?

Richard Strauss (1864–1949)
On Inspiration in Music, 1940

71   The one true comment on a piece of music is another piece of music.

Igor Stravinsky (1882–1971)
Quoted in the *New York Review of Books*, 12 May 1966

72   A good composer does not initiate, he steals.

Igor Stravinsky (1882–1971)
Quoted in Yates, *Twentieth Century Music*, 1967

73   Oh, how difficult it is to make anyone see and feel in music what we see and feel ourselves!

Píotr Ilyich Tchaikovsky (1840–93)
Letter to Nadezhda von Meck, 1878

74   Music is not illusion, but revelation rather. Its triumphant power resides in the fact that it reveals to us beauties we find nowhere else, and that the apprehension of them is not transitory, but a perpetual reconcilement to life.
Píotr Ilyich Tchaikovsky (1840–93)
Quoted in Shapiro, *An Encyclopedia of Quotations about Music,* 1978

75   I compose at the piano and like to feel involved in my work with my hands.
Michael Tippett (1905–   )
Quoted in Schafer, *British Composers in Interview,* 1963

76   There is no avant-garde: only some people a bit behind.
Edgar Varèse (1883–1965)
Attributed

77   Music which should pulsate with life, needs new means of expression, and science alone can infuse it with youthful vigour.
Edgar Varèse (1883–1965)
In 1917, trans Louise Varèse

78   Music is antiquated in the extreme in its medium of expression compared with the other arts. We are waiting for a new notation–a new Guido d'Arezzo–when music will move forward at a bound.
Edgar Varèse (1883–1965)
Quoted in Ewen, *American Composers,* 1982

79   The great men of music close periods; they do not inaugurate them. The pioneer work, the finding of new paths, is left to smaller men.
Ralph Vaughan Williams (1872–1958)
National Music, 1934

80   In the matter of music, and works dealing with music, I have no faith in my own judgment any more than in that of others. Think of the views expressed by Weber, Schumann or Mendelssohn concerning Rossini, Meyerbeer and others, and tell me whether there is any reason to believe in a composer's opinion.
Giuseppe Verdi (1813–1901)
Letter, 1883

81   The language of tones belongs equally to all mankind, and melody is the absolute language in which the musician speaks to every heart.
Richard Wagner (1813–83)
Beethoven, 1870

82   Your ears will always lead you correctly, but you must know why.
Anton von Webern (1883–1945)
Attributed

28 IMPROVISATION

1   It's extraordinary how much gipsy music is like modern counter-point; everyone plays what he likes, but it all comes out together and it sounds all right.
Antonin Dvořák (1841–1904)
Quoted in Robertson, *Dvořák*, 1964

2   Music can never be an abstraction, however thoughtful and objectless – for its object is the living man in time – nor can it be accidental, however improvised . . . because improvisation is not the expression of accident but rather of the accumulated yearnings, dreams and wisdom of our very soul.
Yehudi Menuhin (1916–   )
Theme and Variations, 1972

3   You are welcome home, Mr Dubourg.
George Frideric Handel (1685–1759)
To a violinist who had improvised through a complex series of keys and finally ended in the tonic, quoted in Young, *Handel*, 1947

29 INSPIRATION AND TECHNIQUE

1   You will ask where my ideas come from. I cannot say for certain. They come uncalled, sometimes independently, sometimes in association with other things. It seems to me that I could wrest them from Nature herself with my own hands, as I go walking in the woods. They come to me in the silence of the night or in the early morning, stirred into being by moods which the poet would translate into words, but which I put into sounds; and these go through my head ringing and singing and storming until at last I have them before me as notes.
Ludwig van Beethoven (1770–1827)
Letter to Louis Schlösser, 1823

2   Without craftsmanship, inspiration is a mere reed shaken in the wind.
Johannes Brahms (1833–97)
Quoted in Hopkins, *Music all around me*, 1967

3   Consider it well: each tone of our scale
       in itself is nought;
    It is everywhere in the world—loud,
       soft, and all is said:
    Give it to me to use! I mix it with two
       in my thought:
    And, there! Ye have heard and seen:
       consider and bow the head!
    Robert Browning (1812–89)
    Abt Vogler, 1864

4   Notation, the writing out of compositions, is primarily an ingenious
expedient for catching an inspiration, with the purpose of exploiting it
later. But notation is to improvisation as the portrait to the living model.
It is for the interpreter to resolve the rigidity of the signs into the
primitive emotion.
Ferruccio Busoni (1866–1924)
Sketch of a New Aesthetic of Music, trans 1911

5   Genius is one per cent inspiration and ninety-nine per cent
perspiration.
Thomas Alva Edison (1847–1931)
Life, 1932

6   *Female Admirer:* How do you think of those lovely melodies?
    Gounod: God, Madame, sends me down some of his angels and they
             whisper sweet melodies in my ear.
Quoted in Harding, *Gounod*, 1973

7   If an idea strikes me as beautiful and satisfactory to the ear and heart,
I would far rather overlook a grammatical error than sacrifice what is
beautiful to mere pedantic trifling.
Joseph Haydn (1732–1809)
Quoted in Nohl, *Life of Haydn*, 1883

8   . . . after unconscious creativity follows a period of *quiet
clearsightedness*, in which one renders account of one's situation.
Arnold Schoenberg (1874–1951)
Letter to Busoni, 24 August 1909, trans Beaumont

9   All the inspiration I ever needed was a phonecall from a producer.
Cole Porter (1891–1964)
In 1955, quoted in Green, *Dictionary of Contemporary Quotations*, 1982

10 A composer knows about as little as anyone else about where the
substance of his work comes from.
Edgar Varèse (1883–1965)
Lecture, 1959

30 TEACHING AND TEACHERS

1   The music teacher came twice a week to bridge the awful gap between Dorothy and Chopin.
George Ade (1866–1944)
Quoted in Esar and Bentley, *Treasury of Humorous Quotations*

2   Music has the power of producing a certain effect on the moral character of the soul, and if it has the power to do this, it is clear that the young must be directed to music and must be educated in it.
Aristotle (384–322 BC)
Politics

3   A musicologist is a man who can read music but can't hear it.
Thomas Beecham (1879–1961)
Quoted in Proctor-Gregg, *Beecham Remembered*, 1976

4   You can't teach a young musician to compose any more than you can teach a delicate plant to grow, but you can guide him a little by putting a stick in here and a stick in there.
Frederick Delius (1862–1934)
Quoted in Fenby, *Delius as I knew him*, 1936

5   To teach men's sons and daughters on the virginal and viol, it is as harmless a calling as any man can follow.
Solomon Eccles (1618–83)
A Musick-Lector, 1667

6   Do not try to be a genius in every bar.
Gabriel Fauré (1845–1924)
Advice to students, quoted in Honegger, *I am a Composer*, 1951

7   We have to establish already in schoolchildren the belief that music belongs to everyone and is, with a little effort, available to everyone.
Zoltán Kodály (1882–1967)
Lecture, 1946

> 8   [On the Royal Academy of Music:]
> Here tottered, tipsy e'er the day begun
> That prince of bad composers H. MacCunn
> Here sat, in impotent and senile frenzy
> That doddering old soaker A. MacKenzie
> And here reclines, in ultimate blue ruin,
> That gruff and surly toper J. McEwen.
> Constant Lambert (1905–51)
> *Fragment from a Satire against Scotland*, quoted in Motion, *The Lamberts*, 1986

9   We must teach music in schools; a schoolmaster ought to have skill in music, or I would not regard him; neither should we ordain young men as preachers unless they have been well exercised in music.
Martin Luther (1483–1546)
Table Talk, pub 1566

10   Stuffing birds or playing stringed instruments is an elegant pastime, and a resource to the idle, but it is not education.
Cardinal Newman (1801–90)
The Idea of a University Defined, 1873

11   Education in music is most sovereign, because more than anything else rhythm and harmony find their way to the inmost soul and take strongest hold upon it, bringing with them and imparting grace, if one is rightly trained.
Plato (428–347 BC)
The Republic

12   What will a child learn sooner than a song?
Alexander Pope (1688–1744)
Imitations of Horace, 1738, Epistle II i

13   I would only make you a bad Schoenberg, and you're such a good Gershwin already.
Arnold Schoenberg (1874–1951)
To George Gershwin when asked if he could be accepted as one of Schoenberg's pupils

14   My first teacher in musical theory … took me through a book which I still have, called *The Child's Introduction to Thorough Bass in Conversations of a Fortnight between a Mother and her Daughter aged Ten years old*, London, printed for Baldwin Cradock and Joy, 14 Paternoster Row, 1819. Here is a specimen from conversation 8:

Mary: Mama, have I anything more to learn about the chord of the 7th?
Mother: Yes, you already know how a simple chord of the 7th is formed, but you are also to learn that there are four different kinds of 7th.
Ralph Vaughan Williams (1872–1958)
A Musical Autobiography, 1950

31 WRITING AND MUSIC

1   I would rather write 10000 notes than one letter of the alphabet.
Ludwig van Beethoven (1770–1827)
Letter to Simrock, 28 November 1820

2   [When asked to explain the meaning of the Sonata in D Minor, Op 32 No 2, and the *Appassionata* Sonata:] Read Shakespeare's *Tempest*.
Ludwig van Beethoven (1770–1827)
Quoted in Scott, *Beethoven*, 1934

3   I would have gone to death, yes, ten times to death, for Goethe.
Ludwig van Beethoven (1770–1827)
Letter to J.F. Rochlitz, 1822

4   You know that my pretensions to musical taste, are merely a few of Nature's instincts, untaught and untutored by Art.–For this reason, many musical compositions, particularly when much of the merit lies in Counterpoint, however they may transport and ravish the ears of you connoisseurs, affect my simple lug no otherwise than merely as melodious din.
Robert Burns (1759–96)
Letter, 1792

5   Johnson marched to kettle-drums and trumpets;
Gibbon moved to flutes and hautboys.
George Colman the Younger (1762–1836)
Random Records, 1830

6   If a literary man puts together two words about music, one of them will be wrong.
Aaron Copland (1900–90)
Quoted in *The Penguin Dictionary of Modern Quotations*, 1980

7   Hardly does a composer appear than people start devoting essays to him and weighing his music down with ambitious definitions. They do far greater harm than even the fiercest detractors could do.
Claude Debussy (1862–1918)
Quoted in Calvocoressi, *Musicians' Gallery*, 1933

8   The greatest advantage that a writer can derive from music is, that it teaches most exquisitely the art of development.
Benjamin Disraeli (1804–81)
Contarini Fleming, 1832

9   Music is the most disagreeable and the most widely beloved of all noises.
Théophile Gautier (1811–72)
Le Figaro, October 1863

10   The significance of good music is as real as that of good poetry, you cannot translate one into the other, Palestrina into Dante or Bach into Milton, but each has its own inherent and spiritual truth.
Henry Hadow (1859–1937)
Letter quoted in Foreman (ed), *From Parry to Britten*, 1987

11   Nothing is more futile than theorizing about music. No doubt there are laws, mathematically strict laws, but these laws are not music; they are only its conditions . . .
Heinrich Heine (1797–1856)
Letters on the French Stage, 1837

12   Music soothes us, stirs us up; it puts noble feelings in us; it melts us to tears, we know not how: – it is a language by itself, just as perfect, in its way, as speech, as words; just as divine, just as blessed . . . Music has been called the speech of angels; I will go further, and call it the speech of God himself.
Charles Kingsley (1819–75)
Life and Works, 1903

13   Music, oh how faint, how weak,
Language fades before thy spell!
Why should Feeling ever speak,
When thou canst breathe her soul so well?
Thomas Moore (1779–1852)
On Music

14   Music has been one of the greatest passions in my life. I say *has been*, because now I have scarcely any opportunity of hearing any except in my memories. It has brought me ineffable joys and certitudes – the proof that there exists something other than the void I have encountered on all sides; it runs like a guide-line throughout all my work.
Marcel Proust (1871–1922)
Quoted in Myers, *Modern French Music*, 1971

15   Harley Granville-Barker was not far out when, at a rehearsal of one of my plays, he cried out 'Ladies and gentlemen: will you please remember that this is Italian Opera.'
George Bernard Shaw (1856–1950)
London Music, 1888–9, Preface, 1935

16   I chatter over stony ways
In little sharps and trebles.

Alfred, Lord Tennyson (1809–92)
The Brook

17   Never and never will I write my memoirs. It is enough for the world of music to have had to put up with my notes for so long. I will never condemn it to read my prose.

Giuseppe Verdi (1813–1901)

18   When I re-read my theoretical works, I can no longer understand them.

Richard Wagner (1813–83)
Quoted in Saint-Saëns, *Portraits et Souvenirs*, 1903

LIVES AND WORKS

Nothing is so entertaining or enlightening (if often unedifying) as one composer's opinion of another: usually it tells us more about the perpetrator of the remark. Much of this section consists of such piquant observations; there are also a number of touching personal credos, and some shafts of revealing contemporary light.

32 ALKAN

1 One of the strangest and most unclassifiable figures in all music.
Kaikhosru Shapurji Sorabji (1895–1988)
Mi Contra Fa, 1947

2 Charles Valentin Alkan has just died. It was necessary for him to die in order to suspect his existence.
Obituary in *Le Ménestrel*, 1888

33 ANTHEIL

1 Bad Boy of Music
George Antheil (1900–59)
Title of his autobiography, 1945

2 [On his musical aims:] To warn the age in which I am living of the simultaneous beauty and danger of its unconscious mechanistic philosophy.
George Antheil (1900–59)
Quoted in Ewen, *American Composers*, 1982

34 ARNE

1 A good melody is such a one as would grind about the streets upon the organ.
Thomas Arne (1710–78)
Quoted in Kelly, *Reminiscences*, 1826

2 Arne had kept bad company: he had written for vulgar singers and hearers too long to be able to comport himself properly at the opera-house, in the first circle of taste and fashion.
Charles Burney (1726–1814)
A General History of Music, 1776–89

3 Scarcely had we lost Arne when Irish jigs usurped the musical domain. These having had their day, it was difficult to find a substitute, and now music is decidedly nowhere.
Charles Dibdin (1745–1814)
Quoted in Langley, *Doctor Arne*, 1938

35 AUBER

1 There was a composer named Auber
Who seldom was somber or sauber.
   Yet he held aloof
   From the opera bouffe,
But he lived past life's golden Octauber.
Musical Herald, 1888

36 C.P.E. BACH

1 [C.P.E.] Bach is the father, we the children.
Joseph Haydn (1732–1809)
Quoted in Headington, *The Bodley Head History of Western Music*, 1974

2 It's Prussian blue – it fades!
Johann Sebastian Bach (1685–1750)
On the music of his son Carl Philipp Emanuel (1714–88)

37   J.S. BACH

1   For the glory of the most high God
    alone,
And for my neighbour to learn from.
Johann Sebastian Bach (1685–1750)
Epigraph to the *Little Organ Book*, 1717

2   I find that the duties are by far not so agreeable as they were described to me originally; and that quite a few of the bonuses attached to the post have been withdrawn; that the cost of living is very high here; and that the authorities are rather strangely hostile to music; that I have to live in a state of almost constant struggle; that envy prevails and vexations are numerous.
Johann Sebastian Bach (1685–1750)
Letter to Georg Erdmann, Leipzig, 28 October 1730

3   This can only be the devil or Bach himself!
A village organist on finding Bach playing on his organ, quoted in Geiringer, *The Bach Family*, 1954

4   Too much counterpoint; what is worse, Protestant counterpoint.
Thomas Beecham (1879–1961)
Quoted by N. Cardus, *Guardian*, 8 March 1971

5   I would give the whole of Bach's Brandenburg Concertos for Massenet's *Manon* and would think I had vastly profited by the exchange.
Thomas Beecham (1879–1961)
Quoted in Harding, *Massenet*, 1970

6   Though full of great musical lore
Old Bach is a terrible bore
A fugue without a tune
He thought was a boon
So he wrote seventeen thousand or more.
Musical Herald, 1884

7   The immortal god of harmony.
Ludwig van Beethoven (1770–1827)
Letter to Christoph Breitkopf, 1801

8   There is one god – Bach – and Mendelssohn is his prophet.
Hector Berlioz (1803–69)
Quoted in Elliot, *Berlioz*, 1967

9   I need Bach at the beginning of the day almost more than I need food and water.

Pablo Casals (1876–1973)
Lloyd Webber (ed), *Joys and Sorrows*, 1985

10   When the old Saxon cantor has no ideas, he sets off on anything and is truly merciless. In short, he is unbearable except when he is admirable . . . However, had he had a friend – an editor, perhaps – who would have gently advised him not to write one day a week, for example, we might have been spared several hundred pages in which we must wander through a thicket of joyless measures which unwind pitilessly with ever the same little rascal of a 'subject' and 'countersubject'.

Claude Debussy (1862–1916)
Letter to Jacques Durand, 1917

11   Bach almost persuades me to be a Christian.

Roger Fry (1866–1934)
Quoted in Woolf, *Roger Fry*, 1940

12   I don't know how, with no vibrato, Bach could have so many sons.

Paul Hindemith (1895–1963)
Quoted in Jacobson, *Reverberations*, 1975

13   You play Bach your way and I'll play him *his* way.

Wanda Landowska (1879–1959)
Attributed

14   [On appointing Bach as cantor at Leipzig, Graupner having refused the post:] Since the best cannot be had, one must take the next best.

Mayor Abraham Platz
In 1723, quoted in Neuman, *Bach*, 1961

15   'Here! None of that mathematical music!'
Said the Kommandant when Munch offered Bach to the regiment.

Ezra Pound (1885–1972)
Canto, LXXX

16   In the course of time the distance between sources diminishes. Beethoven, for instance, did not need to study all that Mozart studied – Mozart, not all that Handel – Handel, not all that Palestrina – because these had already absorbed the knowledge of their predecessors. But there is one source which inexhaustibly provides new ideas – Johann Sebastian Bach.

Robert Schumann (1810–56)
Music and Musicians, trans Ritter, 1878

17   Lamented Bach! Your touch upon the
          organ's keys
      Long since has earned you company among the
          great,
      And what your quill upon the music-sheet has
          writ
      Has filled hearts with delight, though some
          did envy seize.

Georg Philipp Telemann (1681–1767)
Sonnet, trans de Hann

18   Handel was a man of the world; Bach a world of a man.

Ronald Stevenson (1828–)
Western Music, 1971

---

38 BALAKIREV

---

1   The part he played in the development of Russian music is
incomparably important, and after Glinka first place in the history of
Russian music should be allotted to Mily Alexeyevich Balakirev.

S.M. Lyapunov
1910

2   In time he will be a second Glinka.

Mikhail Glinka (1803–57)
Quoted in Garden, *Balakirev*, 1967

---

39 BARTÓK

---

1   For my own part, all my life, in every sphere, always and in every way,
I shall have one objective: the good of Hungary and the Hungarian
nation.

Béla Bartók (1881–1945)
Letter to his family, 1903

2   My kingdom is one of discord!

Béla Bartók (1881–1945)
Letter to Stefi Geyer, 1907

3   Mr Nielsen, do you think my music is modern enough?
Béla Bartók (1881–1945)
Remark, 1920, quoted in Simpson, *Carl Nielsen*, 1952

4   The extremes of variation, which is so characteristic of our folk music, is at the same time the expression of my own nature.
Béla Bartók (1881–1945)
In 1927, quoted in Ujfalussy, *Béla Bartók*, 1971

5   [On birdsong:] How well I understand that those people whose lives are lived in close proximity with nature, and far away from so-called civilization, from the questionable blessing of doctors and hospitals, are still entrusting their fate to those rituals of healing song.
Béla Bartók (1881–1945)
In 1945, quoted in Fassett, *The Naked Face of Genius*, 1958

6   Bartók ... was completely inhuman. He hardly existed as a personality, but his impersonality was tremendous–he was the living incarnation and embodiment of the spirit of music. He was pure spirit, in fact, and his frail, intense and delicate physique gave the impression of something ethereal and disembodied, like a flame burning in oxygen.
Cecil Gray (1895–1951)
Musical Chairs, 1948

7   Every art has the right to strike its roots in the art of the previous age; it not only has the right to but it must stem from it.
Béla Bartók (1881–1945)
Essays, 1976

8   Bartók's name ... stands for the principle of and the demand for regeneration stemming from the people, both in art and in politics.
Zoltán Kodály (1882–1967)
Address, 1956

40 BEETHOVEN

1   O my fellow men, who consider me, or describe me as unfriendly, peevish or even misanthropic, how greatly do you wrong me. For you do not know the secret reason why I appear to you to be so. Ever since my childhood my heart and soul have been imbued with the tender feeling of goodwill. But just think, for the last six years I have been afflicted with an incurable complaint which has been made worse by incompetent doctors. From year to year my hopes of being cured have gradually been shattered and finally I have been forced to accept the prospect of a *permanent infirmity* . . . Yet I could not bring myself to say to people: 'Speak up, shout, for I am deaf.' Alas! how could I possibly refer to the impairing *of a sense* which in me should be more perfectly developed than in other people . . . How humiliated I have felt if somebody standing beside me heard the sound of a flute in the distance and *I heard nothing,* or if somebody heard *a shepherd sing* and again I heard nothing. Such experiences almost made me despair, and I was on the point of putting an end to my life. The only thing that held me back was *my art* . . .

Ludwig van Beethoven (1770–1827)
From a letter to his brothers Carl and Johann, 6 October 1802, found among his papers after his death, and known as the *Heiligenstadt Testament.*

2   *From* the heart –
May it go again
to the heart.

Ludwig van Beethoven (1770–1827)
On the score of his *Missa Solemnis,* 1824

3   *Power* is the moral principle of those who excel others, and it is also mine.

Ludwig van Beethoven (1770–1827)
Letter to Freiherr Zmeskall von Domanowecz, 1798

4   Music is a higher revelation than all wisdom and philosophy, it is the wine of a new procreation, and I am Bacchus who presses out this glorious wine for men and makes them drunk with the spirit.

Ludwig van Beethoven (1770–1827)
Quoted in Scott, *Beethoven,* 1934

5   I will seize Fate by the throat; it shall certainly not bend and crush me completely.

Ludwig van Beethoven (1770–1827)
Letter to F.G. Wegeler, 1801

6   I must confess that I live a miserable life . . . I live entirely in my music.

Ludwig van Beethoven (1770–1827)
Ibid

7   You may be a man no longer, not for yourself, only for others, for you there is no longer happiness except in yourself, in your art – O God, give me strength to conquer myself, nothing must chain me to life.

Ludwig van Beethoven (1770–1827)
Journal, 1812

8   I carry my thoughts about with me for a long time, before I write them down. Meanwhile my memory is so tenacious that I am sure never to forget, not even in years, a theme that has once occurred to me. I change many things, discard and try again until I am satisfied. Then, however, there begins in my head the development in every direction and, insomuch as I know exactly what I want, the fundamental idea never deserts me – it arises before me, grows – I see and hear the picture in all its extent and dimensions stand before my mind like a cast, and there remains for me nothing but the labour of writing it down, which is quickly accomplished when I have the time, for I sometimes take up other work, but never to the confusion of one with the other.

Ludwig van Beethoven (1770–1827)
Letter to Louis Schlösser, 1823

9   I still hope to create a few great works and then like an old child to finish my earthly course somewhere among kind people.

Ludwig van Beethoven (1770–1827)
Letter to F.G. Wegeler, 1826

10   *Muss es sein? Es muss sein! Es muss sein!*
     Must it be? It must be! It must be!

Ludwig van Beethoven (1770–1827)
Comment written below the opening phrases of the finale of his String Quartet in F Major, Op 135 (his last work)

11   Music is the one incorporeal entrance into the higher world of knowledge which comprehends mankind but which mankind cannot comprehend.

Ludwig van Beethoven (1770–1827)
Quoted by Bettina von Arnim, letter to Goethe, 1810

12   Mistakes—mistakes—you yourselves are one great mistake—I have to keep my copyist and myself perpetually on the rush if I am to prevent my published work from consisting wholly of mistakes.
Ludwig van Beethoven (1770–1827)
Letter to his publishers, Breitkopf und Härtel, 1811

13   Music should strike fire from a man.
Ludwig van Beethoven (1770–1827)
Quoted in Scott, *Beethoven*, 1934

14   Strange, I feel as if up to now I had written no more than a few notes.
Ludwig van Beethoven (1770–1827)
Words on his deathbed

15   *Plaudite, amici, comedia finita est.*
Applaud, my friends, the comedy is over.
Ludwig van Beethoven (1770–1827)
Words on his deathbed, quoting the dying Augustus

16   I shall hear in heaven.
Ludwig van Beethoven (1770–1827)
Attributed last words

17   They are burying the general of the musicians.
Unknown old woman
At Beethoven's funeral, quoted in Scott, *Beethoven*, 1934

18   [Of Beethoven:] His music always reminds one of paintings of battles.
Bertolt Brecht (1898–1956)
Quoted in *Brecht as they knew him*, Witt(ed), 1974

19   [Of Op 111:] The grandeur of Beethoven's thirty-second piano sonata represents the opening of the gates of heaven.
Robert Browning (1812–89)
Quoted in Thomas, *Robert Browning—A Life Within A Life*, 1982

20   The haughty beauty, Beethoven.
Muzio Clementi (1752–1832)
Letter to F.W. Collard, 1807

21   Your genius is centuries in advance, and at the present time there is scarcely one hearer who would be sufficiently enlightened to enjoy the full beauty of this music.
Prince Nicholas Galitsin (1794–1860)
Letter to Beethoven, 1824

22   He is no man; he's a devil. He will play me and all of us to death. And how he improvises!
Joseph Gelinek (1758–1825)
In *c* 1795, quoted in Scott, *Beethoven*, 1934

23   His talent excited my astonishment, but unfortunately his personality is entirely uncontrolled; he is perfectly welcome to think the world detestable, but by that means he does not make it more enjoyable for himself or for others.
Johann Wolfgang von Goethe (1749–1832)
On meeting Beethoven, letter to Carl Friedrich Zelter, 2 September 1812

24   A more self-contained, energetic, sincere artist I never saw.
Johann Wolfgang von Goethe (1749–1832)
Quoted in Scott, *Beethoven*, 1934

25   The thing that impresses me most about Beethoven's Fifth is – *da da da daaa* – it's fate knocking at the door. That's one of the biggest hits in history. There's no video to it, he didn't *need* one.
Billy Joel (1949–   )
Quoted in the *Independent*, 23 May 1990

26   Shame on the blind men who took Beethoven for a deaf man!
Wilhelm von Lenz (1809–83)
Beethoven, 1855–60

27   To us musicians the work of Beethoven parallels the pillars of smoke and fire which led the Israelites through the desert.
Franz Liszt (1811–86)
Letter to Wilhelm von Lenz, 1852

28   *Une fleur entre deux abîmes.*
     A flower between two abysses.
Franz Liszt (1811–86)
Of the middle movement of Beethoven's *Moonlight Sonata*, quoted in Tovey, *Beethoven*, 1944

29   [On the slow movement of the Fourth Piano Concerto:] Orpheus taming the wild beasts.

Franz Liszt (1811–86)
Quoted in Tovey, *Essays in Musical Analysis,* III, 1936

30   [Of Beethoven's Sonata in C Minor, Op 111:] An ego painfully isolated in the absolute, isolated too from sense by the loss of his hearing; lonely prince of a realm of spirits, from whom now only a chilling breath issued to terrify his most willing contemporaries, standing as they did aghast at these communications of which only at moments, only by exception, they could understand anything at all. (Kretschmar)

Thomas Mann (1875–1955)
Doctor Faustus, 1947, trans Lowe-Porter

31   [Of Beethoven's *Pastoral* Symphony:] This is no question of gaily dressed shepherds . . . it is a matter of nature in her simple truth.

Hector Berlioz (1803–69)
A Travers chants, 1862

32   Beethoven always sounds to me like the upsetting of a bag of nails, with here and there an also dropped hammer.

John Ruskin (1819–1900)
Letter, 1881

33   Nature would burst should she attempt to produce nothing save Beethovens.

Robert Schumann (1810–56)
Quoted in Walker (ed), *Robert Schumann: the Man and his Music,* 1972

34   Beethoven's last quartets are not the justification of modern music, but modern music has reached the point at which it justifies the quartets.

Marion M. Scott
Beethoven, 1934

35   I have occasionally remarked that the only entirely creditable incident in English history is the sending of one hundred pounds to Beethoven on his deathbed by the London Philharmonic Society; and it is the only one that historians never mention.

George Bernard Shaw (1856–1950)
Letter to *The Times,* 20 December 1932

36   Beethoven was wanting in aesthetic feeling and in a sense of the beautiful.
Louis Spohr (1784–1859)
Autobiography, 1865

37   [Of Beethoven's Symphony No 9:] The fourth movement is, in my opinion, so monstrous and tasteless and, in its grasp of Schiller's *Ode,* so trivial that I cannot understand how a genius like Beethoven could have written it.
Louis Spohr (1784–1859)
Ibid

38   The fiery, almost incredible inventive faculty which inspires him is attended by so many complications in the arrangement of his ideas that it is only his earlier compositions that interest me; the later ones appear to me a confused chaos, an unintelligible struggle after novelty from which occasionally heavenly flashes of genius dart forth, showing how great he might be if he chose to control his luxuriant fancy.
Carl Maria von Weber (1786–1826)
Letter to H.G. Nageli, 1810

39   The extravagances of Beethoven's genius have reached the *ne plus ultra* in the Seventh Symphony, and he is quite ripe for the madhouse.
Carl Maria von Weber (1786–1826)
Quoted in Hughes and Van Thal, *The Music Lover's Companion,* 1971

41 BERG

1   When I compose I always feel I am like Beethoven; only afterwards do I become aware that at best I am only Bizet.
Alban Berg (1885–1935)
Quoted in Adorno, *Alban Berg,* 1968

2 No one in the audience, no matter how aware he may be of the musical forms contained in the framework of the opera, of the precision and logic with which it has been worked out, no one, from the moment the curtain parts until it closes for the last time, pays any attention to the various fugues, inventions, suites, sonata movements, variations and passacaglias about which so much has been written. No one gives heed to anything but the vast social implications of the work, which by far transcend the personal destiny of *Wozzeck*. This, I believe, is my achievement.

Alban Berg (1885–1935)
Wozzeck, 1925, 'Postscript'

3 Berg's personality is fascinating in more ways than one, but what I find most striking is the combination of immediate expressiveness with outstanding structural powers.

Pierre Boulez (1925–)
Orientations, trans Cooper, 1986

4 Lulu's last victim.

Helene Berg (1885–1976)
Referring to her husband, letter to Heinsheiner, 1937

42 BERLIOZ

1 My life is to me a deeply interesting romance.

Hector Berlioz (1803–69)
Letter to Humbert Ferrand, 1833

2 A young musician of extraordinary sensibility and abundant imagination . . .

Hector Berlioz (1803–69)
Programme for the *Fantastic Symphony*, 1830

3 If I were threatened with the destruction of all my works but one, I would beg mercy for the *Messe des morts*.

Hector Berlioz (1803–69)
Letter to Humbert Ferrand, 1867

4 I ask only for time and tranquillity.

Hector Berlioz (1803–69)
Letter to Adèle Berlioz, 1833

5   I'll sing you something new.
Motto from *Faust* in one of Berlioz's *8 Scenes*, 1829

6   Miss Smithson was married last week, in Paris, to Derlioz [sic], the musical composer. We trust this marriage will insure the happiness of an amiable young woman, as well as secure us against her reappearance on the English boards.
The Court Journal, 1833

7   Berlioz . . . pointed the way for untold generations.
Ferruccio Busoni (1866–1924)
Quoted in Barzun, *Berlioz and the Romantic Century*, 1951

8   If he has failed, he has failed magnificently.
Pierre Scudo (1803–69)
On *Les Troyens à Carthage*, 1863

9   *Lélio, ou le Retour à la vie* must be the craziest work ever sketched out by a composer not actually insane.
J.H. Elliot
Berlioz, 1967

10   Of all the great composers, Berlioz has been the one least understandingly dealt with by criticism.
Ernest Newman (1868–1959)
Berlioz and His Critics, 1949

11   Berlioz says nothing in his music but he says it magnificently.
James Gibbons Huneker (1860–1921)
Old Fogy, 1913

12   The voice of the critic has but a feeble echo. The reverberation of a beautiful score is more powerful than all our phraseology.
Hector Berlioz (1803–69)
In 1846, quoted by Barzun, *Berlioz and the Romantic Century*, 1951

13   He makes me sad, because he is really a cultured, agreeable man and yet composes so very badly.
Felix Mendelssohn (1809–47)
Letter to his mother, 1831

14   [Of Berlioz's overture *Les Francs Juges:*] His orchestration is such
. . . an incongruous mess, that one ought to wash one's hands after
handling one of his scores.
Felix Mendelssohn (1809–47)
Letter, 1834

15   I have now done everything I had to do.
Hector Berlioz (1803–69)
To his son, on completing *Beatrice and Benedict*, 1862

16   Once dead he will live for a long time.
Stephen Heller (1814–88)
In 1844, quoted in Barzun, *Berlioz and the Romantic Century*, 1951

43   BERNSTEIN

1   To be strong of will, but not to offend;
    To be intimate with my fellow man, but not to presume;
    To love, but not to be weakend by loving;
    To serve music, but not to forget humanity for the music;
    To work, but not to destroy oneself in working;
    To rest, but not to be idle;
    To be a proud and grateful American, but also to be a proud and
        grateful Jew;
    To give, but also to receive;
    To create, but also to perform;
    To act, but also to dream;
    To live, but also to be.
    Leonard Bernstein (1918–90)
    From a speech at the American-Israel Cultural Foundation, 2 February 1959

2   Leonard Bernstein has been disclosing musical secrets that have
been well known for over 400 years.
Oscar Levant (1906–72)
Memoirs of an Amnesiac, 1965

3   The epitome of glamour combined with quality, and thank heaven
for him – the heaven of the golden gods of yore.
Ned Rorem (1923–   )
Speech on Bernstein's seventieth birthday, August 1988

4   The Peter Pan of music.
The New York Times, 1960

44 BIZET

1   Bizet has conquered the universe. He has conquered not only by his talent, but also by the sympathy, the warmth, the profoundly human quality of that talent. His soul showed through his music – that sensitive, loyal, generous soul; that spontaneous, kind, uncomplicated character that all those who knew Bizet enjoyed praising.

Reynaldo Hahn (1874–1947)
Le Figaro, 1938

2   I want to do nothing *chic*, I want to have *ideas* before beginning a piece.

Georges Bizet (1838–75)
Letter to Gounod, 1858

3   Let us have fantasy, boldness, unexpectedness, enchantment – above all, tenderness, *morbidezza*.

Georges Bizet (1838–75)
Letter to Edmond Galabert, quoted in Dean, *Bizet*, 1975

4   As a musician I tell you that if you were to suppress adultery, fanaticism, crime, evil, the supernatural, there would no longer be the means for writing one note.

Georges Bizet (1838–75)
Letter to Edmond Galabert, October 1866

5   In order to succeed today you have to be either dead or German.

Georges Bizet (1838–75)
Letter to Louis Gallet, quoted in Dean, *Bizet*, 1975

6   In *Carmen* the composer has made up his mind to show us how learned he is, with the result that he is often dull and obscure.

Léon Escudier (1816–81)
In 1875, quoted in Dean, *Bizet*, 1975

7   Take the Spanish airs and mine out of the score, and there remains nothing to Bizet's credit but the sauce that masks the fish.

Charles Gounod (1818–93)
On the première of *Carmen*, 1875, quoted in Dean, *Bizet*, 1975

8   [On *Carmen:*] Bizet's music seems to me perfect. It comes forward lightly, gracefully, stylishly. It is lovable, it does not sweat. 'All that is good is easy, everything divine runs with light feet': this is the first principle of my aesthetics. This music is wicked, refined, fatalistic: and withal remains popular – it possesses the refinement of a race, not of an individual.

Friedrich Nietzsche (1844 – 1900)
Der Fall Wagner, 1888

45   BLISS

1   There is only a little of the spider about me, spinning his own web from his inner being. I am more of a magpie type. I need what Henry James calls a *'trouvaille'* or a *'donnée'*.

Arthur Bliss (1891 – 1975)
As I Remember, 1970

2   Rebellion is a natural ingredient of youth. It is good that each generation is not born a generation of yes-men, or we should have no progress.

Arthur Bliss (1891 – 1975)
Speech, Princetown N.J., 1968

3   I found myself referring to the programme to find out whether I ought to be seeing red or looking blue at certain moments, and some of it made many of the audience feel green.

The Times, reviewing Bliss's *A Colour Symphony,* 1922

4   Visits to the studios of painters act as a greater incentive to work than any amount of talk with my fellow musicians. In looking at the struggle for realized form in a sculptor's or painter's work I find something that instructs me in my own art.

Arthur Bliss (1891 – 1975)
As I Remember, 1970

46 BORODIN

1   The supreme justification of the amateur in music.
Gerald Abraham (1904–   )
Borodin, 1927

2   I am a composer in search of oblivion; and I'm always slightly ashamed to admit that I compose.
Alexander Borodin (1833–87)
Letter to Lydia Karmalina

3   A score of Borodin's orchestral piece [had] the title [*In the Steppes of Central Asia*] helpfully printed in three languages thus:

IM MITTELASIEN   DANS L'ASIE MOYENNE
                    IN AVERAGE ASIA
Constant Lambert (1905–51)
Quoted in Motion, *The Lamberts*, 1986

---

47 BOULEZ

1   Music is in a state of permanent revolution . . .
Pierre Boulez (1925–   )
Orientations, trans Cooper, 1986

2   Boulez is a great composer. He is also a very intelligent man. He understands all the changes and they make him suffer. There are people who go unperturbed through change. Like Bach. Like Richard Strauss. But Boulez cannot. He thinks that advancing the language is all. He feels he must be in the advance guard and he doesn't like what is happening there.
Olivier Messiaen (1908–   )
Quoted in Peyser, *Boulez*, 1976

3   [On Boulez's *Le Marteau sans maître*:] Like ice cubes clinking in a glass.
Igor Stravinsky (1882–1971)
Attributed

4 [Of Boulez's *Le Marteau sans maître*:] Webern sounding like Debussy.

Heinrich Strobel (1898–1970)
Quoted in Myers, *Modern French Music*, 1971

5 The Elliptical Geometry of Utopia.

Pierre Boulez (1925–   )
Title of speech, 1979

48 BRAHMS

1 My things really are written with an appalling lack of practicability!

Johannes Brahms (1833–97)
Letter to Joachim

2 [Of his *Four Serious Songs*:] Ungodly ditties.

Johannes Brahms (1833–97)
Letter to Mandyczewski, 1896

3 . . . the artist cannot and should not be separated from the man. And in me it happens that the artist is not so arrogant and sensitive as the man, and the latter has but small compensation if the work of the former is not allowed to expiate his sins.

Johannes Brahms (1833–97)
Letter to Clara Schumann, 1893

4 Benjamin Britten claims that he plays through 'the whole of Brahms' at intervals to see whether Brahms is really as bad as he thought, and ends by discovering that he is actually much worse.

Colin Wilson (1931–   )
Brandy of the Damned, 1964

5 Too much beer and beard.

Paul Dukas (1865–1935)
Quoted in Demuth, *Vincent d'Indy*, 1951

6 Brahms knew what Goethe knew: that there can be no development without man, beyond man. As a result he became the arch-enemy of all illusions.

Wilhelm Furtwängler (1886–1954)
Notebooks, trans Whiteside, 1989

7   When Brahms is in extra good spirits, he sings 'The grave is my joy'.
Joseph Hellmesberger (1828–93)
Quoted in Gal, *Johannes Brahms*, 1961

8   One morning at breakfast, [Brahms] gobbled up a whole tin of sardines and made assurance doubly sure by drinking the oil from the tin at a draught.
Liza Lehmann (1862–1918)
Autobiography, 1919

9   Many new and significant talents have arisen; a new power in music seems to announce itself; the intimation has been proved true by many aspiring artists of the last years . . . To me, who followed the progress of these chosen ones with the greatest sympathy, it seemed that there inevitably must appear a musician called to give expression to his times in an ideal fashion; a musician who would reveal his mastery not in a gradual evolution, but like Athene would spring fully armed from Zeus's head. And such a one has appeared, a young man over whose cradle Graces and Heroes have stood watch. His name is Johannes Brahms and he comes from Hamburg . . .
Robert Schumann (1810–56)
Neue Zeitshrift für Musik, 1853

10   I believe Johannes to be the true Apostle, who will also write Revelations.
Robert Schumann (1810–56)
Letter to Joachim

11   Should he only point his magic wand to where those massed forces, both of chorus and of orchestra, may lend him their power, yet more wondrous glimpses into the spirit world await us.
Robert Schumann (1810–56)
1853

12   Brahms's *Requiem* has not the true funeral relish: it is so execrably and ponderously dull that the very flattest of funerals would seem like a ballet, or at least at *danse macabre*, after it.
George Bernard Shaw (1856–1950)
Quoted in *The World*, 1892

13   The Leviathan Maunderer.
George Bernard Shaw (1856–1950)
Quoted in *The Star*, 1892

14   A most remarkable and extraordinary personality was Brahms. Humorous, fearless, far-seeing, sometimes over-rough to his contemporaries, but a worshipper of and worshipped by young children; with a very noble, generous, and ideal side to his character, and a curiously warped and sensual side as well. He could look like Jupiter Olympus at one moment, and like Falstaff the next.

C.V. Stanford (1852–1924)
Studies and Memories, 1908

15   He has no charm for me. I find him cold and obscure, full of pretensions, but without any real depth.

Píotr Ilyich Tchaikovsky (1840–93)
Letter to Nadezhda von Meck

16   I have played over the music of that scoundrel Brahms. What a giftless bastard!

Píotr Ilyich Tchaikovsky (1840–93)
Diary, 1886

17   [Of Brahms's *German Requiem*:] Schumann's Last Thought.

Richard Wagner (1813–83)
On Poetry and Composition, 1879

18   In a single cymbal crash from a work of Liszt there is expressed more spirit and feeling than in all Brahms's symphonies and his serenades besides.

Hugo Wolf (1860–1903)

19   I once sent him a song and asked him to mark a cross wherever he thought it was faulty. Brahms returned it untouched, saying, 'I don't want to make a cemetery of your composition.'

Hugo Wolf (1860–1903)
Quoted in Lebrecht, *Discord*, 1982

49   BRITTEN

1   I remember the first time I tried [composing] the result looked rather like the Forth Bridge.

Benjamin Britten (1913–76)
Quoted in the *Sunday Telegraph*, 1964

2   One day I'll be able to relax a bit, and try and become a good composer.

Benjamin Britten (1913–76)
Letter to Imogen Holst, 1968

3   Night and silence–these are two of the things I cherish most.

Benjamin Britten (1913–76)
Quoted in Headington, *Britten*, 1981

4   I can say with honesty that in every piece I have written, in spite of hard work, there are still passages where I have not quite solved problems. Not once have these passages been noticed, nor of course suggestions made as to how I could have improved them.

Benjamin Britten (1913–76)
On his critics

5   If wind and water could write music, it would sound like Ben's.

Yehudi Menuhin (1916–   )
Quoted in Headington, *Britten*, 1981

50   BRUCKNER

1   I will present to God the score of my *Te Deum*, and He will judge me mercifully.

Anton Bruckner (1824–96)
Attributed

2   I cannot find the words to thank you as I would wish, but if there were an organ here, I could tell you.

Anton Bruckner (1824–96)
On receiving an honorary DPhil, Vienna University, 1891

3   They want me to compose in a different way; I could, but I must not.

Anton Bruckner (1824–96)
Quoted by Cooke, *The Symphony*, ed Simpson, 1966

4   [Of Bruckner's symphonies:] Symphonic boa-constrictors.

Johannes Brahms (1833–97)
Quoted by Specht, *Johannes Brahms*, 1928

5   [Of Bruckner's Symphony No 3:] A vision of Beethoven's Ninth becoming friendly with Wagner's Valkyries and finishing up trampled under their hooves.
Eduard Hanslick (1825–1904)

6   [Of Bruckner's Symphony No 8:] It is not impossible that the future belongs to this nightmarish *Katzenjammer* style, a future which we therefore do not envy.
Eduard Hanslick (1825–1904)
Neue Freie Presse, 1892

7   Yesterday I heard Bruckner's B flat major Symphony, and it moved me to tears. For a long time afterwards I was completely transported. What a strangely profound spirit, formed by a religious sense . . . as something no longer in harmony with our time.
Jean Sibelius (1865–1957)
Quoted by Mellers, *The Listener*, 1 December 1955

8   [Of Bruckner's Symphony No 2:] Very nice.
Richard Wagner (1813–83)
Attributed

9   Bruckner! He is my man!
Richard Wagner (1813–83)
Attributed

51   BULL

1   Her Grace [Queen Elizabeth I] was at that tyme at the virginalls: whereupon . . . Maister Bull did come by stealthe to heare without, and by mischaunce did sprawle intoe the queenes Maiesties Presence, to the queenes great disturbance. Shee demaundinge incontinent the wherefore of suche presumption, Maister Bull with greate skill sayd that wheresoever Maiesty and Musicke so well combyned, no man mighte abase himself too deeplie; whereupon the queenes Maiesty was mollifyde and sayd that so rayre a Bull hath song as sweete as Byrd.
Peter Philips (1561–1628)
On John Bull (1562–1628)

2   Lo, where doth pace in order
    A braver Bull than did Europa carry.

Anonymous
*Parthenia, or the Maydenhead of the first
musicke that ever was printed for the
Virginalls*, 1612

· 52   BUSONI

1   I want to attain the unknown! What I already know is boundless. But I want to go even further. The final word still eludes me.

Ferruccio Busoni (1866–1924)
Der mächtige Zauberer, 1905

2   In matters concerning art my feelings are those of an autocrat.

Ferruccio Busoni (1866–1924)
Letter to Gisella Selden-Goth, 1918

3   ... youth and high spirits, qualities which for me are inseparable from the art of music.

Ferruccio Busoni (1866–1924)
Letter to Heinrich Burkard, 1923

4   Busoni ... always had most lavishly given away money, right and left, to pupils and struggling musicians, and sacrificed much of his time to teaching them and performing their works. If he ever complained of anything, it was that his example had not borne fruit, that younger men, when their successes had made them financially competent, were not in their turn ready to give of what they had acquired, to others less fortunate, whose work might enrich music if not themselves.

Bernard van Dieren (1884–1936)
Down Among The Dead Men, 1935

5   He could never understand selfishness, whether reasoning or unreasoning, and one could not point to a nobler trait in his character, or to one that showed better how loyal and true-hearted an artist he was. His duty, he felt, was to art, and in every sense.

Bernard van Dieren (1884–1936)
Ibid

6 Busoni has been called the prophet of the new music. A better description would be its *conscience*.
Willy Schuh (1900–) Swiss music critic and musicologist
Attributed

7 Busoni's piano-playing signifies the victory of reflection over bravura.
Alfred Brendel (1931–)
Musical Thoughts and Afterthoughts, 1976

8 [Of Busoni:] A kind of musical Leonardo.
Wilhelm Kempff (1895–)
Attributed

9 If one only knows Busoni as a musician, one does not know him. (And who knows him as a musician?)
Alfred Einstein (1880–1952)

10 Couldn't one make it clear to the critics that dissonances *don't exist*? That the term cacophony has no meaning any more?
Ferruccio Busoni (1866–1924)
Letter to H.W. Braber, 1913

53 BYRD

1 For even as among artisans it is shameful in a craftsman to make a rude piece of work from some precious material, so indeed to sacred words in which the praises of God and of the Heavenly host are sung, none but some celestial harmony (so far as our powers avail) will be proper.
William Byrd (1543–1623)
Dedication to *Gradualia*, 1605–7

2 Here is offered unto thy courteous acceptation, music of sundry sorts, and to content diverse humours.
William Byrd (1543–1623)
Introduction to *Psalmes, Sonets and Songs*, 1588

3   List to that sweet recorder;
How daintily this Byrd his notes doth vary,
As if he were the Nightingale's own brother!

Anonymous
Parthenia, or the Maydenhead of the first
musicke that was ever printed for the
Virginalls, 1612

4   *Birde, suos iactet si musa Britanna*
clientes
Signiferum turmis te creet illa suis.
If the British muse should hold a review of her
followers, she would appoint you, master Byrd, as
standard-bearer of her squadrons.

Robert Dow
Comment on one of the part-books he prepared for Christ
Church, Oxford

5   For motets and music of piety and devotion as well as for the honour
of our nation, as the merit of the man, I prefer above all our Phoenix
Mr William Byrd, whom in that kind I know not whether any may
equal.

Henry Peacham (1576?–1643?)
The Compleat Gentleman, 1622

6   [Referring to Byrd:] There be some English songs lately set forth by
a great Master of Music, which for skill and sweetness may content the
most curious.

Nicholas Yonge (d 1619)
Musica Transalpina, 1588

---

54 CAGE

---

1   Schoenberg said I would never be able to compose, because I had no
ear for music; and it's true that I don't hear the relationships of tonality
and harmony. He said: 'You always come to a wall and you won't be able
to go through.' I said, well then, I'll beat my head against that wall; and I
quite literally began hitting things, and developed a music of percussion
that involved noises.

John Cage (1912–   )
Interview in *The Observer* magazine, 1982

2   Before he became infatuated with Zen and employed a technique of rhythmic sequences borrowed from the raga, he wrote interesting works.

Pierre Boulez (1925–)
Orientations, trans Cooper, 1986, 'Oriental Music: A Lost Paradise?', 1967

55   CHERUBINI

1   This harmonic setting seems to me preferable to that one, but the old masters thought otherwise and we must defer to them.

Luigi Cherubini (1760–1842)
Quoted by Berlioz, *Memoirs*

2   True art is imperishable and the true artist feels heartfelt pleasure in grand works of genius, and that is what enchants me when I hear a new composition of yours; in fact I take greater interest in it than in my own; in short, I love and honour you.

Ludwig van Beethoven (1770–1827)
Letter to Cherubini, 1823

3   . . . Beethoven impetuously threw himself at Cherubini's feet, explicitly and personally acknowledging him as his master; a compliment which poor Cherubini could return only by complaining that Beethoven's music made him sneeze.

Donald Francis Tovey (1875–1940)
Essays in Musical Analysis, IV, 1937

4   *Napoleon:*   My dear Cherubini, you are certainly an excellent musician; but really your music is so noisy and complicated, that I can make nothing of it.
   Cherubini: My dear general, you are certainly an excellent soldier; but, in regard to music, you must excuse me if I don't think it necessary to adapt my compositions to your comprehension.

Luigi Cherubini (1760–1842) and Napoleon Bonaparte (1769–1821)
Quoted in Bellasis, *Cherubini*, 1847

56 CHOPIN

1   He was dying all his life.
Hector Berlioz (1803–69)
Quoted in Elliot, *Berlioz*, 1967

2   Only one man knew . . . how to compose quasi-improvised music, or
at least what seems such. That is Chopin. He is a charming personality,
strange, unique, inimitable.
Georges Bizet (1838–75)

3   He is the truest artist I have ever met.
Eugène Delacroix (1798–1863)
Quoted in Hedley, *Chopin*, 1947

4   [Of Chopin's music:] It is the only enthusiasm of my youth which
remains.
Franz Liszt (1811–86)
Remark to his pupils, 1882

5   I love the angelic in his figure, which reminds me of Shelley: the
peculiarly and very mysteriously veiled, unapproachable, withdrawing,
unadventurous flavour of his being, that not wanting to know, that
rejection of material experience, the sublime incest of his fantastically
delicate and seductive art.
(Leverkühn)

Thomas Mann (1875–1955)
Doctor Faustus, 1947, trans Lowe-Porter

6   She had learned in her girlhood to fondle and cherish those long
sinuous phrases of Chopin, so free, so flexible, so tactile, which begin by
reaching out and exploring far outside and away from the direction in
which they started, far beyond the point which one might have expected
their notes to reach, and which divert themselves in those fantastic
bypaths only to return more deliberately – with a more premeditated
reprise, with more precision, as on a crystal bowl that reverberates to the
point of exquisite agony – to clutch at one's heart.
Marcel Proust (1871–1922)
Du côté de chez Swann, trans Scott-Moncrieff and Kilmartin

7   Hats off, gentlemen – a genius!
Robert Schumann (1810–56)
Reviewing Chopin's Op 2 in the *Allgemeine Musikalische Zeitung*, December 1831

8   A composer for the right hand.
Richard Wagner (1813–83)
Quoted in Cardus, *The Delights of Music*, 1966

9   After playing Chopin, I feel as if I had been weeping over sins that I had never committed.
Oscar Wilde (1854–1900)
The Critic as Artist, 1891

57   CORELLI

1   Corelli's excellence consists in the chastity of his composition.
John Gregory (1724–73)
The State and Faculties of Man, 1766

58   COUPERIN

1   I declare in all good faith that I am more pleased with what moves me than with what astonishes me.
François Couperin (1668–1733)
L'Art de toucher le clavecin, 1716

2   As hardly anyone has composed more than myself . . . I hope that my family will find in my wallet something to make them regret my passing.
François Couperin (1668–1733)
Pièces de clavecin, 1730, Bk 4, Preface

3   The artistocracy of Couperin's spirit lived in complete unawareness of is superiority. While the magnificence of Louis XIV was all on the outside, that of Couperin's music lies in its inner richness. For music was the centre of his life.
Wanda Landowska (1879–1959)
Landowska on Music, 1964

4   Why is this music which depicts our despair so comforting too? It is not because it expresses our sorrow, but because it is a sublimation of our distress, and in this sublimation lies the consoling power . . .
Wanda Landowska (1879–1959)
Ibid, 'François Couperin Le Grand'

59 CROTCH

1   The promise was that he would become a second Mozart; he became instead a man of musical learning and the composer of works that, whilst popular in their day, did not rise so high above the level of contemporary production as to secure immortality.

Percy A. Scholes (1877–1958)
Entry on William Crotch (1775–1847), *Oxford Companion to Music*, 1930

60   DEBUSSY

1   Music is a sum total of scattered forces.

Claude Debussy (1862–1918)
Monsieur Croche, antidilettante, 1921

2   French music is still in the position of a pretty widow who, having no one by her side strong enough to direct her, falls, to her cost, into alien arms.

Claude Debussy (1862–1918)
Ibid

3   The colour of my soul is iron-grey and sad bats wheel about the steeple of my dreams.

Claude Debussy (1862–1918)
Letter to Chausson, 1894

4   I shall always prefer a subject where, somehow, action is sacrificed to feeling. It seems to me that music thus becomes more human and real.

Claude Debussy (1862–1918)
Letter to Vasnier, 1885

5   Claude Debussy, if he's not making music, has no reason for existing.

Claude Debussy (1862–1918)
Letter to Jacques Durand, during the First World War

6   All Debussy's work has suffered from our native thurifers, who have choked their idol with poor-quality incense.

Pierre Boulez (1925–   )
Orientations, trans Cooper, 1986

7   Debussy has always remained my favourite composer after Mozart. I could not do without his music. It is my oxygen.

Francis Poulenc (1899–1963)
Quoted in Bernac, *Francis Poulenc*, 1977

8   [Of Debussy's music:] Better not listen to it; you risk getting used to it, and then you would end by liking it.

Nikolai Rimsky-Korsakov (1844–1908)
Quoted in Stravinsky, *Chronicles of my Life*, 1936

9   [On Debussy:] Nothing wrong with him that a few weeks in the open air wouldn't cure.

Carl Ruggles (1876–1971)
Attributed

10   [Of *La Mer*:] The audience seemed rather disappointed; they expected the ocean, something big, something colossal, but they were served instead some agitated water in a saucer.

Louis Schneider
Quoted in *Gil Blas*, 1905

61   DELIUS

1   How can music ever be a mere intellectual speculation or a series of curious combinations of sound that can be classified like the articles of a grocer's shop? Music is an outburst of the soul.

Frederick Delius (1862–1934)
Quoted in Fenby, *Delius as I knew him*, 1936

2   His entire philosophy of life was based upon an ultra-Nietzschean conception of the individual . . . This, of course, means that Frederick from the Anglo-Saxon point of view must be reckoned a supreme and complete egoist, and such he was, unquestionably.

Thomas Beecham (1879–1961)
A Mingled Chime, 1944

3   Strange how often a man's work is the opposite of his human personality. Delius as a man was as hard as nails, cold and cynical, yet his music is as soft as butter, warm and romantic.

Cecil Gray (1895–1951)
Notebooks, Pauline Gray (ed), 1989

4   There was always something incredibly sinister about the Delius
household . . . Even before the onset of the terrible illness from which
he increasingly suffered for so many years, and eventually died . . . I can
only say that I am amazed at Mr Fenby's fortitude in enduring, for
several years, experiences that nearly drove me insane after only a few
days.

Cecil Gray (1895–1951)
Musical Chairs, 1948

5   The musical equivalent of blancmange.

Bernard Levin (1928–   )
Enthusiasms, 1983

6   Delius was ferociously and fanatically anti-Christian. His anti-
Christianity was suspect, it was that of a rabidly and injudicially
prejudiced person who is fiercely opposed to something in which he
subconsciously fears there may be a good deal more after all than he is
willing to admit.

Kaikhosru Shapurji Sorabji (1895–1988)
Mi Contra Fa, 1947

7   As Beethoven is the morning and Wagner the high noon, so Delius is
the sunset of that great period of music which is called Romantic.

Peter Warlock (1894–1930)
Quoted in Machlis, *Introduction to Contemporary Music,* 1963

62   DONIZETTI

1   My heyday is over, and another must take my place. The world wants
something new. Others have ceded their places to us and we must cede
ours to still others . . . I am more than happy to give mine to people of
talent like Verdi.

Gaetano Donizetti (1797–1848)
Letter to Giuseppina Appiani, 1844

2 While his magical tunes bring joy to the world, while everyone sings them and trills them, he himself sits, a terrible picture of insanity in a lunatic asylum near Paris. Until some time ago, he had kept a childish consciousness of clothes: he had to be attired carefully every day in full dress, his tail coat decorated with all his orders; and so, from early in the morning until late at night he sat motionless, his hat in his hand! But even that is over with; he now recognizes no one. Such is the destiny of man.

Heinrich Heine (1797–1856)
On Donizetti's last days

---

63 DOWLAND

1 Dowland to thee is dear, whose heavenly
     touch
   Upon the lute doth ravish human sense.
   Richard Barnfield (1574–1627)
   Sonnet, published in *The Passionate Pilgrim*, 1599

2 *Semper Dowland Semper Dolens.*
   Always Dowland, always sad.
John Dowland (1563–1626)
Title of pavan for solo lute

3 *Dolande misero surripis mentem mihi,*
   Excorsque cordae pectus impulsae premunt.
   Quis tibi deorum tam potenti numine
   Digitos trementes dirigit is inter deos
   Magnos oportet principem obtineat locum . . .
   At O beate siste divinas manus,
   Iam iam parumper siste divinas manus,
   Liquescit anima, quam cave exugas mihi.
   O Dowland, unawares thou stealest my poor mind, the strings thou pluckest quite overwhelm my breast. The god who with such divine power directs thy trembling fingers, among the great gods he should hold the leading place . . . But O thou blest one, stay thy divine hands; now, now, for a moment stay thy divine hands. My soul dissolves, draw it not from me quite.
   Thomas Campion (1567–1620)
   Poemata, 1595

4   The music of Campion and of Dowland does not pretend to achieve anything higher than pleasant little tunes, which have for us a mild exotic charm because of certain archaic elements in their harmony and rhythm.

Donald Francis Tovey (1875–1940)
Words and Music, 1938

64   DVOŘÁK

1   I am just an ordinary Czech musician.

Antonin Dvořák (1841–1904)
Letter, 1886

2   I compose only for my own pleasure.

Antonin Dvořák (1841–1904)
Letter to Simrock, 1893

3   I have composed too much.

Antonin Dvořák (1841–1904)
Letter to Sibelius

4   You do write a bit hastily.

Johannes Brahms (1833–97)
Letter to Dvořák

5   I should be glad if something occurred to me as a main idea that occurs to Dvořák only by the way.

Johannes Brahms (1833–97)
Quoted in Sourek (ed), *Antonin Dvořák: Letters and Reminiscences,* 1954

6   Next to Brahms, the most God-gifted composer of the present day.

Hans von Bülow (1830–94)
Letter to Dvořák, 1877

7   Do you know what it is like when someone takes your words out of your mouth before you speak them? This is how I always felt in Dvořák's company. I can interchange his personality with his work. He has taken his melodies from my heart. Nothing on earth can sever such a bond.

Leoš Janáček (1854–1928)
Uncollected Essays, pub 1989

8   In music, as in joiner's work, you can take the poorest materials and set the public gaping at them by simply covering them with black cloth and coffin-nails.

George Bernard Shaw (1854–1950)
Review of Dvořák's *Requiem*, 9 November 1892

9   This jester.

Bedřich Smetana (1824–84)
Letter to L. Prochazka, 23 December 1879

65   ELGAR

1   [Elgar telling Delius what flying in an aeroplane is like:] To put it poetically, it is not unlike your life and my life. The rising from the ground was a little difficult; you cannot tell exactly how you are going to stand it. When once you have reached the height it is very different. There is a delightful feeling of elation in sailing through gold and silver clouds. It is, Delius, rather like your music–a little intangible sometimes, but always very beautiful. I should have liked to stay there for ever. The descent is like our old age–peaceful, even serene.

Edward Elgar (1857–1934)
Quoted in The *Daily Telegraph*, 1933

2   I like to look on the composer's vocation as the old troubadours and bards did. In those days it was no disgrace for a man to be turned on to step in front of an army and inspire them with a song.

Edward Elgar (1857–1934)
Quoted in the *Strand* magazine, 1904

3   [On Elgar's Symphony No 1:] The musical equivalent of St Pancras Station.

Thomas Beecham (1879–1961)
Quoted in Atkins and Newman, *Beecham Stories*, 1978

4   Look out for this man's music; he has something to say and knows how to say it.

Hubert Parry (1848–1918)
Remark after hearing the first performance of *Enigma Variations*, 1899

5   Gentlemen, let us now rehearse the greatest symphony of modern times, written by the greatest modern composer . . .
Hans Richter (1843–1916)
To the Halle Orchestra, 1908, on Elgar's First Symphony

6   If a German or an Austrian, a Czech or a Bashibazouk, had composed *Gerontius*, the whole world would have by now admitted its qualities.
Neville Cardus (1889–1975)
Quoted in the *Manchester Guardian*, 1939

7   Elgar . . . might have been a great composer if he had thrown all that religious paraphernalia overboard. *Gerontius* is a nauseating work . . .
Frederick Delius (1862–1934)
Quoted in Fenby, *Delius as I knew him*, 1936

8   Elgar loved his rivers . . . the Severn in particular. One could almost label the movements in the Violin Concerto, The Severn, The Thames, and The Wye; for they seem to flow through all his music.
W.H. Reed (1876–1942)
Quoted in *The Listener*, 10 November 1937

9   The first Progressivist in English music.
Richard Strauss (1864–1949)
Quoted in *The Musical Times*, 1931

10   [Of *The Dream of Gerontius*:] My son, that is a sublime masterpiece.
Pope Pius XII (1876–1958)
Remark to John Barbirolli, quoted in Kennedy, *Barbirolli, Conductor Laureate*, 1971

66   FAURÉ

1   I have been reserved all my life . . . and have only been able to let myself go in certain situations.
Gabriel Fauré (1845–1924)
Letter to his wife Marie, 1921

2   Fauré in his *Requiem*, composed for the church of La Madeleine, was perhaps the only one to elevate the church music of his day to the rank of an admirable work of art.
Jacques Chailley (1910–   )
40000 Years of Music, trans Myers, 1964

3   The play of the graceful, fleeting lines described by Fauré's music may be compared to the gesture of a beautiful woman without either suffering from comparison.
Claude Debussy (1862–1918)
Quoted in *Gil Blas*, 1903

4   [The sort of music] a pederast might hum when raping a choirboy.
Marcel Proust (1871–1922)
On Fauré's *Romances sans paroles*, quoted in *Musical Quarterly*, 1924

5   I not only admire, adore and venerate your music, I have been and still am in love with it.
Marcel Proust (1871–1922)
Letter to Fauré, 1897

67 FRANCK

1   [Of César Franck's symphonic works:] Cathedrals in sound.
Alfred Bruneau (1857–1934)
Speech, 1904

2   César Franck was single-minded. To have found a beautiful harmony sufficed to make his day happy.
Claude Debussy (1862–1918)
Monsieur Croche, antidilettante, 1921

68 GERSHWIN

1   [To George Gershwin, on refusing him as a pupil:] You would only lose the spontaneous quality of your melody, and end by writing bad Ravel.
Maurice Ravel (1875–1937)
Quoted in Kendall, *The Tender Tyrant: Nadia Boulanger*, 1976

2   An apochryphal story is that upon meeting Maurice Ravel, George
asked for lessons in composition. Ravel inquired about George's yearly
income and when told that it was $200000 replied, 'You teach me.'

Oscar Levant (1906–72)
Memoirs of an Amnesiac, 1965
(Stravinsky is also attributed with this remark, not Ravel)

69   GESUALDO

1   Related to the great aristocratic families of Italy, Gesualdo was of a
violent nature. In 1590 he ordered the murder of his wife Marie
d'Avalos and her lover Fabrizio Carafa; after which tragic event he
composed six books of madrigals, married Eleonora d'Este, and devoted
himself to music.

Henry Prunière (1886–1942)
A New History of Music, trans Lockspeiser, 1941

70   GIBBONS

1   . . . this Orlando parallels di Lasso:
Whose triple praise would tire a very Tasso.

Anonymous
*Parthenia, or the Maydenhead of the first
musicke that ever was printed for the
Virginalls,* 1612

2   *Inter musas et musicae nato.*
Born among the Muses and Music.

Anonymous
Monument to Orlando Gibbons in Canterbury Cathedral, trans William Boyce

3   . . . the repertoire that I'm fondest of tends to emerge from the pens
of *fin-de-siècle* men. I can't think of anybody who represents the end of
an era better than Orlando Gibbons does, and Gibbons *is* my favourite
composer—always has been.

Glenn Gould (1932–82)
Cott, *Conversations with Glenn Gould,* 1984

71 GLINKA

1 My brother wrote only when something strong and pleasant acted upon him, be it a woman, nature, the climate, or an outstanding work of art. Then he was inspired.

Lyudmila Glinka
Quoted in Brown, *Glinka*, 1974

2 [Of Glinka's *A Life for the Tsar*:] What an opera you can make out of our national tunes! Show me a people who have more songs! ... Glinka's opera is only a beautiful beginning.

Nikolai Gogol (1809–52)
Quoted in *The Contemporary*, 1836

72 GLUCK

1 The pit was so tightly packed that when a man who had his hat on his head was told by the guard to take it off, he replied: 'Come and take it off yourself, for I cannot move my arms'; which caused laughter. I have seen people coming out with their hair bedraggled and their clothes drenched as through they had fallen into a stream. Only Frenchmen would pay so dearly for a pleasure. There are passages in the opera which force the audience to lose their countenance and their composure.

Christoph Willibald von Gluck (1714–87)
Letter to the Countess von Fries, 16 November 1777, Paris, quoted in Gal, *The Musician's World*, 1965

2 Today our celebrated *Kapellmeister* Gluck gives the first performance of his opera *Iphigénie en Aulide*, which Mme la Dauphine will attend. The music has been greatly applauded at the rehearsals, and it is expected to mark an epoch in the reformation of French harmony, for this last is, as you know, very insipid and monotonous.

Count de Mercy-Argenteau
Letter to Empress Maria Theresa of Austria, 19 April 1774

73 GOUNOD

1   Musical ideas sprang to my mind like a flight of butterflies, and all I had to do was to stretch out my hand to catch them.

Charles Gounod (1818–93)
Of his period in Provence, 1863, quoted in Harding, *Gounod*, 1973

2   My humiliating profession of decomposer of music.

Charles Gounod (1818–93)
After demands for alterations to his opera *Mireille*, quoted in Harding, *Gounod*, 1973

3   I fight against the void, I think I've written something acceptable, and then, when I look at it again, I find it execrable.

Charles Gounod (1818–93)
In 1870, quoted in Harding, *Gounod*, 1973

4   To be a great artist it is not necessary to be an honourable man.

Georges Bizet (1838–75)
Quoted in Dean, *Bizet*, 1975

5   You were the beginning of my life as an artist. I spring from you. You are the cause and I am the consequence.

Georges Bizet (1838–75)
Letter to Gounod, 1872

6   Once upon a time an Englishman – or can it possibly have been an American? – was being shown the sights of Weimar and paused for a moment to study the inscription on an imposing statue of Goethe.
   'Who was this Goathy anyway?', he asked. 'I've never heard of him.'
   'He was a great Master,' replied his German guide. 'He wrote *Faust*.'
   Whereupon the now enlightened tourist was able to rejoin: 'Oh yes, of course.' And out of the kindness of his heart he added a piece of gratuitous information: 'In our country we pronounce his name Goono.'

Gervase Hughes (1905–)
Sidelights on a Century of Music, 1969

7   A base soul who poured a sort of bath-water melody down the back of every woman he met. Margaret or Madeleine, it was all the same.

George Moore (1852–1933)
Memoirs of My Dead Life, 1906

74 GRAINGER

1 What an artist, what a man! What a lofty idealist, what a child, and at the same time, what a broad and mature outlook he has on life. A future socialist of the purest water. Wagner's words: '*Aus Mitleid wissend, der reine Thor!*' fit him exactly . . .

Edvard Grieg (1843–1907)
Diary, 5 August 1907

2 The object of my music is not to entertain, but to agonize – to make mankind think of the agony of young men forced to kill each other against their will and all the other thwartments and torturings of the young.

Percy Aldridge Grainger (1882–1961)
Anecdotes, 1949–54, quoted in Bird, *Percy Grainger*, 1976

75 GRIEG

1 The realm of harmonies was always my dream-world.

Edvard Grieg (1843–1907)
Letter to Henry T. Finck

2 If there is in my music anything of lasting value it will live; if not, it will perish. That is my belief, for I am convinced that truth will prevail *ultimately*.

Edvard Grieg (1843–1907)
Letter to Henry T. Finck, 1905

3 One has in one's mouth the bizarre and charming taste of a pink bonbon stuffed with snow.

Claude Debussy (1862–1918)
Quoted in *Gil Blas*, 1903

4 I had wanted to be Grieg's prophet, but instead he became my prophet. I had wanted critically and impersonally to proclaim the still-unsuspected, far-reaching importance of Grieg's compositional innovations, but instead became his protégé.

Percy Grainger (1882–1961)
Notes on Grieg

5   Orpheus with his wondrous tones
    Roused souls in beasts, struck fire from
      stones.

Of stones has Norway not a few,
And beasts she has in plenty too.

Play then, that sparks from rocks may leap!
Play then, and pierce the brutes' hides deep!

Henrik Ibsen (1828–1906)
Verse written in Grieg's album, trans Horton

6   I ventured to say the coda of one of the movements seemed not quite
up to the level of the rest. 'Ah yes!' he said, shrugging his shoulders, 'at
that point inspiration gave out and I had to finish without!'

Dame Ethel Smyth (1858–1944)
Impressions That Remained, II

7   What charm, what inimitable and rich musical imagery! . . . What
interest, novelty, and independence!

Píotr Ilyich Tchaikovsky (1840–93)
Quoted in Finck, *Grieg and his Music*, 1906

76 HANDEL

1   I did think I did see all Heaven before me, and the great God
Himself.

George Frideric Handel (1685–1759)
Words to his servant, who found him alone and weeping, after completing Part II of
Messiah with the 'Hallelujah Chorus',

2   I should be sorry, my Lord, if I have only succeeded in entertaining
them; I wished to make them better.

George Frideric Handel (1685–1759)
To Lord Kinnoull after the first London performance of *Messiah*

3   [Accused of borrowing music written by Bononcini:] It's much too
good for him; he did not know what to do with it.

George Frideric Handel (1685–1759)
Attributed in Lang, *George Friderich Handel*, 1967

4   Conceive the highest you can of his abilities, and they are far beyond anything you can conceive.
Dr John Arbuthnot (1667–1735)
Quoted in Young, *Handel*, 1947

5   I sat close by [Beethoven] and heard him assert very distinctly in German, 'Handel is the greatest composer that ever lived.' I cannot describe to you with what pathos, and I am inclined to say, with what sublimity of language, he spoke of the *Messiah* of this immortal genius. Every one of us was moved when he said, 'I would uncover my head, and kneel down at his tomb!'
Edward Schulz
On a visit to Beethoven, in *The Harmonicon*, January 1824

6   [Of an edition of Handel's works:] There is the truth.
Ludwig van Beethoven (1770–1827)
Remark on his deathbed, quoted in Young, *Handel*, 1947

7   A tub of pork and beer.
Hector Berlioz (1803–69)
Quoted in Elliot, *Berlioz*, 1967

8   Handel's general look was somewhat heavy and sour; but when he did smile, it was his sire the sun, bursting out of a black cloud.
Charles Burney (1726–1814)
An Account of the Musical Performances . . . in Commemoration of Handel, 1785

9   Handel and Shakespeare have left us the best that any have left us; yet, in spite of this, how much of their lives was wasted. Fancy Handel expending himself upon the Moabites and Ammonites, or even the Jews themselves, year after year, as he did in the fullness of his power.
Samuel Butler (1835–1902)
Note-books, pub 1912

10   Handel is so great and so simple that no one but a professional musician is unable to understand him.
Samuel Butler (1835–1902)
Ibid

11   Some say, that Signor Bononcini,
Compar'd to Handel's a mere ninny;
Others aver, to him, that Handel
Is scarcely fit to hold a candle.
Strange! that such high dispute shou'd be
'Twixt Tweedledum and Tweedledee.
John Byrom (1692–1763)
Epigram on the feuds between Handel and Bononcini

12   Remember Handel? Who, that was not
      born
    Deaf as the dead to harmony, forgets,
    Or can, the more than Homer of his age?

William Cowper (1731–1800)
The Task, 1785, VI

13 I think Handel never gets out of his wig, that is, out of his age: his Hallelujah Chorus is a chorus, not of angels, but of well-fed earthly choristers, ranged tier above tier in a Gothic cathedral, with princes for audience, and their military trumpets flourishing over the full volume of the organ. Handel's gods are like Homer's, and his sublimes never reached beyond the region of the clouds.

Edward Fitzgerald (1809–83)
Letter, 1842

14 A good old pagan at heart.

Edward Fitzgerald (1809–83)
Quoted in Young, *Handel*, 1947

15   There *Hendel* strikes the strings, the
      melting strain
    Transports the soul, and thrills through
      every vein.

John Gay (1685–1732)
Trivia, 1716

16 The inspired master of our art.

Christoph Willibald von Gluck (1714–87)
Quoted in Kelly, *Reminiscences*, 1826

17 [On hearing the Hallelujah Chorus:] He is the master of us all.

Joseph Haydn (1732–1809)
Quoted in Headington, *The Bodley Head History of Western Music*, 1974

18 Handel was the Jupiter of music; ... his hallelujahs open the heavens. He utters the word 'Wonderful', as if all their trumpets spoke together. And then, when he comes to earth, to make love amidst nymphs and shepherds (for the beauties of all religions find room in his breast), his strains drop milk and honey, and his love is the youthfulness of the Golden Age.

Leigh Hunt (1784–1859)
Table Talk, 1851

19   Handel understands effect better than any of us – when he chooses, he strikes like a thunderbolt.

Wolfgang Amadeus Mozart (1756–91)
Quoted in Young, *Handel*, 1947

20   [Of Handel's playing:] I found . . . nothing worthy to remark but the elasticity of his fingers.

Isaac Newton (1642–1727)
Quoted in Hawkins, *Life of Johnson*, 1787

21   Handel is only fourth rate. He is not even interesting.

Píotr Ilyich Tchaikovsky (1840–93)

22   It was part of Handel's misfortune, and part too of his glory, that his music should readily have become an integral part of an Englishman's religion.

Percy M. Young (1912–   )
Handel, 1947

23   Bach invaded the *Himmelreich*; Handel found *Lebensraum* on earth.

Percy M. Young (1912–   )
Handel, 1947

77   HAYDN

1   [Of his youthful compositions:] I thought then that everything was all right if only the paper was chock-full of notes.

Joseph Haydn (1732–1809)
Quoted in Hughes, *Haydn*, 1970

2   [Of his period as *Kapellmeister* at the Esterházy court:] I was cut off from the world. There was no one to confuse or torment me, and I was forced to become original.

Joseph Haydn (1732–1809)
Quoted in Hadden, *Haydn*, 1934

3   The said Joseph Haydn must see that both he himself and all his musicians will obey the regulations and appear in white stockings, white linen and powdered hair, either tied in a bow or with a wig.

Article 2 of Haydn's contract with Prince Nicholas Esterházy

4 The said Joseph Haydn will present himself daily in the ante-chamber before and after noon, to receive instructions from His Highness as to whether or not the orchestra's services will be required. After receiving his orders, he will communicate them to the other musicians and see that they are punctually carried out . . .

Ibid, Article 5

5 The master of music, Mr Haydn, is reminded to apply himself more assiduously to composition than he has done so far, especially with respect to pieces for the gamba [the 'barytone', the Prince's favourite instrument], of which we have seen very little up to now; and, to show his zeal, he will hand in the first piece of every composition in a clean, tidy copy.

Prince Nicholas Esterházy (1714–90)
Gal, *The Musician's World*, 1965

6 It is a sad thing always to be a slave, but Providence will have it so, poor wretch that I am!

Joseph Haydn (1732–1809)
Letter to Marianne von Genzinger, 1790

7 I had a kind Prince but was at times dependent upon mean spirits. I often sighed for deliverance, now I have it after a fashion . . . although my spirit is oppressed with much work. The knowledge that I am not a bondsman makes up for all my toil . . .

Joseph Haydn (1732–1809)
Letter, 17 September 1791

8 This is my wife; she has often enraged me.

Joseph Haydn (1732–1809)
Haydn's words to a friend, before a picture of his late wife

9 I get up early, and as soon as I have dressed I go down on my knees and pray God and the Blessed Virgin that I may have another successful day. Then when I've had some breakfast I sit down at the clavier and begin my search. If I hit on an idea quickly, it goes ahead easily and without much trouble. But if I can't get on, I know that I must have forfeited God's grace by some fault of mine, and then I pray once more for grace until I feel I'm forgiven.

Joseph Haydn (1732–1809)
Quoted in Hughes, *Haydn*, 1970

10 That will make the ladies scream.

Joseph Haydn (1732–1809)
Of the 'Surprise' Symphony, quoted in Gyrowetz, *Memoirs*, 1848

11 [At a performance of *The Creation*:] Not from me – it came from above.

Joseph Haydn (1732 – 1809)
Headington, *The Bodley Head History of Western Music*, 1974

12 I was never so devout as when I was at work on *The Creation*.

Joseph Haydn (1732 – 1809)
Quoted in Hughes, *Haydn*, 1970

13 Oh God, how much is still to be done in this splendid art, even by such a man as I have been!

Joseph Haydn (1732 – 1809)
Letter to Georg August Griesinger, 1799

14 Don't be frightened, children, where Haydn is no harm can come to you.

Joseph Haydn (1732 – 1809)
To his terrified servants during the French bombardment of Vienna, 1809, quoted in Hughes, *Haydn*, 1970

15 Often when I was wrestling with obstacles of every kind, when my physical and mental strength alike were running low and it was hard for me to persevere in the path on which I had set my feet, a secret feeling within me whispered: 'There are so few happy and contented people here below, sorrow and anxiety pursue them everywhere; perhaps your work may, some day, become a spring from which the careworn may draw a few moments' rest and refreshment.' And that was a powerful motive for pressing onward

Joseph Haydn (1732 – 1809)
Letter to a group of music-lovers in Bergen

16 Though I had some instruction from Haydn, I never learned anything from him.

Ludwig van Beethoven (1770 – 1827)
Quoted in Scott, *Beethoven*, 1934

17 I have had the great Haydn here, I think him as good a creature as great musician.

Charles Burney (1726 – 1814)
Letter to Arthur Young, 1791

18   Among other observations His Majesty [George III] said: 'Dr Haydn, you have written a good deal.' Haydn modestly replied: 'Yes, Sire, a great deal more than is good.' His Majesty neatly rejoined: 'Oh, no, the world contradicts that.'

A. Gyrowetz
Memoirs, 1848

19   It has been said that if the opening phrase of a classical minuet can be fitted to the words 'Are you the O'Reilly who owns this hotel' then it was composed by Haydn; if they can't then it wasn't.

Gervase Hughes (1905–)
Sidelights on a Century of Music, 1969

20   Whoever studies music, let his daily bread be Haydn. Beethoven indeed is admirable, he is incomparable, but he has not the same usefulness as Haydn: he is not a necessity . . . Haydn the great musician, the first who created everything, discovered everything, taught everything to the rest!

Jean Ingres (1780–1867)

21   To my dear friend Haydn: A father who had decided to send his sons into the great world, thought it his duty to entrust them to the protection and guidance of a man who was very celebrated at the time and who, moreover, happened to be his best friend.

Wolfgang Amadeus Mozart (1756–91)
Dedicating *Six String Quartets* to Haydn, 1785

22   So far as genius can exist in a man who is merely virtuous, Haydn had it. He went as far as the limits that morality sets to intellect.

Friedrich Nietzsche (1844–1900)
All-Too-Human, 1878

78   HINDEMITH

1   *Er komponiert nicht, er musiziert.*
    He doesn't compose, he makes music.

Paul Bekker (1882–1937)
Attributed

2 [Hindemith's] blood may be purely German, but this only provides drastic confirmation of how deeply the Jewish intellectual infection has eaten into the body of our own people.

Joseph Goebbels (1897–1945)
Speech, 1935

3 I am gradually beginning to feel like a cornerstone on which every passerby can pass the water of his artistic opinion.

Paul Hindemith (1895–1963)
Letter to Willy Strecker, 1946

4 Hindemith's music does not bore many people, though it annoys some. He is never very long, he thumps no tubs, and his attitudes are not solemn. He is manifestly humorous, and he makes the best of modern life ... Neither with Hindemith nor with Haydn can I undertake to preserve a solemn countenance while I discuss their works ...

Donald Francis Tovey (1875–1940)
Essays and Lectures on Music, 1949

79 HOLST

1 Holst was a visionary but, at the same time, in all essentials a very practical man. He himself used to say that only second-rate artists were unbusinesslike. It is the blend of the visionary with the realist that gives Holst's music its distinctive character.

Ralph Vaughan Williams (1872–1958)
Radio broadcast quoted in Shore, *The Orchestra Speaks,* 1938

80 HONEGGER

See also 95 Milhaud

1 I am like a steam engine: I need to be stoked up, it takes me a long time to get ready for genuine work.

Arthur Honegger (1892–1956)
I am a Composer, 1951

2   Starting from objective contemplation … the speed increases steadily and reaches lyrical ecstacy at seventy-five miles an hour, with 300 tons hurtling down the track.
Arthur Honegger (1892–1956)
On his *Pacific 231*, 1924

3   My inclination and my effort have always been to write music which would be comprehensible to the great mass of listeners and at the same time sufficiently free of banality to interest genuine music lovers.
Arthur Honegger (1892–1956)
I am a Composer, 1951

81   HUMMEL

1   Never come near me again! You are a faithless cur, and may the hangman take all faithless curs.
(Beethoven here uses the insulting third person 'er' for 'you'.)
Ludwig van Beethoven (1770–1827)
Letter to Hummel, Vienna 1799, quoted in Gal, *The Musician's World*, 1965

2   It was a serious moment for me when Beethoven appeared. Was I to try to follow in the footsteps of such a genius? For a while I did not know what I stood on; but finally I said to myself that it was best to remain true to myself and my own nature.
Johann Nepomuk Hummel (1778–1837)
Quoted in Bie, *A History of the Pianoforte*, 1899

82   IVES

1   Every dissonance doesn't have to resolve if it doesn't happen to feel like it, any more than every horse should have its tail bobbed just because it's the prevailing fashion.
Georges Ives
Remark to his son Charles, quoted in Wooldridge, *Charles Ives*, 1974

2   Not sung by Caruso, Jenny Lind, John McCormack, Harry Lauder or the Village Nightingale.

Charles Ives (1874–1954)
Inscription on a song

3   Please don't try to make things nice! All the wrong notes are *right*. Just copy as I have – I want it that way.

Charles Ives (1874–1954)
MS note to his copyist on score of *The Fourth of July*

4   Four men – who converse, discuss, argue . . . fight, shake hands, shut up – then walk up the mountainside to view the firmament!

Charles Ives (1874–1954)
Programme for String Quartet No 2

5   These prefatory essays were written by the composer for those who can't stand his music – and the music for those who can't stand his essays; to those who can't stand either, the whole is respectfully dedicated.

Charles Ives (1874–1954)
Essays before a Sonata, 1920

6   An Old Testament prophet crying a New Mythology in the American wilderness.

David Wooldridge
Charles Ives, 1974

7   There is a great Man Living in this Country – a composer.
He has solved the problem of how to preserve one's self and to learn.
He responds to negligence by contempt.
He is not forced to accept praise or blame.
His name is Ives.

Arnold Schoenberg (1874–1951)
MS note, *c* 1945, quoted in Cowell, *Charles Ives*, 1955

83   JANÁČEK

1   I do not play about with empty melodies. I dip them in life and nature. I find work very difficult and serious – perhaps for this reason.

Leoš Janáček (1854–1928)
Letter to K.E. Sokol, 1925

2   Let our composers grow wings large enough to carry them far,
     That they may drink the waters of all the Slavs.
     Perhaps only this can satisfy the composer's soul.

Leoš Janáček (1854–1928)
Questions and Answers, 1922

3   Composing music is not as easy as an innocent mind would have it. To create an image through music is, in large part, one of the graphic arts. It becomes such an art when, as if by a miracle, the vision catches a glimpse of itself in a real being.

Leoš Janáček (1854–1928)
Uncollected Essays, pub 1989

4   If I grow at all, it is only out of folk-music, out of human speech . . .

Leoš Janáček (1854–1928)
Ibid

5   *Jenůfa* is tied with the black ribbon of the long illness, pains and cries of my daughter Olga.

Leoš Janáček (1854–1928)
Quoted in Brod, *Leoš Janáček*, 1956

6   I want to be in direct contact with the clouds, I want to feast my eyes on the blue of the sky, I want to gather the sun's rays into my hands, I want to plunge myself in shadow, I want to pour out my longings to the full: all directly.

Leoš Janáček (1854–1928)
Lidove Noviny, 1927

84 HENRY LAWES

1   I confess the Italian Language may have some advantage by being better smooth'd and *vowell'd* for Musick . . . and our English seems a little over-clogg'd with *Consonants*; but that's much the *Composer's* fault, who by judicious setting and right tuning the words may make it smooth enough.

Henry Lawes (1596–1662)
Ayres and Dialogues, 1653, Preface

2   Harry, whose tuneful and well measured
        song
    First taught our English music how to span
    Words with just note and accent, not to scan
    With Midas ears, committing short and long.

John Milton (1608–74)
To Mr H Lawes on the Publishing of his Airs

3   Thou honour'st Verse, and Verse must
        lend her wing
    To honour thee, the Priest of *Phoebus* Quire,
    That tun'st their happiest Lines in hymn or
        story.

John Milton (1608–74)
Ibid

4   But you alone may truly boast
    That not a syllable is lost;
    The writer's, and the setter's skill
    At once the ravished ears do fill.

Edmund Waller (1606–87)
To Mr Henry Lawes

5   You by the help of tune and time,
    Can make that song that was but rhyme.

Edmund Waller (1606–87)
Ibid

85 WILLIAM LAWES

1   *Concord* is conquer'd; in this urn
        there lies
    The master of great Music's mysteries;
    And in it is a riddle like the cause,
    Will Lawes was slain by those whose *Will* are
        Lawes.

Epitaph for William Lawes (b 1602, d in the siege of Chester, 1645)

86 LIGETI

1 *Interviewer:* I'm intrigued by one title from 1951, your *Grand Symphonie Militaire* Op 69.

   Ligeti: Oh that was a joke. The Opus number refers of course to the sexual position.

Paul Griffiths
Györgi Ligeti, 1983

87 LISZT

1 *Le concert c'est moi.*
Franz Liszt (1811–86)
On his innovation of the solo recital, 1839

2 Everyone is against me. Catholics, because they find my church music profane, Protestants because to them my music is Catholic, Freemasons because they think my music too clerical; to conservatives I am a revolutionary, to the 'Futurists' an old Jacobin. As for the Italians . . . if they support Garibaldi they detest me as a hypocrite; if they are on the Vatican side, I am accused of bringing Venus's grotto into the Church. To Bayreuth I am not a composer but a publicity agent. Germans reject my music as French, the French as German, to the Austrians I write Gypsy music, to the Hungarians foreign music. And the Jews loathe me, my music and myself, for no reason at all.
Franz Liszt (1811–86)
Letter to Ödön Mihalovich from his last years, *New Hungarian Quarterly*, autumn 1986

3 Music herself should be silent when Nicholas speaks.
Franz Liszt (1811–86)
On being asked why he stopped playing when Czar Nicholas I was talking

4 Anyone who cannot tell sentimentality from true feeling, or false pathos from the genuine kind, will ruin Liszt's music, even if he does not ruin his own reputation. Anyone who does not play Liszt with nobility passes sentence on himself.
Alfred Brendel (1931–)
The Times, 3 November 1986

5   Yesterday saw Liszt . . . he was getting out of a hackney carriage, his black silk cassock fluttering ironically behind him—Mephistopheles disguised as an Abbé. Such is the end of Lovelace!

Ferdinand Gregorovius (1821–91)
The Roman Journals, 1852–74, trans Hamilton, 1910

6   [On Liszt's playing:] One no longer thinks of difficulty overcome; the piano vanishes and—music appears.

Heinrich Heine (1797–1856)
Quoted in Beckett, *Liszt*, 1956

7   He is without doubt the artist who finds in Paris the most unreserved enthusiasm, as well as the keenest opposition. It is significant that no one speaks of him with indifference. A man who lacks positive stature, cannot in this world arouse favourable or antagonistic passions. It takes fire to kindle men, whether to hate or to love. What speaks most for Liszt is the respect with which even his enemies recognize his personal merits. He is a man of unruly but noble character, unself-seeking and without falseness.

Heinrich Heine (1797–1856)
Letters on the French Stage, 1837, quoted by Barzun, *Pleasures of Music*, 1952

8   Liszt never charged a fee from any of his pupils, and we all looked upon him with a feeling akin to adoration. Felix Weingartner . . . once said to me 'Liszt was the decentest of them all.' The word decent seems a strange one to apply to this extraordinary personality, but the more I think of it, the more I realize it's the right epithet for Liszt. Indeed I go further than that. Liszt was the good Samaritan of his day and generation.

Frederic Lamond (1868–1948)
Memoirs, 1949

9   *Ich kann warten.*
    I can wait.

Franz Liszt (1811–86)
On the neglect of his music, quoted by Lamond, *Memoirs*, 1949

10   While young the unabashed Franz
     Embarked on a Periode Glanze.
     His honour-sheathed swords
     Entangled in chords
     Nearly caused him his own Totentanz.

     A Bellagio room with a view
     Of Lake Como with Countess d'Agoult
     Caused him quickly to learn
     Life with Daniel Stern
     Would yield moments of peace far and few.

     Bernard P. Langley (1929–)
     Lisztrionics

11   I began to love and admire you in Vienna in 1822, a recollection so
dear to me! The succeeding years have only increased my affection for
you. Your determination to enter on an ecclesiastical career has not
surprised me. Rather it has inspired me. Oh, my dearest Abbé Liszt,
allow me to offer my sincere felicitations on the *holy* road you have taken,
which assures you the best possible future. However, I am sure that you
will not abandon music in which God has so richly endowed you that the
harmony of Heaven will ever be your best escort on this earth.

Gioachino Rossini (1792–1868)
Letter to Liszt, 1865

12   [On Liszt:] The incontestable incarnation of the modern piano.
Camille Saint-Saëns (1835–1921)
Portraits et Souvenirs, 1899

13   [Of Liszt:] The world persisted to the end in calling him the
greatest pianist in order to avoid the trouble of considering his claims as
one of the most remarkable of composers.
Camille Saint-Saëns (1835–1921)
Harmonie et Mélodie, 1885

14   A young lady pianist had announced a recital, advertising herself (in the hope of attracting a larger audience) as a 'pupil of Liszt'. As she had never laid eyes on him in her life, she was horrified to read in the papers on the morning of her concert that the Abbé had arrived in the city. The only thing to be done was to make a clean breast of it; she went to his hotel and asked for an interview. When she was shown in she confessed with many tears, and asked for absolution. Liszt asked her the name of the pieces she was going to play, chose one and made her sit down at the piano and play it. Then he gave her some hints about her performance, and dismissed her with a pat on the cheek, and the remark, 'Now, my dear, you can call yourself a pupil of Liszt.'

Charles Villiers Stanford (1852–1924)
Pages from an Unwritten Diary, 1914

88   LULLY

1   He merits with good reason the title of Prince of French Musicians, being regarded as the inventor of this beautiful and great French music.

Evrard Titon du Tillet (1677–1762)
Quoted in Mellers, *François Couperin*, 1950

2   After Lulli, all other musicians such as Colasse, Campra, Destouches, and the rest, simply imitated him until Rameau came, when, by the depth of his harmony, he surpassed them and made of music a new art.

Voltaire (1694–1778)
The Age of Louis XIV, 1752–56

89   MAHLER

1   My music is, throughout and always, but a sound of nature.

Gustav Mahler (1860–1911)
Quoted in Machlis, *Introduction to Contemporary Music*, 1963

2   Only when I experience do I compose – only when I compose do I experience.

Gustav Mahler (1860–1911)
Letter to Anton Seidl, 17 February 1897

3 I am three times homeless: a native of Bohemia in Austria; an Austrian among Germans; a Jew throughout the whole world.
Gustav Mahler (1860–1911)
Quoted in Yates, *Twentieth Century Music*, 1968

4 [On seeing Niagara Falls:]
   Endlich fortissimo!
   Fortissimo at last!
Gustav Mahler (1860–1911)
Quoted in Blaukopf, *Gustav Mahler*, 1973

5 For the first time in musical history, music is interrogating itself about the reasons for its existence and about its nature . . . it is a knowing music, with the same tragic consciousness as Freud, Kafka, Musil.
Hans Werner Henze (1926–   )
Music and Politics, 1982, 'Gustav Mahler', 1975

90 MASCAGNI

1 It was a pity I wrote *Cavalleria* first. I was crowned before I was king.
Pietro Mascagni (1863–1945)
Quoted in Carner, *Puccini*, 1974

91 MASSENET

1 We must pay attention to this little chap, he's going to leave us standing.
Georges Bizet (1838–75)
Quoted in Dean, *Bizet*, 1975

2 The vulgar, impassioned whinings of Massenet.
Gabriel Fauré (1845–1924)
Letter to his wife, 1909

3   It's very odd! When I hear Massenet's operas I always long for
Saint-Saëns's. I should add that hearing Saint-Saëns's operas makes
me long for Massenet's.

Henri Gauthier-Villars
Quoted in Harding, *Massenet,* 1970

4   Massenet is to Gounod what Schumann is to Mendelssohn.

Camille Saint-Saëns (1835–1921)
Attributed

---

92   MENDELSSOHN

---

1   Ever since I began to compose, I have remained true to my starting
principle: not to write a page because no matter what public, or what
pretty girl wanted it to be thus or thus; but to write solely as I myself
thought best, and as it gave me pleasure.

Felix Mendelssohn (1809–47)
Letter, 1843

2   Mendelssohn has shown us that a Jew may have the amplest of
talents, the finest and most varied culture, the highest and tenderest
sense of honour, yet these qualities cannot help him even once to evoke
in us the deep heart-searching effect which we expect from art.

Richard Wagner (1813–83)
Judaism in Music, 1850

3   To the Noble Artist who, surrounded by the Baal-worship of
debased art, has been able, by his genius and science, to preserve
faithfully, like another Elijah, the worship of true art . . .

Albert, Prince Consort (1819–61)
Inscription in Mendelssohn's libretto of *Elijah*

4   A wonderful genius . . . so pleasing and amiable.

Queen Victoria (1819–1901)
Journal, 1842

93 MESSIAEN

1 Among the artistic hierarchy, the birds are probably the greatest musicians to inhabit our planet.

Olivier Messiaen (1908–)
Quoted in Sherlaw Johnson, *Messiaen*, 1975

2 Melody is the point of departure. May it remain supreme! And whatever complexities there may be in our rhythms or harmonies, they shall not dominate it, but, on the contrary . . . be subject to it like faithful servants.

Olivier Messiaen (1908–)
Technique de mon langage musical, 1950

3 In Messiaen I see very clearly the musical reflection of stalactites: a succession of fourths, perfect or augmented, tumbling down or mounting again in pyramids, from low to high, in a ladder of sound.

Arthur Honegger (1892–1956)
I am a Composer, 1951

4 [Of Messiaen's *Turangalíla-symphonie*:] Little more can be required to write such things than a plentiful supply of ink.

Igor Stravinsky (1882–1971)
Themes and Conclusions, 1972

94 MEYERBEER

1 [Of Meyerbeer:] The luck of having talent was not enough; he also had a talent for luck.

Hector Berlioz (1803–69)

2 He left opera a distinctly more perfected large-scale musical form than he found it.

Bernard van Dieren (1884–1936)
Down Among the Dead Men, 1935

3 Meyerbeer's music, as a witty woman once remarked to me, is like stage scenery–it should not be scrutinized too closely.

Camille Saint-Saëns (1835–1921)
Musical Memories

4   As I listened to the music, I could not find a single inspired idea. Meyerbeer's skill and intelligence are incredible, but neither skill nor intelligence can simulate the human heart. *The greatest craftsman is still not a poet.*

Alexander Dargomizhsky (1813–69)

95   MILHAUD

1   Darius Milhaud is the most gifted of us all.

Arthur Honegger (1892–1956)
Quoted in Harding, *The Ox on the Roof,* 1972

2   Honegger's career is a fine example of success rapidly reached in all fields. Whereas at every one of my new works the critics bared their teeth, they accepted his at first hearing; they treated me as a leg-puller and joker incapable of serious thought, but they regarded Arthur as both serious and profound.

Darius Milhaud (1892–1974)
Notes without Music, trans Evans, 1952

96   MONTEVERDI

1   I am aware that contrasts are what stir our souls, and that such stirring is the aim of all good music.

Claudio Monteverdi (1567–1643)
Madrigals of War and Love, 1638, Preface

2   [Of his *seconda prattica*:] The modern composer builds his works on the basis of truth.

Claudio Monteverdi (1567–1643)
Fifth Book of Madrigals, 1605, Preface

97 MOZART

1   A man of ordinary talent will always be ordinary, whether he travels or not; but a man of superior talent (which I cannot deny myself to be without being impious) will go to pieces if he remains for ever in the same place.

Wolfgang Amadeus Mozart (1756–91)
Letter, 1778

2   If I have time, I shall rearrange some of my violin concertos and shorten them. In Germany we rather like length, but after all it is better to be short and good.

Wolfgang Amadeus Mozart (1756–91)
Letter, 1778

3   *Emperor Joseph II:* Very many notes, my dear Mozart.
    Mozart: Exactly the necessary number, your Majesty.

An exchange after the première of *Die Entführung aus dem Serail,* 1782

4   Whether the angels play only Bach in praising God I am not quite sure; I am sure, however, that *en famille* they play Mozart.

Karl Barth (1886–1968)
Quoted in his *New York Times* obituary

5   In *Cosi fan tutte* the dying eighteenth century casts a backward glance over a period outstanding in European life for grace and charm and, averting its eyes from a new age suckled in a creed of iconoclasm, sings its swan-song in praise of a civilization that has passed away for ever.

Thomas Beecham (1879–1961)
A Mingled Chime, 1944

6   I could not compose operas like *Don Giovanni* and *Figaro.* I hold them both in aversion. I could not have chosen such subjects; they are too frivolous for me.

Ludwig van Beethoven (1770–1827)
Beethoven: Impressions of Contemporaries, Sonneck (ed), 1926

7   Raphael is the same man as Mozart.

Georges Bizet (1838–75)
Letter to Hector Gruyer, 1858

8   He has light and shade at his disposal; but his light does not blind and his darkness still shows a definite outline.

In the most tragic situation he still has a joke ready – in the most lighthearted he can frown philosophically.

His smile is not that of a diplomat or an actor, but that of a pure soul – and yet worldly-wise.

He is the perfect and rounded figure, the sum total, an end not a beginning.

He is young as a youth and wise as an old man – never ancient and never modern, has been carried to the grave, yet lives still. His transfigured human smile still radiates to us . . .

Ferruccio Busoni (1866–1924)
35 Aphorisms on Mozart, 1906, trans Stevenson

9   [Of *The Magic Flute*:] The opera . . . is the only one in existence that might conceivably have been composed by God.

Neville Cardus (1889–1975)
Quoted in the *Manchester Guardian*, 1961

10   Mozart in his music was probably the most reasonable of the world's great composers. It is the happy balance between flight and control, between sensibility and self-discipline, simplicity and sophistication of style that is his particular province . . . Mozart tapped once again the source from which all music flows, expressing himself with a spontaneity and refinement and breath-taking rightness that has never since been duplicated.

Aaron Copland (1900–90)
Copland on Music, 1960

11   Mozart is sunshine.

Antonín Dvořák (1841–1904)
Quoted in Sourek (ed), *Antonin Dvořák: Letters and Reminiscences*, 1954

12   Mozart should have composed *Faust*.

Johann Wolfgang von Goethe (1749–1832)
Conversations with Eckermann, 1827

13   In Bach, Beethoven and Wagner we admire principally the depth and energy of the human mind; in Mozart, the divine instinct. His highest inspirations seem untouched by human labour. Unlike the masters cited, no trace of struggle remains in the forms on which he moulded his material. Mozart has the childish, happy, Aladdin nature which overcomes all difficulties as in play. He creates like a god, without pain . . .

Edvard Grieg (1843–1907)

14   [Of the fifteen-year-old Mozart:] This boy will cause us all to be forgotten.
Johann Adolf Hasse (1699–1783)
Quoted in Headington, *The Bodley Head History of Western Music*, 1974

15   Before God, and as an honest man, I tell you that your son is the greatest composer known to me.
Joseph Haydn (1732–1809)
Remark to Leopold Mozart, 1785

16   I only wish I could instil in every friend of music, and in great men in particular, the depth of musical sympathy and profound appreciation of Mozart's inimitable music that I myself feel and enjoy. Then nations would vie with each other to possess such a jewel within their frontiers.
Joseph Haydn (1732–1809)
Letter to Franz Rott, 1787

17   I was quite beside myself for a long while because of his [Mozart's] death, and could not believe that Providence would have so rapidly despatched an irreplaceable man to the other world. I only regret that he could not first have convinced the English, who are still in the dark, of what I had been daily preaching to them . . .
Joseph Haydn (1732–1809)
Letter to Michael Puchberg, January 1792, quoted in Gal, *The Musician's World*, 1965

18   The world will not have such a talent again in a hundred years!
Joseph Haydn (1732–1809)
Letter to Frau von Genziger, 20 December 1791, after Mozart's death, quoted in Gal, *The Musician's World*, 1965

19   I am in love with Mozart like a young girl. Immortal Mozart! I owe you everything . . . I have you to thank that I did not die without having loved.
Sören Kierkegaard (1813–55)
Either/Or, 1843

20   It is sobering to consider that when Mozart was my age he had already been dead for a year.
Tom Lehrer (1928–   )

21   He roused my admiration when I was young; he caused me to despair when I reached maturity; he is now the comfort of my old age.
Gioachino Rossini (1792–1868)

22   From Mozart I learnt to say important things in a conversational way.

George Bernard Shaw (1856–1950)
Conversation with Busoni, *c* 1922

23   The sonatas of Mozart are unique; they are too easy for children, and too difficult for artists.

Arthur Schnabel (1882–1951)
Quoted in Shapiro, *Encyclopedia of Quotations about Music*, 1978

24   O Mozart, immortal Mozart, how many, how infinitely many inspiring suggestions of a finer, better life have you left in our souls!

Franz Schubert (1797–1828)
Diary, 1816

25   What Mozart did, that is, composed up to his thirty-sixth year, the best copyist of today could not write down in the same amount of time.

Franz Strauss (1842–1905)
Quoted by his son, Richard, *Melodic Inspiration*, 1940

98   MUSSORGSKY

1   This is what I would like: my stage people should speak like living people; but besides this, their character and power of intonation, supported by the orchestra, which forms the musical pattern of their speech, must achieve their aim directly, that is, my music should be an artistic reproduction of human speech in all its finest shades.

Modest Mussorgsky (1835–81)
Letter to L. Shestakova, 1868

2   Mussorgsky typifies the genius of Russia: a gigantic untrained child, strong and playful and spontaneous, manifesting itself with a magnificently original energy, and yet with all the child's naive simplicity, sweet and enormous . . .

Havelock Ellis (1859–1939)
Impressions and Comments, 1914

3   It seems easy enough to correct Mussorgsky's defects; but when this is done, it is impossible not to feel that the result is no longer Mussorgsky.

Anatol Liadov (1855–1914)
Quoted in Morgenstern, *Composers on Music,* 1958

4   Mussorgsky was an amateur with moments of genius.

Ernest Newman (1868–1959)
Quoted in *The Nation,* 1914

5   His nature is not of the finest quality; he likes what is coarse, unpolished, and ugly.

Píotr Ilyich Tchaikovsky (1840–93)
Letter to Nadezhda von Meck, 1878

99   OFFENBACH

1   What else is *opéra comique*, in fact, but sung vaudeville?

Jacques Offenbach (1819–80)
Quoted in *Le Ménestrel,* 1856

2   It occurred to me that *opéra comique* was no longer to be found at the Opéra-Comique; that really funny, gay, witty, lively music was gradually being forgotten . . .

Jacques Offenbach (1819–80)
On his reasons for founding the Bouffes-Parisiens, 1855

3   The Mozart of the Champs-Elysées.

Gioachino Rossini (1792–1868)
Quoted in Faris, *Jacques Offenbach,* 1980

4   Offenbach's music is wicked. It is abandoned stuff; every accent is a snap of the fingers in the face of moral responsibility.

George Bernard Shaw (1856–1950)
Ibid

100   ORFF

1   In all my work, my final concern is not with musical but with spiritual exposition.
Carl Orff (1895–1982)
Quoted in Liess, *Carl Orff*, 1968

101   PAGANINI

1   The wildest reports of his appearance were exceeded when the eyes beheld him. He was so thin that he seemed tall, and so dark that even his haggard features left him ageless. His body was completely fleshless and his limbs were mere bones, everything being sacrificed, so it seemed, for his long hands and talon-like fingers. In his portraits ... we have but a ghost of this strange being, for his music was an inseparable part of him and, without it, his is the soundless body of a cricket or a cicada, dead, and with no shrill and vibrant tones, but only the implements of its song.
Sacheverell Sitwell (1897–1988), describing Paganini
Liszt, 1934

2   No one ever asks if you have heard Paganini, but if you have seen him.
Nicolò Paganini (1782–1840)
Letter to Germi, 1832

102   PALESTRINA

1   Worldly cares of any kind ... are adverse to the Muses, and particularly those which arise from a lack of private means.
Giovanni Pierluigi da Palestrina (1525–94)
Dedication to *Lamentations*, 1588

2   There exists a vast mass of love songs of the poets, written in a fashion entirely foreign to the profession and name of Christian. They are the songs of men ruled by passion, and a great number of musicians, corrupters of youth, make them the concern of their art and their industry; in proportion as they flourish through praise of their skill, so do they offend good and serious-minded men by the depraved taste of their work. I blush and grieve to think that once I was of their number.

Giovanni Pierluigi da Palestrina (1525–94)
Dedication to *Fourth Book of Motets*, 1584

3   It is . . . a delusion to suppose that Palestrina set his sacred texts in this way with the deliberate purpose of attaining as nearly as possible to a kind of ideal sanctity of expression. Those who believe so cannot be familiar with his madrigals, in which a very similar style is yoked to the most light-hearted and suggestive texts . . . The truth is, he could not write any other sort of music; and so far was he from aspiring to an unearthly perfection that his works are full of formulas and conundrums taken over from the contrapuntists who preceded him, whose great antagonist he is supposed to have been.

Hector Berlioz (1803–69)
Memoirs, trans Cairns

4   He is the real king of sacred music, and the Eternal Father of Italian music.

Giuseppe Verdi (1813–1901)
Letter to Giuseppe Callignani, 1891

103   PARRY

1   I cannot stand Parry's orchestration: it's dead and is never more than an organ part arranged.

Edward Elgar (1857–1934)
Quoted in *The Elgar Society Newsletter*, 1978

2   We pupils of Parry have, if we have been wise, inherited . . . the great English choral tradition which Tallis passed on to Byrd, Byrd to Gibbons, Gibbons to Purcell, Purcell to Battishill and Greene, and they in their turn through the Wesleys to Parry. He has passed on the torch to us and it is our duty to keep it alight.

Ralph Vaughan Williams (1872–1958)
A Musical Autobiography, 1950

104 POULENC

1   My music is my portrait.
Francis Poulenc (1899–1963)
Quoted in Bernac, *Francis Poulenc*, 1977

2   On the radio a lady has just been caterwauling for a quarter of an hour some songs which may very well have been mine!
Francis Poulenc (1899–1963)
Diary of My Songs, trans Radford, 1985

3   It is always necessary to repudiate for a time, at the age of twenty, those whom you have idolized, for fear of being overgrown with ivy.
Francis Poulenc (1899–1963)
Quoted in Bernac, *Francis Poulenc: The Man and His Songs*, 1972

105 PUCCINI

1   [On the story of *Manon Lescaut*:] Massenet feels it as a Frenchman, with powder and minuets. I shall feel it as an Italian, with desperate passion.
Giacomo Puccini (1858–1924)
Quoted in Carner, *Puccini*, 1974

2   I act as executioner to these poor frail creatures. The Neronian instinct manifests and fulfils itself.
Giacomo Puccini (1858–1924)
On his operatic heroines

3   *Shostakovich:* What do you think of Puccini?
Britten: I think his operas are dreadful.
Shostakovich: No, Ben, you are wrong. He wrote marvellous operas, but dreadful music.
Quoted in Harewood, *The Tongs and the Bones*, 1981

4   I have heard the composer Puccini well spoken of . . . He follows modern trends, which is natural, but remains attached to melody, which is above passing fashions.
Giuseppe Verdi (1813–1901)
Letter to O. Arrivabene, June 1884

5   [After the London première of *Manon Lescaut*:] Puccini looks to me more like the heir of Verdi than any of his rivals.
George Bernard Shaw (1856–1950)
Quoted in *The World*, 1894

106   PURCELL

1   Here lyes Henry Purcell Esqre, who left this Lyfe and is gone to that Blessed Place where only his Harmony can be exceeded.
Purcell's epitaph in Westminster Abbey

2   [Of Purcell:] One of the most celebrated masters of the service of music in the kingdom, and scarce inferior to any in Europe.
Obituary in the *Flying-Post*, 1695

3   Mr Purcell in whose person we have at length found an Englishman equal with the best abroad.
John Dryden (1631–1700)
Dedication to *Amphitryon*, 1690

4   It is recorded that Purcell, when composing one of his odes, could hear a chorister being rehearsed in one of his songs in another room. The singing master kept stopping the boy and trying to make him sing the ornaments exactly as Purcell had put them down on paper. Purcell called out, 'Leave the boy alone. He will ornament by nature better than you or I can tell him.'
Alfred Deller (1912–79)
Quoted in Hardwick, *A Singularity of Voice*, 1980

5   In one way Purcell is a finer stage composer than Wagner: his music is full of movement, of dance. His is the easiest music in all the world to act.
Gustav Holst (1874–1934)
The Heritage of Music, 1928

6   [Of *Dido and Aeneas*:] The only perfect English opera ever written.
Gustav Holst (1874–1934)
Ibid

107 RACHMANINOV

1   Rachmaninov was a little braver than I, and yet he too was excited, and his hands were quite cold. He whispered in my ear, 'If they ask me to play I don't honestly know if I'll be able to. My hands are like ice.' And Tolstoy did ask him to play. I can't recall what he played, I only know of my own worrying thought: 'Suppose he asks me to sing.' My heart went further into my boots, when Tolstoy looked Rachmaninov straight in the eye and asked, 'Tell me, does anyone want this kind of music?'
Fyodor Chaliapin (1873 – 1938)
A Visit to Tolstoy with Sergei Rachmaninov, trans Froud and Hanley

2   [Of Rachmaninov's playing:] Even an ordinary broken chord is made to disclose rare beauties; we are reminded of the fairies' hazelnuts in which diamonds were concealed but you could break the shell only if your hands were blessed.
Neville Cardus (1889 – 1975)
In the *Manchester Guardian,* 1939

3   The whole world is open to me, and success awaits me everywhere. Only one place is closed to me, and that is my own country – Russia. . . .
Sergei Rachmaninov (1873 – 1943)
In *The Musical Times,* June 1930

108 RAVEL

1   [Of *Bolero*:] A piece for orchestra without music.
Maurice Ravel (1875 – 1937)
Quoted in Nichols, *Ravel,* 1977

2   [Nearing his death:] I still have so much music in my head. I have said nothing. I have so much more to say.
Maurice Ravel (1875 – 1937)
Quoted in Jourdan-Morhange, *Ravel et nous,* 1945

3   I think and feel in sounds.
Maurice Ravel (1875 – 1937)
Quoted in Renard, *Journal,* 1907

109 REGER

1 The American music critic Irving Kolodin ... pointed out that
Reger's name is the same either forward or backward, and that his music
displays the same characteristic.
Gervase Hughes (1905–)
Sidelights on a Century of Music, 1969

110 RIMSKY-KORSAKOV

1 Rimsky was ... deeply and unshowingly generous, and unkind only
to admirers of Tchaikovsky.
Igor Stravinsky (1882–1971)
Memories and Commentaries, 1960

2 A cultured aromatist.
Neville Cardus (1889–1975)
In the *Manchester Guardian*, 1935

3 [Of Rimsky-Korsakov's *Scheherazade*:] It reminds one more of a
bazaar than of the Orient.
Claude Debussy (1862–1918)
Letter to Raoul Bardac, 1906

111 ROSSINI

1 Thou knowest, O Lord, as well as I, that really I am only a composer
of *opera buffa*.
Gioachino Rossini (1792–1868)
Dedication to the *Petite Messe solennelle*, 1864

2 Give me a laundry list and I will set it to music.
Gioachino Rossini (1792–1868)
Attributed

3   Rossini ... directed his letters to his mother as 'mother of the famous composer'.

Robert Browning (1812–89)
Letter, 1846

4   Like Verdi, when, at his worst opera's
         end
      (The thing they gave at Florence, what's its
         name?)
      While the mad houseful's plaudits near
         outbang
      His orchestra of salt-box, tongs and bones,
      He looks through all the roaring and the
         wreaths
      Where sits Rossini patient in his stall.

      Robert Browning (1812–89)
      Bishop Blougram's Apology

5   Rossini wrote the first and last acts of *William Tell*. God wrote the second act.

Gaetano Donizetti (1797–1848)
Quoted in Osborne, *Rossini*, 1986

6   Rossini, in music, is the genius of sheer animal spirits. It is a species as inferior to that of Mozart, as the cleverness of a smart boy is to that of a man of sentiment; but it is genius nevertheless.

Leigh Hunt (1784–1859)
Going to the Play Again, 1828

7   The first characteristic of Rossini's music is speed – a speed which removes from the soul all the sombre emotions that are so powerfully evoked within us by the slow strains in Mozart. I find also in Rossini a cool freshness, which, measure by measure, makes us smile with delight.

Stendhal (1783–1842)
Life of Rossini, 1824

8   André Previn asked William whom he considered to be the finest composer. 'Rossini,' said William without hesitation.

Susanna Walton (1926–   )
William Walton: Behind the Façade, 1988

9   Who would not gladly listen to Rossini's lively flights of fancy, to the piquant titillation of his melodies? But who could be so blind as to attribute to him dramatic truth?

Carl Maria von Weber (1786–1826)
In 1820, quoted in Morgenstern, *Composers on Music*, 1958

---

112   SAINT-SAËNS

1   It is possible to be as much of a musician as Saint-Saëns; it is impossible to be more of one!

Franz Liszt (1811–86)
In 1866, quoted in Williams, *Portrait of Liszt*, 1990

2   His skill lies in having the good sense not to involve himself in problems beyond his technical ability. And to climb a precipice of thought with an elegant gesture.

Ferruccio Busoni (1866–1924)
Letter to Emile Blanchet, 17 March 1915, trans Beaumont

3   Does no one care sufficiently for Saint-Saëns to tell him he has written music enough? . . .

Claude Debussy (1862–1918)
Monsieur Croche, antidilettante, 1921

4   Saint-Saëns has informed a delighted public that since the war began he has composed music for the stage, melodies, an elegy, and a piece for the trombone. If he'd been making shell-cases instead it might have been all the better for music.

Maurice Ravel (1875–1937)
Letter, 1916

---

113   SATIE

1   Before I compose a piece, I walk round it several times, accompanied by myself.

Erik Satie (1866–1925)
Quoted in *Bulletin des éditions musicales,* 1913

2   Throughout his life, Satie never knew the meaning of compromise, courageously overcoming the miseries of man's lot and drawing his strength from his own inward resources.

Darius Milhaud (1892–1974)
Notes without Music, trans Evans, 1952

3   He was a composer who feared no man, but ever did what was right in his own eyes–unless, perhaps, the motive might be stated a little differently, to do what was wrong in the eyes of other people . . . He influenced certain contemporaries. It is commonly said (but also denied) that Debussy, with whom he was intimate and who encouraged him, was one of these . . . His mad whimsicality was one thing that stood in the way of any wide recognition–writing his scores in red ink without bar lines, and giving his compositions incomprehensible titles such as *Pieces in the shape of a Pear* and *Limp Preludes for a Dog.* It is to be feared that his humour was usually of the kind that finds a rather small audience.

Percy A. Scholes (1877–1958)
Oxford Companion to Music, 1938

4   My brother was always difficult to understand. He doesn't seem to have been quite normal.

Olga Satie
Quoted in Harding, *Erik Satie,* 1975

5   Satie gave comic titles to his music in order to protect his works from persons obsessed with the sublime.

Jean Cocteau (1889–1963)
Quoted in Myers, *Modern French Music,* 1971

6   For Erik Satie, the sweet medieval musician who has strayed into this century for the joy of his very friendly Claude Debussy.

Claude Debussy (1862–1918)
Dedication on a copy of his *Cinq poèmes de Baudelaire*

114   DOMENICO SCARLATTI

1   This son of mine is an eagle whose wings are grown; he ought not to stay idle in the nest and I ought not to hinder his flight.

Alessandro Scarlatti (1660–1725)
Letter to Ferdinand de Medici, 1705

2 It is time to consider how Domenico
     Scarlatti
   condensed so much music into so few
     bars
   with never a crabbed turn or congested
     cadence,
   never a boast or a see-here.

Basil Bunting (1900–85)
Briggflatts, 1966

3 When we hear Scarlatti's music, we know that we are in the climate
of sunlight and warmth. It is Italy, it is Spain – the spirit of the Latin
countries and the god of the Mediterranean; we are in the presence of
that deity who has been truly called 'the god who dances'.

Wanda Landowska (1879–1959)
Landowska on Music, trans Restout, 1964

115 SCHOENBERG

See also 24 Serialism

1 But there is nothing I long for more intensely . . . than to be taken for
a better sort of Tchaikovsky – for heaven's sake; a bit better, but really
that's all. Or if anything more, then that people should know my tunes
and whistle them.

Arnold Schoenberg (1874–1951)
Letter to Hans Rosbaud, 1947

2 Very well, I can wait.

Arnold Schoenberg (1874–1951)
Attributed remark on being told that his Violin Concerto required a player with six fingers

3 [Of Richard Strauss:] He is no longer of the slightest artistic interest
to me, and whatever I may once have learned from him, I am thankful to
say I misunderstood.

Arnold Schoenberg (1874–1951)
Quoted in Rosen, *Schoenberg*, 1976

4 Only a psychiatrist can help poor Schoenberg now . . . He would do better to shovel snow instead of scribbling on music paper . . . Better give him the grant [from the Mahler Memorial Foundation] anyway . . . You can never tell what posterity will say.
Richard Strauss (1864–1949)
Letter to Alma Mahler, 1913

5 I am a conservative who was forced to become a revolutionary.
Arnold Schoenberg (1874–1951)
Quoted in Reich, *Schoenberg,* 1971

6 Why is Schoenberg's Music so Hard to Understand?
Alban Berg (1885–1935)
Title of essay, 1924

7 [On being asked why he no longer composed music like *Verklärte Nacht:*] I still do, but nobody notices.
Arnold Schoenberg (1874–1951)
Quoted in MacDonald, *Schoenberg,* 1975

8 My music is not modern, it is merely badly played.
Arnold Schoenberg (1874–1951)
Ibid

9 Schoenberg is too melodious for me, too sweet.
Bertolt Brecht (1898–1956)
Quoted in *Brecht as they knew him,* Witt (ed), 1974

10 There is still much good music to be written in C major.
Arnold Schoenberg (1874–1951)
Quoted in Machlis, *Introduction to Contemporary Music,* 1963

11 A great deal of the liveliest music today, when not in fact at sea, is, more or less, in C.
Glenn Gould (1932–82)
Vindicating Schoenberg's statement (*see above*) in the late 1960s
Page (ed), *The Glenn Gould Reader,* 1984, 'Terry Riley'

12 Other masters may conceivably w 'te
Even yet in C major,
But we–we take the perhaps 'primrose path'
To the dodecaphonic bonfire.
Hugh MacDiarmid (1892–1978)
In Memoriam James Joyce, 1955

13   [Of *Gurrelieder*:] A proof if you want it . . . that Schoenberg could, as they used to say about Piccaso, draw when he wanted to.
Lord Harewood (1923–)
The Tongs and the Bones, 1981

14   He is young and perhaps he is right. Maybe my ear is not sensitive enough.
Gustav Mahler (1860–1911)
Quoted in Lebrecht, *Discord*, 1982

15   Not the lunatic he is generally taken for.
Ernest Newman (1868–1959)
In the *Birmingham Post*, 1912

16   Today I have discovered something which will assure the supremacy of German music for the next hundred years.
Arnold Schoenberg (1874–1951)
In conversation with his pupil Josef Rufer in July 1921, concerning his development of the 'twelve-note' compositional system, dodecaphony or serialism

17   It comes to a sort of composing before composition. The whole disposition and organization of the material would have to be ready when the actual work should begin, and all one asks is: which is the actual work?
(Zeitblom)
Thomas Mann (1875–1955)
Doctor Faustus, 1947, trans Lowe-Porter

18   Schoenberg is dead.
Pierre Boulez (1925–)
Title of essay, 1951

19   Harmony! Harmony!
Arnold Schoenberg (1874–1951)
Last words

116   SCHUBERT

1   The art of music here entombed a rich possession, but even far fairer hopes.
Franz Grillparzer (1791–1872)
Schubert's epitaph in Wahring cemetery

2   Such is the spell of your emotional world that it very nearly blinds us to the greatness of your craftsmanship.

Franz Liszt (1811–86)

3   There is a curious English musical dictionary, published in 1827, which may sometimes be found in the fourpenny box outside a second-hand bookshop; and in this dictionary Beethoven is given one of the largest articles and treated as unquestionably the greatest composer of the day (though on the evidence only of his less dangerous works). Such was Beethoven's fame in the year of his death. Schubert died in the next year. There are five Schuberts in this dictionary, but Franz Schubert is not among them.

Donald Francis Tovey (1875–1940)
Essays and Lectures on Music, 1927, 'Franz Schubert'

4   His character was a mixture of tenderness and coarseness, sensuality and candour, sociability and melancholy.

Johann Mayrhofer (1787–1836)
Quoted in Westrup, *Schubert Chamber Music,* 1969

5   Where other people keep diaries in which they record their momentary feelings, etc, Schubert simply kept sheets of music by him and confided his changing moods to them; and his soul being steeped in music, he put down notes when another man would resort to words.

Robert Schumann (1810–56)
Letter to Friedrich Wieck, 6 November 1829, quoted in Gal, *The Musician's World,* 1965

6   Heavenly length.

Robert Schumann (1810–56)
In 1839 on Schubert's 'Great' C major Symphony

7   [Of Schubert:] All of my life his music has been perhaps nearer to my heart than any other–that crystal stream welling and welling for ever.

Ethel Smyth (1858–1944)
Impressions That Remained, 1919

8   In his larger forms, Schubert is a wanderer. He likes to move at the edge of the precipice, and does so with the assurance of a sleepwalker. To wander is the Romantic condition; one yields to it enraptured, or is driven and plagued by the terror of finding no escape. More often than not, happiness is but the surface of despair.

Alfred Brendel (1931–   )
'Schubert's Last Sonatas', *Music Sounded Out,* 1990

9 'My peace is gone, my heart is sore, I shall find it never and nevermore,' I may well sing every day now, for each night, on retiring to bed, I hope I may not wake again, and each morning but recalls yesterday's grief.

Franz Schubert (1797–1828)
Letter to Kupelwieser, 1824

10   Dear Schober,
     I am ill. I have had nothing to eat or drink for eleven days now, and can only stagger feebly and uncertainly between armchair and bed. So please be good enough to help me out in this desperate state with something to read. I have read Cooper's *Last of the Mohicans, The Spy, The Pilot* and *The Pioneers.* If by any chance you have anything else of him, do please leave it for me at the coffeehouse . . .

Franz Schubert (1797–1828)
Schubert's last letter, to Franz von Schober, 12 November 1828

117 SCHUMANN

1   During the night of October 17, 1833, I suddenly had the most frightful thought a human being can possibly conceive – the most terrible that Heaven could inflict – that I might lose my reason. This thought took possession of me with such violence that all comfort, all prayer vanished as if it were idle mockery. This fear drove me from place to place – my breath stopped at the thought: 'What if you were no longer able to think?' Clara, anyone who has once been crushed like that knows no worse suffering, or illness, or despair, that could possibly happen to him.

Robert Schumann (1810–56)
Letter to Clara Wieck, 11 February 1838

2   I have been composing so much that it really seems quite uncanny at times. I cannot help it, and should like to sing myself to death, like a nightingale.

Robert Schumann (1810–56)
Letter to Clara Wieck, 1840

3   For me Wagner is impossible . . . he talks without ever stopping. One just can't talk all the time.

Robert Schumann (1810–56)
Quoted in Gal, *Johannes Brahms*, 1961

4   It is impossible to communicate with Schumann. The man is hopeless; he does not talk at all.

Richard Wagner (1813–83)
Ibid

5   [Of his 'Spring' Symphony:] The music is not intended to describe or paint anything definite, but I believe the season did much to shape the particular form it took.

Robert Schumann (1810–56)
Letter to Ludwig Spohr

6   Schumann is *the* composer of childhood . . . both because he created a children's imaginative world and because children learn some of their first music in his marvellous piano albums.

Igor Stravinsky (1882–1971)
Themes and Conclusions, pub 1972

7   Schumann's our music-maker now.

Robert Browning (1812–89)
Dis aliter visum

8   Today Johannes [Brahms] set the stone over my dear one's grave – my whole soul went with him.

Clara Schumann (1819–96)
Diary, 7 June 1857

118   SCHÜTZ

1   [On Heinrich Schütz (1585–1672):] The most spiritual musician the world has ever seen.

Alfred Einstein (1880–1952)
Heinrich Shütz, 1928

2   In the person of Heinrich Schütz, German art itself crossed the Alps.

Albert Schweitzer (1875–1965)
J.S. Bach, 1911

119 SCRIABIN

1 I was once a Chopinist, then a Wagnerist, now I am only a Scriabinist.
Alexander Scriabin (1872–1915)
In 1903, quoted in Bowers, *Scriabin*, 1969

2 I shall go to tell people that they are strong and powerful!
Alexander Scriabin (1872–1915)
Comment on his Third Symphony, 1905

3 [Of Scriabin's *Poem of Ecstasy*:] The obscenest piece of music ever written.
Anonymous
Quoted in Macdonald, *Skryabin*, 1978

4 Scriabin is near to us because he embraces in his work that fascination of revolution.
Anatol Lunacharsky (1875–1933)
Revolutionary Silhouettes, 1925

5 Just as Dostoyevsky is not only a novelist and Blok not only a poet, so Scriabin is not only a composer, but a cause for everlasting celebration, a festival of Russian culture and the embodiment of its triumph.
Boris Pasternak (1890–1960)
About Scriabin and Chopin, pub 1967

6 Scriabin's *Prometheus* is the product of a once-fine composer suffering from mental derangement, and Schoenberg's lucubrations are simply nothing at all. You cannot expect either a journalist or his public to see any difference between a lunatic and an idiot.
Frederick Corder (1852–1932)
In the *Musical Quarterly*, July 1915

7 The wind that blows through the music is the veritable wind of the cosmos itself. The cries of desire and passion and ecstasy are a sort of quintessential sublimation of all the yearnings, not merely of humanity but of all nature.
Ernest Newman (1868–1959)
Reviewing *Prometheus* in *The Nation*, 1913

8   Scriabin's music sounds like I think—sometimes. Has that far off cosmic itch. Divinely fouled up. All fire and air . . . It was like a bath of ice, cocaine and rainbows.

Henry Miller (1891–1980)
Nexus, 1945

9   [On Scriabin:] A musical traveller without a passport.

Igor Stravinsky (1882–1971)

120   SHOSTAKOVICH

1   Creative reply of a Soviet artist to just criticism.

Dmitri Shostakovich (1906–75)
Note on score of his Symphony No 5, 1937

2   I scribble a page in a single breath.
    I listen to my whistling with an accustomed
        ear.
    I torment the ears of the world around me.
    Then I get into print, and bang into
        oblivion!

Dmitri Shostakovich (1906–75)
Paraphrasing Pushkin, *Preface to the Complete Collection of my Works, Op 123*, 1966

3   [On his Fourteenth Symphony:] The entire symphony is my protest against death.

Dmitri Shostakovich (1906–75)
Quoted in Norris (ed), *Shostakovich*, 1982

4   [Of *Lady Macbeth of Mtsensk*:] It is a leftist bedlam instead of human music. The inspiring quality of good music is sacrificed in favour of petty-bourgeois clowning. This game may end badly.

Pravda, 1936

121 SIBELIUS

1 I believe that music alone – that is to say, absolute music – cannot by itself satisfy.

Jean Sibelius (1865–1957)
Letter to J.J. Erkko, 1893

2 Give me the loneliness either of the Finnish forest or of a big city.

Jean Sibelius (1865–1957)
Quoted in Layton, *Sibelius*, 1965

3 Look at the great nations of Europe and what they have endured. No savage could have stood so much. I do believe in civilization.

Jean Sibelius (1865–1957)
Quoted by Mellers in *The Listener*, 1 December 1955

4 Whatever path you choose, Glorious Ego – don't sacrifice the life-giving warmth and vitality that lies at the heart of your music. You won't be any 'greater' by outdoing . . . your contemporaries in terms of a revolutionary 'profile'. Let's not join in any race.

Jean Sibelius (1865–1957)
Diary, June 1912, quoted in Tawaststjerna, *Sibelius II*, trans Layton, 1986

5 Sibelius justified the austerity of his old age by saying that while other composers were engaged in manufacturing cocktails he offered the public pure cold water.

Neville Cardus (1888–1975)
In the *Manchester Guardian*, 1958

6 [Of a passage in Sibelius's Symphony No 6:] I think he must have been drunk when he wrote that.

Benjamin Britten (1913–76)
Quoted in Headington, *Britten*, 1981

7 A polonaise for polar bears.

Donald Francis Tovey (1875–1940)
On the rondo theme of Sibelius's Violin Concerto

122 SMETANA

1 *The Bartered Bride* is only a toy and composing it was merely child's
play! ... At the time of writing, it was my opinion that not even
Offenbach could compete with it.
Bedřich Smetana (1824–84)
On the opera's hundredth performance, 1882

2 The long insistent note in the finale ... is the fateful ringing in my
ears of the high-pitched tones which, in 1874, announced the beginning
of my deafness. I permitted myself this little joke because it was so
disastrous to me.
Bedřich Smetana (1824–84) on his quartet
From my Life, 1878

3   Smetana's music found in every
     phenomenon a spot
        Where there would be fire, wailing,
           Longing,
              joy,
                 angry pressure
                    prophecy–all through song.
        Leoš Janáček (1854–1929)
        Uncollected Essays, pub 1989

4 Here is a composer with a genuine Czech heart, an artist by the
Grace of God!
Franz Liszt (1811–86)
In 1857, quoted in Clapham, *Smetana*, 1972

5 In haste I write to tell you that the death of Smetana has deeply
affected me. He was indeed a genius!
Franz Liszt (1811–86)
Letter to K. Navratil, 1884

123 SPOHR

1   There was a composer named Spohr
Whose works were a hundred or mohr.
His great work *Jessonda*
Long time was a wonda
But now his successes are o'hr.

Musical Herald, 1888

2   An academic pedant of the first rank.

Edvard Grieg (1843–1907)
Quoted in Finck, *Grieg and his Music,* 1906

124 STOCKHAUSEN

1   Look, down there you can see the ocean of light that is Vienna. In a few years' time I will have progressed so far that, with a single electronic bang, I'll be able to blow the whole city sky-high!

Karlheinz Stockhausen (1928–)
In the early 1950s, quoted in Henze, *Music and Politics,* 1982

2   'Have you heard any Stockhausen?' Sir Thomas Beecham was asked. 'No,' he replied, 'but I believe I have trodden in some.'

Attributed
Lebrecht, *The Book of Musical Anecdotes,* 1985

3   Think NOTHING
Wait until it is absolutely still within you
When you have attained this
Begin to play
As soon as you start to think stop
And try to retain
The state of NON-THINKING
Then continue playing.

Karlheinz Stockhausen (1928–)
Instructions for performing *Es*

4   In Stockhausen's good period I came to trust his music more than anything else. I felt he could solve all the problems, that it was no longer necessary for me to address myself to them.

Pierre Boulez (1925–)
Quoted in Peyser, *Boulez*, 1976

5   [Of Stockhausen's works:] More boring than the most boring of eighteenth-century music.

Igor Stravinsky (1882–1971)
Quoted in Druskin, *Igor Stravinsky*, 1983

125   RICHARD STRAUSS

1   A *human being* of the great order.

Percy Grainger (1882–1961)
Richard Strauss: Seer and Idealist, 1917

2   I may not be a first-rate composer, but I *am* a first-class second-rate composer!

Richard Strauss (1864–1949)
Quoted in Del Mar, *Richard Strauss*, 1962

3   I can assure you that there is sunshine in the music of Strauss . . . it is not possible to withstand his irresistible domination.

Claude Debussy (1862–1918)
Monsieur Croche, antidilettante, 1921

4   Haven't I the right, after all, to write what music I please? I cannot bear the tragedy of the present time. I want to create joy. I need it.

Richard Strauss (1864–1949)
Remark in 1924

5   His absurd cacophony will not be music even in the thirtieth century.

César Cui (1835–1918)
Letter, 1904

6   [After the band of the Grenadier Guards had just played an *Elektra* pot-pourri] His Majesty does not know what the Band has just played, but it is *never* to be played again.

King George V (1865–1936)
Quoted in Reid, *Thomas Beecham*, 1961

7   This Meyerbeer of the twentieth century.
Gian Francesco Malipiero (1882–1973)
L'Orchestra, 1920

8   [Of *Salome*:] From time to time the cruellest discords are succeeded
by exquisite suavities that caress the ear with delight. While listening to
it all I thought of those lovely princesses in Sacher Masoch who lavished
upon young men the most voluptuous kisses while drawing red-hot
irons over their lovers' ribs.
Camille Saint-Saëns (1835–1921)
Quoted in Harding, *Saint-Saëns*, 1965

9   The most extroverted of extroverts.
Kaikhosru Shapurji Sorabji (1895–1988)
Mi Contra Fa, 1947

10   I really like this fellow Strauss, but *Salome* will do him a lot of
damage.
Kaiser Wilhelm II (1859–1941)
Attributed

11   [On Strauss's *Salome*:] That's a nice snake I've reared in my bosom.
Kaiser Wilhelm II (1859–1941)
Attributed

12   Well, it [*Salome*] paid for my villa at Garmisch.
Richard Strauss (1864–1949)
Attributed

13   The last great event in European music.
Romain Rolland (1866–1944)
On the work of Richard Strauss

14   At the end of April 1945 American troops occupied Garmisch.
When they were about to enter his house the old man of eighty-one
confronted them, saying in English 'I am Richard Strauss, the composer
of the *Rosenkavalier*!' At that they left the house.
Ernst Krause
Richard Strauss, 1964

126 STRAVINSKY

1   The greatest crisis in my life as a composer was the loss of Russia, and its language not only of music but of words.
Igor Stravinsky (1882–1971)
Themes and Conclusions, 1972

2   I am the vessel through which *Le Sacré* passed.
Igor Stravinsky (1882–1971)
Recorded talk, 1962

3   My music is best understood by children and animals.
Igor Stravinsky (1882–1971)
In *The Observer*, 1961

4   Stravinsky's 'neo-classicism' was no new classicism at all, but a primitivism-romanticism, if for no other reason than that Stravinsky so violently opposed all limiting rules except those which he made and destroyed daily for himself.
George Antheil (1900–59)
Bad Boy of Music, 1945

5   [*The Rite of Spring*:] The twentieth century's Ninth Symphony.
Serge Diaghilev (1872–1929)
Quoted in Headington, *The Bodley Head History of Western Music*, 1974

6   Stravinsky is a cave man of music.
W.J. Henderson (1855–1937)
In the *New York Sun*, 1924

7   Stravinsky looks like a man who has potty-trained too early and that music proves it as far as I'm concerned.
Russell Hoban (1925–   )
Turtle Diary, 1975

8   Stravinsky was commissioned by the Venice Festival to write them an original work. His contribution turned out to be fifteen minutes long. The officials of the festival complained to Stravinsky that this was too short. 'Well then,' Stravinsky replied calmly, 'play it again.' Since that time, Virgil Thomson has christened him 'the Merchant of Venice'.
Oscar Levant (1906–72)
The Unimportance of Being Oscar, 1968

9   In the forties the late Billy Rose produced a Broadway show, *The Seven Lively Arts,* for which Stravinsky wrote a ballet. After the opening Billy sent a telegram to Stravinsky. 'Ballet great success. Would be greater if you reorchestrate it.'

Stravinsky wired back: 'Content with great success.'

Oscar Levant (1906 – 72)
Ibid

10   An unflattering piece about Stravinsky was written for a magazine sometime ago by the composer-songwriter Vernon Duke ... Stravinsky's angry reply was in the form of an article in the same magazine. His opening line was: Obliterate V.D.!

Oscar Levant (1906 – 72)
Ibid

11   I did not like *Le Sacré* then. I have conducted it fifty times since. I do not like it now.

Pierre Monteux (1875 – 1964)
Quoted in Reid, *Thomas Beecham,* 1961

12   Rather a *Massacre du Printemps*.

H. Moreno
In *Le Ménestrel,* 1914

13   Stravinsky's symphony for wind instruments was written in memory of Debussy; if my own memories of a friend were as painful as Stravinsky's seem to be, I would try to forget it.

Ernest Newman (1868 – 1959)
Quoted in Hughes and Van Thal, *The Music Lover's Companion,* 1971

14   His music used to be original. Now it is aboriginal.

Ernest Newman (1868 – 1959)
In *The Musical Times,* 1921

15   I went to hear the *Sacré du Printemps:* the choreography is ridiculous, the music sheer cacophony. There is some originality, however, and a certain amount of talent. But taken altogether, it might be the creation of a madman. The public hissed, laughed, and – applauded.

Giacomo Puccini (1858 – 1924)
Letter to Tito Ricordi, 1913

16   [Of Stravinsky's *The Firebird*:] Lord, how much more than genius this is—it is real Russia!

Sergei Rachmaninov (1873–1943)
Quoted in Bertensson and Leyda, *Sergei Rachmaninoff,* 1965

17   Who's that drumming away there?
     Why, it's little Modernsky!
     he's got himself a pig-tail,
     suits him quite well!
     like real false hair—
     like a wig,
     just (as little Modernsky imagines)
     just like old Bach.

Arnold Schoenberg (1874–1951)
3 Satires for Mixed Chorus, 1925

18   . . . like the later works of its composer's 'advanced' contemporaries, it shows him fettered fast and immovable to his own monomanias of melodic and rhythmic *ostinati*. How this sort of thing ever came to have the fantastic claim made for it, can only be explained on the hypothesis that musicians, like orthodox economists, are, on their own pet subject, vegetable cretins.

Kaikhosru Shapurji Sorabji (1892–1988)
On Stravinsky's *Les Noces, The English Weekly,* 1949

19   He who could write the *Rite of Spring*
     If I be right, by right should swing!

Boston Herald, 1924

20   Stravinsky said that music does not 'say' anything, and tried to make his art as impersonal as a block of ice cream.

Colin Wilson (1931–   )
Brandy of the Damned, 1964

127 SULLIVAN

1   A giant may play at times, but Mr Sullivan is always playing.

Figaro, London, 1878

2   [On falling from a punt] I've always been a contrapuntalist.

Arthur Sullivan (1842–1900)
Quoted in Brahms, *Gilbert and Sullivan,* 1975

128 TALLIS

1 As he did live, so also did he die,
In mild and quiet sort,
(O! happy man).

Epitaph for Thomas Tallis (*c* 1505–85), St Alfege, Greenwich

129 TAVERNER

1 [On Taverner's possession of heretical books:] Cardinal Wolsey for his music excused him, saying he was but a musician, and so he escaped.

On John Taverner (*c* 1490–1545), quoted in John Foxe (1516–87)
Actes and Monuments, 1563

130 TCHAIKOVSKY

1 In you I see the greatest, or rather the only, hope for our musical future.

Henry Laroche (1845–1904)
(Fellow student of Tchaikovsky; later a distinguished Russian critic)

2 You are needed by us . . . by Russia.

Nicolai Rubinstein (1835–81)
Quoted in Strutte, *Tchaikovsky*, 1979

3 I like listening to it [Tchaikovsky's Fifth] just as I like looking at a fuchsia drenched with rain.

James Agate (1877–1947)
Ego 8, 1947

4   On my word of honour, I have never felt such self-satisfaction, such pride, such happiness, as in the knowledge that I have created a good thing.
Píotr Ilyich Tchaikovsky (1840–93)
Letter to P. Jurgenson, August 1893, on his sixth Symphony

5   How shallow Tchaikovsky appears by the side of Franck! Almost an imposter!
Havergal Brian (1876–1972)
Letter to Granville Bantock, 1915

6   Tchaikovsky's violin concerto poses for the first time the appalling notion that there can be works of music that stink to the ear.
Eduard Hanslick (1825–1904)
In 1881, quoted in Lebrecht, *Discord*, 1982

7   [On Tchaikovsky:] We know butter comes from cream, but must we watch the churning arm?
Charles Ives (1874–1954)
Attributed

131   TELEMANN

1   I have always aimed at facility. Music ought not to be an effort.
Georg Philipp Telemann (1681–1767)
Quoted in Headington, *The Bodley Head History of Western Music*, 1974

2   [Telemann] could write a motet for eight voices more quickly than one could write a letter.
George Frideric Handel (1685–1759)
Quoted in Young, *Handel*, 1946

132   VIRGIL THOMSON

1   In former times no publisher or conductor would even go to the trouble of reading my music. Now that I am a famous and terrifying music critic, they are all eager to publish and to play. They still don't bother to read it.
Virgil Thomson (1896–1989)

2   The way to write American music is simple. All you have to do is be an American and then write any kind of music you wish.
Virgil Thomson (1896–1989)
Quoted in Machlis, *Introduction to Contemporary Music,* 1963

133   TIPPETT

1   If, in the music I write, I can create a world of sound wherein some, at least, of my generation can find refreshment for the inner life, then I am doing my work properly.
Michael Tippett (1905–)
Moving into Aquarius, 1959

2   That art will speak again entire is as sure as the Zodiac.
Michael Tippett (1905–)
Ibid

3   Opera, just because of its music, may be the most suitable medium to hand now to renew the Greek attitude.
Michael Tippett (1905–)
Ibid

4   Whenever I come back to the places where the great seas meet the primeval granite, I am curiously refreshed.
Michael Tippett (1905–)
Ibid

5   Deep within me, I know that part of the artist's job is to renew our sense of the comely and the beautiful. To create a dream. Every human being has this need to dream.
Michael Tippett (1905–)
Ibid

6   My epistemology is an endless agnosticism.
Michael Tippett (1905–)
Quoted in Bowen, *Michael Tippett,* 1982

134 TOVEY

1 It is an honour for any of us to stand on the same platform with him.
Pablo Casals (1876–1973)

2 The most learned musician that ever lived.
Joseph Joachim (1831–1907)
Attributed

3 It seemed to last as long as my first term at school.
Constant Lambert (1905–51)
On the first movement of Tovey's Cello Concerto

135 VARÈSE

1 I dream of instruments obedient to my thought and which with their contribution of a whole new world of unsuspected sounds, will lend themselves to the exigencies of my inner rhythm.
Edgard Varèse (1885–1965)
Trans Louise Varèse, 1917

136 VAUGHAN WILLIAMS

1 Well, I don't know if I like it, but it's what I meant.
Ralph Vaughan Williams (1872–1958)
On hearing his own Fourth Symphony
Attributed

2 I realize now it is not as boring as I thought it was.
Ralph Vaughan Williams (1872–1958)
On his London Symphony, quoted by Adrian Boult in a broadcast, 1 August 1965

3 [Of a passage in his Fourth Symphony:] It looks wrong, and it sounds wrong, but it's right.
Ralph Vaughan Williams (1872–1958)
Attributed

4   [Vaughan Williams] looks like a farmer . . . on his way to judge the shorthorns at an agricultural fair.

Stephen Williams
Quoted in Machlis, *Introduction to Contemporary Music*, 1963

137   VERDI

1   It may be a good thing to copy reality; but to invent reality is much, much better.

Giuseppe Verdi (1813–1901)
Letter to Clarina Maffie, 1876

2   [On press notices of *Aida*:] Stupid criticism and still more stupid praise.

Giuseppe Verdi (1813–1901)

3   I know *Don Carlos* is all the rage in Milan; I am delighted, for your sake and Verdi's. Tell the latter that if he comes to Paris again he must ask a lot of money, for he is the only man capable of composing a *Grand Opera* (may our colleagues forgive me for saying so).

Gioachino Rossini (1792–1868)
Letter to Tito Ricordi, 21 April 1868, quoted in Gal, *The Musician's World*, 1965

4   Verdi . . . has bursts of marvellous passion. His passion is brutal, it is true, but it is better to be impassioned in this way than not at all. His music is at times exasperating, but is never boring.

Georges Bizet (1838–75)
Letter to his mother, 1859

5   When the rough edges of Verdi's raging passion had been smoothed by the experience and refinements of ripe age, there remained undimmed the humorous sympathy embodied in his latest works. They conclusively show how increasing wisdom brings tolerant irony and generous laughter.

Bernard van Dieren (1884–1936)
Down Among the Dead Men, 1935

6   Of all composers, past and present, I am the least learned. I mean
what I say in all seriousness, and by *learning* I do not mean *knowledge* of
music.
Giuseppe Verdi (1813–1901)
Letter to Filippi, 1869

> 7   Once more La Traviata sighs
> Another sadder song.
> Once more Il Trovatore cries
> A tale of deeper wrong.
> Alfred Noyes (1880–1958)
> *The Barrel-Organ*

8   [Of *Ernani:*] It's organ grinder's stuff.
Charles Gounod (1818–93)
Quoted in Harding, *Gounod*, 1973

9   *Otello* is a masterpiece. Go on your knees, Mother, and say 'Viva
Verdi'.
Arturo Toscanini (1867–1957)
Following the première in which he played second cello

138   VIVALDI

1   [Vivaldi] is an old man, who has a prodigious fury for composition.
I heard him undertake to compose a concerto, with all the parts, with
greater dispatch than a copyist can copy it.
Charles de Brosses (1709–77)
Letter, 1739

2   An excellent violinist and a mediocre composer.
Carlo Goldoni (1707–93)
Quoted in Kendall, *Vivaldi*, 1978

3   The peculiar characteristic of Vivaldi's music . . . is, that it is wild
and irregular.
John Hawkins (1719–89)
General History of the Science and Practice of Music, 1776

4   Vivaldi is greatly overrated – a dull fellow who could compose the
same form over and so many times over.
Igor Stravinsky (1882–1971)
Craft, *Conversations*, 1958

139 WAGNER

1   I am a different kind of organism, I have hyper-sensitive nerves, I must have beauty, splendour and light. The world ought to give me what I need! I cannot live the wretched life of a town organist like your Meister Bach! Is it such a shocking demand, if I believe that I am due the little bit of luxury I enjoy? I, who have so much enjoyment to give to the world and to thousands of people!

Richard Wagner (1813–83)
Quoted in Eliza Wille, *Erinnerungen*, 1894

2   Child! This *Tristan* is turning into something *frightful*! That last act!!! I fear the opera will be forbidden – unless the whole thing is turned into a parody by bad production – nothing but mediocre performances can save me! Completely good ones are bound to drive people crazy, – I can't imagine what else would happen! To such a state have things come!!! Alas! –

Richard Wagner (1813–83)
Letter to Mathilde Wesendonck, April 1859

3   His is the art of translating, by subtle gradations, all that is excessive, immense, ambitious in spiritual and natural mankind. On listening to this ardent and despotic music one feels at times as though one discovered again, painted in the depths of a gathering darkness torn asunder by dreams, the dizzy imaginations induced by opium.

Charles Baudelaire (1821–67)
Richard Wagner et Tannhäuser à Paris, 1861

4   It is the fate of great geniuses to be misunderstood by their contemporaries. Wagner is no friend of mine and I am fairly indifferent to him, yet I cannot forget the immeasurable enjoyment which I owe to this original genius. The charm of his muse is inexpressible. Here are voluptuousness, tenderness, love.

Georges Bizet (1838–75)
To Mme Halévy, 1871

5   I once told Wagner himself that I was the best Wagnerian of our time.

Johannes Brahms (1833–97)
Quoted in Specht, *Johannes Brahms*, 1928

6　It's a highbrow axiom that Wagner was responsible for the rise of Nazism. If you want to be in the fashion you must refer darkly to the evil workings of the *Ring* in the Teutonic mentality – though as the whole cycle of operas is devoted to showing that even the gods can't break an agreement without bringing the whole universe crashing about their ears, I've never been able to see what possible encourgement *Hitler* can have got out of it . . .

Edmund Crispin (1921–78)
Swan Song, 1947
(Crispin was the pseudonym of the composer, Bruce Montgomery, best known for his film scores, novels and short stories. *Swan Song* is a classic detective story, set among a touring opera company who are producing Wagner's *Die Meistersinger*.)

7　That old poisoner.

Claude Debussy (1862–1918)
Letter to Pierre Louÿs, 1896

8　If one has not heard Wagner at Bayreuth, one *has heard nothing!* Take lots of handkerchiefs because you will cry a great deal! Also take a sedative because you will be exalted to the point of delirium!

Gabriel Fauré (1845–1924)
Letter to Marguérite Baugnies, 1884

9　Wagner is the Marat of music, and Berlioz is its Robespierre.

Auguste de Gasperini (1825–69)
In *Le Siècle*, 1858

10　I would rather hear Annie Laurie sung with feeling than the greatest singer in the world declaiming a scene from *Tristan and Isolde*.

W.S. Gilbert (1836–1911)
Quoted in Pearson, *Gilbert and Sullivan*, 1935

11　God give me a failure like that!

Charles Gounod (1818–93)
After the failure of the 'Paris version' of *Tannhäuser*, 1861

12　Wagner's art recognizes only superlatives, and a superlative has no future. It is an end, not a beginning.

Eduard Hanslick (1825–1904)
Pleasants (ed), *Hanslick's Music Criticism*, 1950

13   The overture is hardly calculated to win the listener. All the leitmotives of the opera are dumped consecutively into a chromatic flood and finally tossed about in a kind of tonal typhoon . . . The only thing which prevents one from declaring it to be the world's most unpleasant overture is the even more horrible Prelude to *Tristan and Isolde.* The latter reminds me of the old Italian painting of that martyr whose intestines were slowly unwound from his body on to a reel.

Eduard Hanslick (1825–1904)
On Wagner's overture to *Die Meistersinger,* 1868

14   The motives at work in *Das Rheingold* are exclusively deceit, prevarication, violence, and animal sensuality. Even the gods are characterized by covetousness, cunning and breach of contract. Not a single ray of noble moral feeling penetrates this suffocating mist. *Die Walküre* stands out among the four episodes by virtue of its great dramatic and musical beauties; but we will never overcome the moral repulsion of so ecstatic a revelation of incest.

Eduard Hanslick (1825–1904)
Reviewing Wagner's *Der Ring des Nibelungen,* 1876

15   Like the Babylonian ruler who had his monogram burned into every single brick of new public buildings, so also has the author of *Parsifal* impressed an invisible R.W. upon every bar.

Eduard Hanslick (1825–1904)
On Wagner's *Parsifal,* 1882

16   Today I read out, from a Berlin paper, the news of the death, at Bayreuth, where *The Ring* was being performed for the first time, of a member of the Wagner orchestra. '*The first corpse*', said Brahms dryly . . .

George Henschel (1850–1934)
Personal Recollections of Johannes Brahms, 1907

17   Not until the turn of the century did the outlines of the new world discovered in *Tristan* begin to take shape. Music reacted to it as a human body to an injected serum, which it at first strives to exclude as a poison, and only afterwards learns to accept as necessary and even wholesome.

Paul Hindemith (1895–1963)
The Craft of Musical Composition, 1937

18   What I write is the absolute truth.
I hired a professional sleuth
For a year to unknot
All the tangled up plot
Ere I sat through the *Ring* at Bayreuth.

The opera really should float an
Enterprise willing to quote an
Insurance for fire
Should the singers perspire
Through too reckless a magic by Wotan.

Bernard P. Langley (1929–)
Wagneriana

19   A passion for Wagner's enchanted *oeuvre* has been a part of my life ever since I first became aware of it and set out to make it my own, to invest it with understanding. What it has given me in terms of enjoyment and instruction I can never forget, nor the hours of deep and solitary happiness amidst the theatre throng, hours filled with frissons and delights for the nerves and the intellect alike, with sudden glimpses into things of profound and moving significance, such as only this art can afford.

Thomas Mann (1875–1955)
The Sorrows and Grandeur of Richard Wagner, 1933

20   Wagner is the Puccini of music.

J.B. Morton (1893–1979)
Attributed

21   Is Wagner a human being at all? Is he not rather a disease? He contaminates everything he touches–he has made music sick. I postulate this viewpoint: Wagner's art is diseased.

Friedrich Nietzsche (1844–1900)
Der Fall Wagner, 1888

22   [Of *Parsifal*:] Christianity arranged for Wagnerians.

Friedrich Nietzsche (1844–1900)
Quoted in Headington, *The Bodley Head History of Western Music*, 1974

23 The American composer Silas Gamaliel Pratt deserves im-
mortality, if only for the alleged conversation with Wagner, when
Wagner said, 'You are the Richard Wagner of the United States', and
the polite rejoinder was made, 'And you, Sir, are the Silas G. Pratt of
Germany.'
Percy A. Scholes (1877–1958)
Oxford Companion to Music, 1938
(Pratt (1846–1916) studied with Liszt and wrote operas and orchestral music)

24 *Monsieur Wagner a de beaux moments, mais de mauvais quart-d'heures!*
Gioachino Rossini (1792–1868)
Attributed

25 Of all the affected, sapless, soulless, beginningless, endless,
topless, bottomless, topsiturviest, scrannel-pipiest, tongs and boniest
doggerel of sounds I ever endured the deadliest of, that eternity of
nothing was the deadliest . . .
John Ruskin (1819–1900)
On attending *Die Meistersinger,* letter to Mrs Burne-Jones, 30 June 1882

26 Had Wagner been the mere musical epicure and political
mug-wump that the term 'artist' seems to suggest to so many critics and
amateurs–that is, a creature in their own lazy likeness–he need have
taken no more part in the political struggles of his day than Bishop took
in the English Reform agitation of 1832, or Sterndale Bennett in the
Chartist or Free Trade movements.
George Bernard Shaw (1856–1950)
The Perfect Wagnerite, 1898

27 After the last notes of *Götterdämmerung* I felt as though I had been
let out of prison.
Píotr Ilyich Tchaikovsky (1840–93)
Letter to his brother Modeste, after attending the first Bayreuth Festival, 20 August 1876,
quoted in Gal, *The Musician's World,* 1965

28 Wagner's music is better than it sounds.
Mark Twain (1835–1910)
Autobiography, pub 1924

29 [Of *Parsifal:*] The first act of the three occupied two hours, and I
enjoyed that in spite of the singing.
Mark Twain (1835–1910)
At the Shrine of Wagner, 1891

30   Sad, sad, sad.
                         Wagner is dead!

When I read the news yesterday, I may truly say that I was completely crushed. Let us not discuss it. It is a great personality that has disappeared. A name which leaves a mighty imprint upon the history of art.

Giuseppe Verdi (1813–1901)
To Giulio Ricordi, 14 February 1883

31   *Et, Ô ces voix d'enfants chantants dans*
        la coupole!
     And, O those voices of children singing
        under the dome!

     Paul Verlaine (1844–96)
     Parsifal, À Jules Tellier

32   I like Wagner's music better than anybody's. It is so loud that one can talk the whole time without other people hearing what one says.

Oscar Wilde (1854–1900)
The Picture of Dorian Gray, 1891

33   What remains for me to do? He has left me no room, like a mighty tree that chokes with its shade the sprouting young growths under its widely spreading branches.

Hugo Wolf (1860–1903)
Letter, 1883

140   WALTON

1   [A] favourite saying of his was that to compose music was far worse for him than to bear children is for a woman, as it took longer than nine months and was much more painful. He would love to perplex interviewers with remarks such as that his eraser was more important than his pencil, or that he lived abroad to prevent people in England from finding out that he couldn't read or write!

Susanna Walton (1926–   )
William Walton: Behind the Façade

2 I seriously advise all sensitive composers to die at the age of thirty-seven. I know I've gone through the first halcyon period, and am just about ripe for my critical damnation.

William Walton (1902–82)
Letter, 1939

3 You have a happy inclination to polyphonic lines; this will lead you safely through the Waters and Fires which stand between you and the Parnassus.

Ferruccio Busoni (1866–1924)
To the young William Walton, 5 July 1920, unpublished letter, Ronald Stevenson Private Collection

4 Willie Walton, in his symphony particularly, uses pedals so continuously that if it were a bicycle he would have crossed America from the Atlantic to the Pacific. Advice to composers: keep your bowels open and your basses moving. Beware of the costive pedal point.

Cecil Gray (1895–1951)
Notebooks, Pauline Gray (ed), 1989

141 WARLOCK (PHILIP HESELTINE)

1 He who has heard the cry of the curlew on a lone and desolate moor has heard the music of this richly gifted personality. It is the saddest music I know.

Eric Fenby (1906–)
Delius as I knew him, 1936

2 Heseltine was gentle and shy of women; Warlock roughly undressed them; Heseltine wrote dreamy and desolate songs to words by Yeats; Warlock wrote roistering songs about drink and sex.

Colin Wilson (1931–)
Brandy of the Damned, 1964

142 WEBER

1 [Of *Der Freischütz*:] I never could have believed it of the poor weak little mannikin. Weber must write operas now; nothing but operas, one after another.
Ludwig van Beethoven (1770–1827)
Quoted in Saunders, *Weber*, 1940

2 Weber, who seems to whisper in my ear like a familiar spirit, inhabiting a happy sphere where he awaits to console me.
Hector Berlioz (1803–69)
Letter to Ferdinand Hiller, March 1830

3 Behold, the Briton does you justice, the Frenchman admires you, but only the German can love you. You are his own, a bright day in his life, a drop of his blood, a particle of his heart.
Richard Wagner (1813–83)
Speech at Weber's grave

143 WEBERN

1 [Of his own music:] In fifty years one will find it obvious, children will understand it and sing it.
Anton von Webern (1883–1945)
Quoted in Kolneder, *Anton Webern*, 1968

2 Webern's Five Pieces for Orchestra required of the listener the utmost concentration of attention. Inevitably these faint rustlings, these tiny squeaks and titterings called to mind the activities of insects.
W.S. Smith
In the *Boston Post*, 1913, quoted in Slonimsky, 'Lexicon of Musical Invective'

3 We must hail not only this great composer but a real hero. Doomed to a total failure in a deaf world of ignorance and indifference, he inexorably kept on cutting out his diamonds, his dazzling diamonds, the mines of which he knew to perfection.
Igor Stravinsky (1882–1971)
Quoted in Kilnoder, *Anton Webern*, 1968

4 A perpetual pentecost.
Igor Stravinsky (1882–1971)
Quoted in Carner, *Alban Berg*, 1983

144 WEELKES

1 Thomas Weelkes . . . divers times and very often comes so disguised either from the tavern or alehouse into the choir as is much to be lamented, for in these humours he will both curse and swear most dreadfully.

William Lawes (1602–45)
Sub-chanter of Chichester Cathedral, quoted in Brown, *Thomas Weelkes*, 1969

145 WEILL

1 I am not struggling for new forms or new theories. I am struggling for a new public.

Kurt Weill (1900–50)
Quoted in Green, *The World of Musical Comedy*, 1974

2 What Liszt did for Wagner, Busoni did for me.

Kurt Weill (1900–50)
Interview, 1936

3 I never felt the oneness with my native country that I do with the United States; the moment I landed here I felt as though I'd come home.

Kurt Weill (1900–50)
Interview, 1943

4 In much the same way that Handel can be claimed as Britain's greatest opera composer, Kurt Weill might be claimed as America's: a master musician, master musical dramatist, and large soul who found song for the people of his adopted country, learned its idioms, joined them to his own, and composed music of international importance.

Andrew Porter (1928–   )
In *The New Yorker*, 1978

146 WOLF

1   Today two new songs . . . have occurred to me, of which one sounds so weird and strange that I am quite afraid of it. God help the unfortunate people who will one day hear it!

Hugo Wolf (1860–1903)
Letter, 1888

2   If only I were Hugo Wolf.

Hugo Wolf (1860–1903)
In his last days, quoted in Walker, *Hugo Wolf,* 1968

MUSICAL INSTRUMENTS

Wagner wrote as a young man of his distaste for the visible scraping and blowing and banging that accompanies instrumental performance. As an old man he designed a theatre that submerged his orchestra into invisibility. Here, however, are loud claims, flattering and otherwise, for a motley assortment of music's inanimate sources.

147 ACCORDION

1 Accordion, n. An instrument in harmony with the sentiments of an assassin.
Ambrose Bierce (1842–1914?)
The Devil's Dictionary, 1911

2 The vile belchings of lunatic accordions.
Arthur Honegger (1892–1956)
I am a Composer, 1951

148 AEOLIAN HARP

1 The breeze warbles, and the mute still
    air
   Is Music slumbering on her instrument.
   Samuel Taylor Coleridge (1772–1834)
   The Aeolian Harp, 1795

2 A certain Music, never known before,
   Here soothed the pensive melancholy Mind;
   The God of Winds drew Sounds of deep Delight:
   Whence, with just Cause, The Harp of Aeolus
     it Light.
   Ah me! what hand can touch the strings so fine?
   Who up the lofty Diapason roll
   Such sweet, such sad, such solemn Airs
     divine,
   Then let them down again into the Soul?
   James Thomson (1700–48)
   Castle of Indolence, 1748

149 BAGPIPE

1   Twelve Highlanders and a bagpipe make a rebellion.

Proverb, cited by Walter Scott, quoted in Collinson, *The Bagpipe*, 1975

2   We had the music of the bagpipe every day at Armadale, Dunvegan and Col. Dr Johnson appeared fond of it, and used often to stand for some time with his ear close to the great drone.

James Boswell (1740–95)
The Journal of a Tour of the Hebrides, 1785

3   I got to try the bagpipes. It was like trying to blow an octopus.

James Galway (1939–   )
An Autobiography, 1978

4   Plant, what are you then? Your leafs
Mind me o' the pipes lood drone
– And a' your purple tops
Are the pirly-wirly notes
That gang staggerin' owre them as they groan.

Hugh MacDiarmid (1892–1978)
A Drunk Man Looks at the Thistle, 1926

5   Let me play to you tunes without measure
or end,
Tunes that are born to die without a herald,
As a flight of storks rises from a marsh,
circles,
And alights on the spot from which it rose.

Hugh MacDiarmid (1892–1978)
Bagpipe Music, 1943

6   The bagpipes – they are screaming and
they are sorrowful.
There is a wail in their merriment, and
cruelty in their triumph.
They rise and fall like a weight swung in the
air at the end of a string.

Hugh MacDiarmid (1892–1978)
Ibid

7 *Falstaff:*   ... 'Sblood, I am as melancholy as a gib cat or a
                     lugged bear.
   Prince Henry: Or an old lion or a lover's lute.
   Falstaff: Yea, or the drone of a Lincolnshire bagpipe.

William Shakespeare (1564–1616)
Henry IV Pt I, 1589–90, Act I, Sc II

8 And others, when the bagpipe sings i' th'
       nose,
   Cannot containe their urine.
   (Shylock)

   William Shakespeare (1564–1616)
   The Merchant of Venice, 1598–8, Act IV, Sc I

150 BARREL ORGAN

1 In this unmusical country [England] there are dreadful barrel organs
which go up and down the streets – there is one playing under my
windows right now, which is so out of tune that it almost makes me weep
and I find it nearly impossible to continue this letter to you.

Princess Lieven
Letter to Metternich, 11 July 1820, quoted in Barzun, *Pleasures of Music*, 1952

151 BASSOON

1 The Wedding-Guest here beat his breast,
   For he heard the loud bassoon.

   Samuel Taylor Coleridge (1772–1834)
   The Ancient Mariner, 1798, Pt I

2 The bassoon in the orchestra plays the same role as Gorgonzola
among cheeses – a figure of fun. Actually the bassoon can be the most
romantic and passionate of instruments and Gorgonzola can be the
finest of cheeses – but they must both be treated properly.

Cecil Gray (1891–1951)
Notebooks, Pauline Gray (ed), 1989

3   It is a bass instrument without proper bass strength, oddly weak in sound, bleating burlesque.
Thomas Mann (1875–1955)
Doctor Faustus, 1947, trans Lowe-Porter

152   BELLS

1   Is it not fine to dance and sing
When the bells of death do ring.
Anonymous
Quoted in Lee, *Music of the People,* 1970

2   Bells are booming down the bohreens,
White the mist along the grass.
John Betjeman (1906–84)
Ireland with Emily, 1945

3   Bells, the poor man's only music.
Samuel Taylor Coleridge (1772–1834)
Frost at Midnight

4   Bells are music's laughter.
Thomas Hood (1799–1845)
Miss Kilmansegg: Her Marriage, 1827

5   Bells, the music nighest bordering upon heaven.
Charles Lamb (1775–1834)
Essays of Elia, 1823

6   The mellow lin-lan-lone of evening bells.
Alfred, Lord Tennyson (1809–92)
Far-Far-Away

153 BUGLE

1   Blow, bugle, blow, set the wild echoes
      flying,
    Blow, bugle; answer echoes, dying, dying,
      dying.
    Alfred, Lord Tennyson (1809–92)
    The Princess, 1847, IV

154 CELLO

1   Madam, you have between your legs an instrument capable of giving
pleasure to thousands – and all you can do is scratch it.
Attributed remark of Thomas Beecham (1879–1961) to a lady cellist in rehearsal

2   The cello is like a beautiful woman who has not grown older, but
younger with time, more slender, more supple, more graceful.
Pablo Casals (1876–1973)
In *Time*, 29 April 1957

155 CLARINET

1   Clarionet, n. An instrument of torture operated by a person with
cotton in his ears. There are two instruments that are worse than a
clarionet – two clarionets.
Ambrose Bierce (1842–1914?)
The Devil's Dictionary, 1911

2   The many-keyed clarinet, which can sound so ghostly in the deep
chalumeau register but higher up can gleam in silvery blossoming
harmony.
Thomas Mann (1875–1955)
Doctor Faustus, 1947, trans Lowe-Porter

156 CLAVICHORD

1   The clavichord gives a fretful waspish kind of sound, not at all suited to tender expression.

John Robison (1739–1805)
Supplement to the *Encyclopaedia Britannica*, 1801

157 CORNET

1   What can yield a tone so like an eunuch's voice as a true cornet pipe?

Roger North (1653–1734)
The Musicall Gramarian, 1728

158 FLUTE

1   The flute is not an instrument that has a good moral effect – it is too exciting.

Aristotle (384–322 BC)
Politics

2   Blowing is not playing the flute; you must make use of your fingers.

Johann Wolfgang von Goethe (1749–1832)
Sprüche in Prosa, 1819

3   When the young men serenaded only the flute was forbidden. Why, I asked. Because it was bad for the girls to hear the flute at night.

Ernest Hemingway (1898–1961)
On the customs of the Abruzzi in *A Farewell to Arms*, 1929

4   Anon they move
In perfect phalanx to the Dorian mood
Of flutes and soft recorders.

John Milton (1608–74)
Paradise Lost, 1667, I

5   ... the vile squeaking of the wry-necked
fife.

(Shylock)

William Shakespeare (1564–1616)
The Merchant of Venice, 1596–8, Act II, Sc V

159 GLASS HARMONICA

1   When Dr [Benjamin] Franklin invented the [glass] Harmonica, he concealed it from his wife till the instrument was fit to play; and then woke her with it one night, when she took it for the music of angels.
Leigh Hunt (1784–1859)
Autobiography, 1850, 'Musical Memories'

2   Cherubim in a box.
Thomas Gray (1716–71)

160 GUITAR

1   To use a woman or a guitar, one must know how to tune them.
Spanish proverb

2   Never having thought of writing for the guitar, I asked Julian [Bream] for a chart which would explain what the guitar could do. I managed to write some rather pretty pieces for him, except that the first six notes of the first piece all need to be played on open strings. So when he begins to play, the audience will probably think he's tuning the bloody thing up.
William Walton (1902–83)

161 HARMONIUM

1   'Strings for ever!' said little Jimmy. 'Strings alone would have held their ground against all the newcomers in creation. But clar'nets was death.' ('Death they was!' said Mr Penny.) 'And harmoniums,' William continued in a louder voice, and getting excited by these signs of approval, 'harmoniums and barrel organs . . . be miserable – what shall I call 'em – miserable –' 'Sinners,' suggested Jimmy, who made large strides like the men and did not lag behind like the other little boys. 'Miserable machines for such a divine thing as music!'
Thomas Hardy (1840–1928)
Under the Greenwood Tree, 1873

162 HARP

1   Bifor the king he sat adoun
    And tok his harpe so miri of soun,
    And trempreth his harp as he wele can,
    And blisseful notes he ther gan.

Anonymous
Orfeo and Heurodis, fourteenth century

2   Hold golden hands a moment to the harp,
    be happy and content:
    music in sweet measurement
    will charm away your torment.

William Thomas (sixteenth century)
Trans Keith Bosley

3 Hang the harpers wherever found.

Queen Elizabeth I (1533–1603)
Proclamation of 1603, quoted in Boyle, *The Irish Song Tradition,* 1976

4   Leave strumming at the doors of inns
    To vagabonds and sharpers.
    Where men seek minstrels for their sins
    They shall not lack for harpers.

Laurence Housman (1865–1959)
Farewell to Town

5   Then, crowned again, their golden harps
     they took,
    Harps ever tuned, that glittering by their
     side
    Like quivers hung: and with preamble sweet
    Of charming symphony they introduce
    Their sacred song, and waken raptures high;
    No voice exempt, no voice but well could join
    Melodious part; such concord is in heaven.

John Milton (1608–74)
Paradise Lost, 1667, III

6   The harp that once through Tara's halls
    The sound of music shed,
    Now hangs as mute on Tara's walls
    As if that soul were fled.

Thomas Moore (1779–1852)

7   And it came to pass when the evil spirit from God was upon Saul that David took up a harp and played with his hand; so that Saul was refreshed and was well and the evil spirit departed from him.

Bible, Authorized Version
I Samuel, Ch 16, v 23

8   Hearken, my minstrels! which of ye all
Touched his harp with that dying fall,
So sweet, so soft, so faint,
It seemed an angel's whispered call
To an expiring saint?

Walter Scott (1771–1832)
The Bridal of Triermain, 1813

9   Then will I go unto the altar of God, unto God my exceeding joy: yea, upon the harp will I praise thee, O God my God.

Bible, Authorized Version
Psalms, Ch 43, v 4

10   Harp not on that string, madam.
(Richard)

William Shakespeare (1564–1616)
Richard III, 1592–3, Act IV, Sc IV

11   Harping always upon love, till you be as blind as a harper.

John Lyly (1554–1606)
Sapho and Phao, c 1584, Act IV, Sc III

163   HARPSICHORD

1   Sounds like two skeletons copulating on a corrugated tin roof.

Thomas Beecham (1879–1961)
Quoted in Atkins and Newman, *Beecham Stories*, 1978

2   The harpsichord, however it may sound in a small room – and to my mind it never has a pleasant sound – in a large concert room sounds just like the ticking of a sewing machine.

Ralph Vaughan Williams (1872–1958)
Broadcast talk, *Bach, the Great Bourgeois*, 1950

3   The harpsichord is perfect as to its compass, and brilliant in itself, but as it is impossible to swell out or diminish the volume of its sound, I shall always feel grateful to any who, by the exercise of infinite art supported by fine taste, contrive to render this instrument capable of expression.

François Couperin (1668–1733)
Pièces de clavecin, 1713, Book I, Preface

> 4   Two harpsichords playing—
> and there's a robust heaven:
> no lackadaisical boredom of the infinite
>   here,
> no epicene angels being languid,
> not a golden pavement in sight.
> The logic of passion made articulate,
> invents fibres in the listening mind
> that shape it from shapelessness.
>
> Norman MacCaig (1910–   )
> *Down-to-earth heaven*, 1977

5   A performance on a bird-cage with a toasting fork.

An opinion of the harpsichord quoted by Percy A. Scholes (1877–1958), *The Oxford Companion to Music*, 1938

164 HORN

> 1   With eyes up-rais'd, as one inspir'd
> Pale Melancholy sate retir'd
> And from her wild sequester'd seat,
> In notes by distance made more sweet,
> Pour'd thro' the mellow horn her pensive
>   soul.
>
> William Collins (1721–59)
> *The Passions, an Ode for Music*

> 2   The horn, the horn, the lusty horn
> Is not a thing to laugh to scorn.
>
> William Shakespeare (1564–1616)
> *As You Like It*, 1599, Act IV, Sc II

3   O hark, O hear! how thin and clear,
    And thinner, clearer, farther going!
    O sweet and far from cliff and scar
    The horns of Elfland faintly blowing!

Alfred, Lord Tennyson (1809–92)
The Princess, 1847

4   *Dieu! que le son du cor est triste au fond de bois!*
    God, how sad is the sound of the horn in the depths of the wood!

Alfred de Vigny (1797–1863)
Le Cor

165 LUTE

1   Like as the lute delights, or else
        dislikes,
    As is his art that plays upon the same,
    So sounds my Muse according as she strikes
    On my heart strings, high tuned unto her
        fame.

Samuel Danyel (1562/3–1619)
Song, 1606

2   In a sadly pleasing strain
    Let the warbling lute complain.

Alexander Pope (1688–1744)
Ode for Musick, on St Cecilia's Day, c 1708

3   He capers nimbly in a lady's chamber
    To the lascivious pleasing of a lute.
    (Richard)

William Shakespeare (1564–1616)
Richard III, 1592–3, Act I, Sc I

4   My lute awake! Perform the last
    Labour that you and I shall waste,
    The end that I have now begun;
    For when this song is sung and past,
    My lute be still, for I have done . . .

Thomas Wyatt (1503–42)

166 LYRE

1   *Dapibus supremi*
    Grata testudo Jovis.
    The lyre is welcome at the feasts of supreme
      Jupiter.
    Horace (Quintus Horatius Flaccus 65–8 BC)
    Odes, 1, 32

167 MANDOLIN

1   The pleasant whining of a mandoline.
T.S. Eliot (1888–1965)
The Waste Land, 1922

168 OBOE

1   All first oboists are gangsters. They are tough, irascible, double-reed roosters, feared by colleagues and conductors.
Harry Ellis Dickson
Gentlemen, More Dolce Please, 1969

2   I used to compose like the devil in those days, chiefly for the hautboy, which was my favourite instrument.
George Frideric Handel (1685–1759)
On being shown, in old age, chamber works composed when he was eleven

169 ORGAN

1   Whence hath the Church so many Organs and Musicall Instruments? To what purpose, I pray you, is that terrible blowing of Belloes, expressing rather the crakes of Thunder, than the sweetness of the voyce?
Aelred, Abbot of Rievaulx
Speculum Charitatis, twelfth century, trans William Prynne (1600–69)

2   Hence from their resounding prison the docile winds are loosed, and repay a melody for their liberty received.

Jean Baptiste de Santeul (1630–97)
Inscription on an organ

3   There is nothing to it. You only have to hit the right notes at the right time and the instrument plays itself.

Johann Sebastian Bach (1685–1750)
On playing the organ, quoted in Geiringer, *The Bach Family*, 1954

> 4   But O! what art can teach
> What human voice can reach,
> The sacred organ's praise?
>
> John Dryden (1631–1700)
> *A Song for St Cecilia's Day*, 1687

5   If 'tis Pedals for two martel hours of practice I never complain; and he has plenty of vagaries. When 'tis hot summer weather there's nothing will do for him but Choir, Great and Swell together, till yer face is but a vapour; and on a frosty winter night he'll keep me there while he tweedles upon the Twelfth and Sixteenth till my arms be scrammed for want of motion.
(The Organblower)

Thomas Hardy (1840–1928)
The Hand of Ethelberta, 1876

6   Joking apart, Prince Albert asked me to go to him on Saturday at two o'clock so that I may try his organ.

Felix Mendelssohn (1801–47)
Quoted in Bonavia, *Musicians on Music*, 1956

7   *Dryfat:*   The organs of the body, as some term them.
   Mrs Purge: Organs! fie, fie, they have a most abominable sound in mine ears; they edify not a whit, I detest 'em. I hope my body has no organs.

Thomas Middleton (*c* 1570–1627)
The Family of Love, 1608, Act III, Sc II

> 8   There let the pealing Organ blow,
> To the full voic'd Quire below,
> In Service high, with Anthems cleer,
> As may with sweetnes, through mine ear,
> Dissolve me into extasies,
> And bring all Heav'n before mine eyes.
>
> John Milton (1608–74)
> *Il Penseroso*, 1632

9   In my eyes and ears the organ will ever be the King of instruments.
Wolfgang Amadeus Mozart (1756–91)
Letter, 1777

10   When the full organ joins the tuneful
        choir,
     Th' Immortal Pow'rs incline their ear.
        Alexander Pope (1688–1744)
        Ode for Musick, on St Cecilia's Day, c 1708

11   Lose no opportunity of practising on the organ; there is no instrument which takes a swifter revenge on anything unclear or sloppy in composition and playing.
Robert Schumann (1810–56)
Aphorisms, c 1833

12   It's organ organ organ all the time with him.
(Mrs Organ Morgan)
Dylan Thomas (1914–53)
Under Milk Wood, pub 1954

13   [Of the organ for St Paul's:] A confounded box of whistles.
Christopher Wren (1632–1723)
Quoted in Phillips, *The Singing Church,* 1968

14   I, too, played the organ frequently in my youth, but my nerves could not withstand the power of this gigantic instrument. I should place an organist who is master of his instrument at the very head of all virtuosi.
Ludwig van Beethoven (1770–1827)
To the Breslau organist, K.G. Freudenberg, *c* 1825

170   PERCUSSION

1   In what unison sounded the drums and
        bells!
     What joy was there in the hall with its
        circlet of water!
     The lizard-skin drums rolled harmonious,
     As the blind musicians performed their parts.
        Chinese Ode, c 1135 BC

2   In the orchestra, percussion instruments are effective in inverse proportion to their number.
Charles Villiers Stanford (1852–1924)

3   Effects: a term used in dance-band parlance, etc, for imitative instruments such as various forms of whistle and anvil, baby cry, bantam rooster, bear growl, calf bawl, cuckoo, dog bark, duck quack, pig grunt, hen cackle, cock crow, drum call, glass crash, horse trot, lion roar, locomotive, nose blow, peacock, pop-gun, rain, siren, sleigh-bells, steam exhaust, surf and thunder, typewriter effect, whip crack, etc.
Percy A. Scholes (1877–1958)
Oxford Companion to Music, 1963

4   The noisy drum hath nothing in it, but mere air.
Thomas Fuller (1608–61)

5   There is no instrument the sound of which proclaims such vast internal satisfaction as the drum.
George Meredith (1828–1909)
Sandra Belloni, 1886

6   I have a reasonable good ear in music. Let's have the tongs and the bones.
(Bottom)
William Shakespeare (1564–1616)
A Midsummer Night's Dream, 1595, Act IV, Sc I

7   Let's march without the noise of threatening drum.
(Bolingbroke)
William Shakespeare (1564–1616)
Richard II, 1595, Act III, Sc III

8   In strains more exalted the salt-box
        shall join,
    And clattering and battering and clapping
        combine;
    With a rap and a tap while the hollow side
        sounds,
    Up and down leaps the flap, and with rattling
        rebounds.

Bonnell Thornton (1724–68)
From the burlesque *Ode on St Cecilia's Day,* adapted to the ancient British *musick, viz the salt-box, the jew's harp, the marrow-bones and cleaver, the hum-strum or hurdy-gurdy, &c,* 1749

171 PIANOFORTE

1   Old piano players never die, they simply fake away.
Anonymous

2   The piano is the social instrument par excellence. It is drawing-room furniture, a sign of bourgeois prosperity, the most massive of the devices by which the young are tortured in the name of education and the grown-up in the name of entertainment.
Jacques Barzun (1907–)
Loesser, *Men, Women and Pianos,* 1954, Preface

3   My father would not let me take up the piano; otherwise I should no doubt have turned into a formidable pianist in company with forty thousand others.
Hector Berlioz (1803–69)
Memoirs

4   Piano, n. A parlour utensil for subduing the impenitent visitor. It is operated by depressing the keys of the machine and the spirits of the audience.
Ambrose Bierce (1842–1914?)
The Devil's Dictionary, 1911

5   Whoever really wants to know what Liszt has done for the piano should study his old operatic Fantasies. They represent the classicism of piano technique.
Johannes Brahms (1833–97)
Quoted by Friedheim, *Life and Liszt,* 1961

6   A piano-forte is a fine resource,
All Balzac's novels occupy one shelf,
The new edition fifty volumes long.
Robert Browning (1812–89)
Bishop Blougram's Apology

7   Bach is the foundation of piano playing, Liszt the summit. The two make Beethoven possible.
Ferruccio Busoni (1866–1924)
Letter to Woltersdorf, 1898

8   Take it for granted from the beginning that everything is possible on the piano, even when it seems impossible to you, or really is so.
Ferruccio Busoni (1866–1924)
Ibid

9   I find piano practising a great effort, yet one dare not ignore it. It's like an animal whose heads are continually growing again, however many one cuts off.
Ferruccio Busoni (1866–1924)
Letter to Gerda Busoni, 1907

10   Respect the pianoforte! It gives a single man command over something complete: in its ability to go from very soft to very loud in one and the same register it excels all other instruments. The trumpet can blare, but not sigh; the flute is contrary; the pianoforte can do both. Its range embraces the highest and lowest practicable notes. Respect the pianoforte!
Ferruccio Busoni (1866–1924)
Sketch of a New Aesthetic of Music, trans 1911

11   'Tis wonderful how soon a piano gets into a log-hut on the frontier.
Ralph Waldo Emerson (1803–82)
Civilization, 1870

12   A harp in a box.
Leigh Hunt (1784–1859)
The Seer, 1840

13   A piano is a lot more useful than a synthesizer. You can make a synthesizer sound like a piano, you can get a sample which produces an exact replica of the noise. But you can't *stand* on a synthesizer, you can't jump up and down on a synthesizer, you can't do a back-flip off a synthesizer. A piano comes in handy for that kind of stuff.
Billy Joel (1949–   )
Quoted in the *Independent*, 23 May 1990

14·   So how it is vain for the singer to
        burst into clamour
    With the great black piano appassionato.
        D.H. Lawrence (1885–1930)
        Piano

15   [Of *Vingt regards sur l'enfant Jésus:*] It is possible to make sounds on a piano that are more orchestral than those of an orchestra.
Olivier Messiaen (1908–   )
Nichols, *Messiaen*, 1975

16   A man of brains is like a virtuoso who can give a concert all by himself. Or he is like a piano, which is in itself a small orchestra.
Arthur Schopenhauer (1788–1860)
Maxims of Worldly Wisdom, quoted in Barzun, *Pleasures of Music*, 1952

17   The pianoforte is the most important of all musical instruments: its invention was to music what the invention of printing was to poetry.

George Bernard Shaw (1856–1950)
Fortnightly review, 1894, 'The Religion of the Pianoforte'

18   Over the piano was printed a notice: 'Please do not shoot the pianist. He is doing his best.'

Oscar Wilde (1854–1900)
Impressions of America: Leadville

19   In spite of myself, the insidious
        mastery of song
     Betrays me back, till the heart of me weeps
        to belong
     To the old Sunday evenings at home, with
        winter outside
     And hymns in the cosy parlour, the tinkling
        piano our guide.

   D.H. Lawrence (1885–1930)
   Piano

172   RECORDER

1   To Drumbleby's and did there talk a great deal about pipes, and did buy a recorder which I do intend to learn to play on, the sound of it being of all sounds in the world most pleasing to me.

Samuel Pepys (1633–1703)
Diary, 1668

2   It is as easy as lying. Govern these vantages with your fingers and thumb, give it breath with your mouth, and it will discourse most eloquent music.
(Hamlet to Guildenstern)

William Shakespeare (1564–1616)
Hamlet, 1600–1, Act III, Sc II

173 SAXOPHONE

1   The saxophone is the embodied spirit of beer.
Arnold Bennett (1867–1931)
Attributed

2   Wagner did not like the saxophone. He said it 'sounds like the word *Reckankreuzungsklankewerkzeuge*'.
Recounted by Nicolas Slonimsky (1894–   )
A Thing or Two about Music, 1948

174 TROMBONE

1   The trombones are too sacred for frequent use.
Felix Mendelssohn (1809–47)

2   Many a sinner has played himself into heaven on the trombone, thanks to the [Salvation] Army.
George Bernard Shaw (1856–1950)
Major Barbara, 1905

175 TRUMPET

1   For if the trumpet give an uncertain sound, who shall prepare himself to the battle?
Bible, Authorized Version
I Corinthians, Ch 14, v 8

2   He promptly made a trumpet of his arse.
Dante (1265–1321)
Inferno, Canto XXI

3   Blowing one's own trumpet.
Diogenianus (second century AD)

4   At the round earth's imagined corners,
       blow
    Your trumpets, angels.
    John Donne (1572?–1631)
    Holy Sonnets, 7

   5   The Trumpet's loud clangour
       Excites us to arms
       With shrill notes of anger
       And mortal alarms.
       John Dryden (1631–1700)
       A Song for St Cecilia's Day, 1687, set by Handel

6   *At tuba terribili sonitu taratantara dixit.*
    And the trumpet with a terrible noise went 'taratantara'.
Ennius (*c* 239–169 BC)
Annals

7   It came to pass when the people heard the sound of the trumpet, and
the people shouted with a great shout, that the wall fell down flat, so that
the people went up into the city.
Bible, Authorized Version
Joshua, Ch 6, v 20

8   The Spirit of the Lord came upon Gideon, and he blew a trumpet.
Bible, Authorized Version
Judges, Ch 6, v 34

9   The silver, snarling trumpets 'gan to chide.
John Keats (1795–1821)
The Eve of St Agnes, 1819

10   [My] idea of heaven is eating *pâtés de foie gras* to the sound of
trumpets.
Sydney Smith (1771–1845)
Quoted in Pearson, *The Smith of Smiths,* 1934

176   TUBA

1   The tuba is certainly the most intestinal of instruments, the very
lower bowel of music.
Peter De Vries (1910–   )
The Glory of the Hummingbird, 1974

2   One day ... my wife and I were walking, and as we passed a second-hand music shop, there in the window stood the one thing which I had wanted to own and play ever since I could remember. There it stood: fat, solid, charming in every way – a tuba! The next thing I knew was that I had bought him, and my wife and I were carrying him across Piccadilly Circus in the pouring rain. At home we gave him a nice bath and a rub. For the next three days I produced a series of noises so dreadful and so sordid that a rumour went about in the neighbourhood that we were keeping a live elephant in the bath. But on the fourth day I was able to make some quite nice noises ...

Gerard Hoffnung (1925 – 59)
Music Club, BBC broadcast, 1954

177   VIOLA

1   That instrument of mixed sex ... this hermaphrodite of the orchestra.

Thomas Beecham (1879 – 1961)
A Mingled Chime, 1944

2   Despite Mozart's gifts as a pianist, his favourite instrument was the viola – appropriately enough, for it lies at the heart of the string quartet.

Alec Hyatt King (1911 –   )
Mozart Chamber Music, 1968

178   VIOLIN

1   Old King Cole was a merry old soul,
       And a merry old soul was he;
       He called for his pipe and he called for his
          bowl,
       And he called for his fiddlers three.

Anonymous
Nursery rhyme

2   Fiddle, n. An instrument to tickle human ears by friction of a horse's tail on the entrails of a cat.

Ambrose Bierce (1842–1914?)
The Devil's Dictionary, 1911

3   I live by twa trades, sir ... fiddle, sir, and spade; filling the world, and emptying of it.

Walter Scott (1771–1832)
The Bride of Lammermoor, 1819

4   There's many a good tune played on an old fiddle.

Samuel Butler (1835–1902)
The Way of All Flesh, 1903

5   The manner of the conveyance of sounds, which is as it were the basis of music, is unintelligible. For what can be more strange, than that the rubbing of a little *Hair* and *Cat-gut* together, should make such a mighty alteration in a Man that sits at a distance?

Jeremy Collier (1650–1726)
An Essay of Musick, 1702

6   In came a fiddler – and tuned like fifty stomach-aches.

Charles Dickens (1812–70)
A Christmas Carol, 1843

7   Entry of the violinists, dancing ...

Stage direction in a *divertissement* by Lully and Molière

8   Difficult do you call it, sir? I wish it were impossible.

Dr Samuel Johnson (1709–84)
Attributed remark on a violinist's playing

9   I am quite at your service to play second fiddle in all your laudable enterprises.

Alain René Lesage (1668–1747)
Gil Blas, 1715–35, trans Malkin, 1809

10   From this did Paganini comb the fierce
     Electric sparks, or to tenuity
     Pull forth the inmost wailing of the *wire*
     No cat-gut could swoon out so much of soul!

Robert Browning (1812–89)
Red Cotton Night-Cap Country, 1873

11   There are in the music of the violin ... accents so closely akin to those of certain contralto voices that one has the illusion that a singer has taken her place amid the orchestra. One raises one's eyes, and sees only the wooden case, delicate as a Chinese box, but at moments, one is still tricked by the Siren's deceiving call; at times too, one thinks one is listening to a captive genie struggling in the darkness of the sapient, quivering and enchanted box, like a devil immersed in a stoup of holy water; sometimes, again, it is in the air, at large, like a pure and supernatural being that unfolds its invisible message as it goes by.
(Swann in Love)

Marcel Proust (1871–1922)
Remembrance of Things Past, trans Scott Moncrieff and Kilmartin

12   The Devil rides upon a fiddlestick.
(Prince Henry)

William Shakespeare (1564–1616)
Henry IV Pt I, 1596, Act II, Sc IV

13   When a man is not disposed to hear music, there is not a more disagreeable sound in harmony than that of the violin.

Richard Steele (1672–1729)
In the *Tatler*, 1 April 1712

14   The gentlemen in private meeting ... played three, four and five parts with viols ... and they esteemed a violin to be an instrument only belonging to a common fiddler, and could not endure that it should come among them for fear of making their meetings to be vain and fiddling.

Anthony Wood (1632–95)
Antiquities, 1674

15   Is it not strange that sheeps' guts should hale souls out of men's bodies?
(Benedict)

William Shakespeare (1564–1616)
Much Ado About Nothing, 1598, Act II, Sc III

179   VIOLS

1   And from henceforth, the stateful instrument gambo viol shall with
ease yield full various and as deviceful musics as the lute.

Tobias Hume (d 1645)
The First Part of Ayres, 1605

2   The viol, the violet and the vine.

Edgar Allan Poe (1809–49)
The City in the Sea

PLAYERS

Just as female composers had a long struggle for a hearing, outnumbered as they were historically by their male counterparts, so women players were, until modern times, all too easily elbowed aside and overshadowed. This is no longer so, but section 182 should be seen in this light, rather than as an exercise in misogyny.

180   MUSICIANS IN GENERAL

1   Sing unto the Lord with the harp; with the harp, and the voice of a psalm. With trumpets and sound of cornet make a joyful noise before the Lord, the King.
Bible, Authorized Version
Psalms 5, Ch 98, v 5

2   These three take crooked ways: carts, boats, and musicians.
Hindu proverb, quoted in Mencken, *Dictionary of Quotations*, 1942

3   Hell is full of musical amateurs, music is the brandy of the damned. (Don Juan)
George Bernard Shaw (1856–1950)
Man and Superman, 1902

4   [Of musicians:] Our business is emotion and sensitivity–to be the sensors of the human race.
Janet Baker (1933–   )
Interview in *The Observer*, 1982

5   Ah music! What a beautiful art! But what a wretched profession!
Georges Bizet (1838–75)
Attributed, 1867

6   But God has a few of us whom he whispers
          in the ear;
     The rest may reason and be welcome; 'tis we
          musicians know.
     Robert Browning (1812–89)
     Abt Vogler, 1864

7 A taste of sculpture and painting is in my mind as becoming as a taste of fiddling and piping is unbecoming a man of fashion. The former is connected with history and poetry, the latter, with nothing that I know of but bad company.

Lord Chesterfield (1696–1773)
Letter to his son, 1749

8 Some men are like musical glasses—to produce their finest tones you must keep them wet.

Samuel Taylor Coleridge (1772–1834)
Table Talk, 1834

9 A certain skilful action of his fingers as he hummed some bars and beat time on the seat beside him seemed to denote the musician; and the extraordinary satisfaction he derived from humming something very slow and long, which had no recognizable tune, seemed to denote that he was a scientific one.

Charles Dickens (1812–70)
Dombey and Son, 1846

10 As to Mr Feeder, BA, Doctor Blimber's assistant, he was a kind of human barrel-organ, with a little list of tunes at which he was continually working, over and over again, without any variation.

Charles Dickens (1812–70)
Ibid

11 Music might tame and civilize wild beasts, but 'tis evident it never yet could tame and civilize musicians.

John Gay (1685–1732)
Polly, 1729

12 The fundamental evil in music is the necessity of reproduction of its artistic creations by performance.

Ferdinand Hiller (1811–85)

13 Music-making as a means of getting money is hell.

Gustav Holst (1874–1934)
Quoted in Imogen Holst, *Holst,* 1974

14 'Tis the common disease of all your musicians, that they know no mean to be entreated either to begin or end.
(Julia)

Ben Jonson (1572–1637)
The Poetaster, Act II Sc II

15   King Henry the Eighth could not only sing his part sure, but of himself composed a service of four, five, and six parts.
Henry Peacham (1576?–1643?)
The Compleat Gentleman, 1622

16   The professional musician, as such, can have no special social status whatever, because he may be anything, from an ex-drummer boy to an artist and philosopher of world-wide reputation.
George Bernard Shaw (1856–1950)
In *The World,* 19 January 1893

17   The chief objection to playing wind instruments is that it prolongs the life of the player.
George Bernard Shaw (1856–1950)

18   The Scots are all musicians. Every man you meet plays on the flute, the violin or the violincello, and there is one nobleman [Thomas Erskine, Earl of Kelly] whose compositions are universally admired.
Tobias Smollet (1721–71)
Letter, 1756

19   Musical people are so very unreasonable. They always want one to be perfectly dumb at the very moment when one is longing to be absolutely deaf.
(Mabel Chiltern)
Oscar Wilde (1854–1900)
An Ideal Husband, 1895, Act II

20   I play a musical instrument some, but only for my own amazement.
Fred Allen (1894–1956)
Quoted in the *Reader's Digest,* 1936

181   SOLOISTS

1   Brahms–what a pianist! One of ten thumbs!
Philip Hale (1854–1934)
In the *Boston Herald*

2   He would attack the piano not only with his hands but also with his elbows, his forehead, his stomach and even his feet, thereby producing the most unusual effects and a volume of sound akin to that of a ferocious storm; he would only relax when the unfortunate instrument was itself reeling on its legs like a drunken man.

A description of the playing of Emmanuel Chabrier (1841–94) by André Messager (1853–1929), quoted in Hughes, *Sidelights on a Century of Music*, 1969

3   [Corelli] was requested one evening to play, to a large and polite company, a fine solo which he had lately composed. Just as he was in the midst of his performance, some of the number began to discourse together a little unseasonably; Corelli gently lays down his instrument. Being asked if there was anything the matter with him? Nothing, he replied, he was only afraid that he interrupted conversation.

John Mainwaring (c 1724–1807)
Memoirs of the Life of the Late George Frederic Handel, 1760

4   When you are playing, do not be concerned about who is listening to you. Always play as though a master were listening to you.

Zoltán Kodály (1882–1967)
Address to the Budapest Academy of Music, 1953

5   Fair-haired, blue-eyed, his aspect blithe
       His figure tall and straight and lithe,
       And every feature of his face
       Revealing his Norwegian race;
       A radiance, streaming from within
       Around his eyes and forehead beamed;
       The angel with his violin
       Painted by Raphael he seemed.

       Henry Wadsworth Longfellow (1807–82)
       On Ole Bull, *Tales of a Wayside Inn*

6   I have wept only three times in my life: the first time when my earliest opera failed, the second time when, with a boating party, a truffled turkey fell into the water, and the third time when I first heard Paganini play.

Gioachino Rossini (1792–1868)
Quoted in Pulver, *Paganini*, 1936

7   [On refusing to play encores:] Applause is a receipt, not a bill.

Artur Schnabel (1882–1951)
Quoted in Kolodin, *The Musical Life*, 1958

8   [Asked the secret of piano-playing:] I always make sure that the lid over the keyboard is open before I start to play.
Artur Schnabel (1882–1951)
Attributed

9   I don't play accurately – anyone can play accurately – but I play with wonderful expression. As far as the piano is concerned, sentiment is my forte. I keep science for Life.
(Algernon Moncrieff)
Oscar Wilde (1854–1900)
The Importance of Being Earnest, 1895, Act I

182   WOMEN PLAYERS

1   All the daughters of musick shall be brought low.
Bible, Authorized Version
Ecclesiastes, Ch 12, v 4

2   I think, Miss Woodhouse, you and I must establish a musical club and have regular weekly meetings at your house or ours . . . for married women, you know – there is a sad story against them, in general. They are but too apt to give up music.
(Mrs Elton)
Jane Austen (1775–1817)
Emma, 1815

3   *Byron:*   [to his childhood friend, Elizabeth Pigot:]
                      'I don't know how it is, I sing a great deal better to
                      your playing than to other people's.'
    Elizabeth Pigot: 'That's because I play to your singing, while others
                      make you sing to their playing.'
Thomas Moore (1779–1852)
Notes for the Life of Byron, c 1820

4   A certain Fräulein P. played the *Mazeppa* Study in frightful style. Bülow, to the delight of the others, told her that she had only one qualification for performing this piece – she had the soul of a horse.
Ernest Newman (1868–1959)
Quoting pupils of a Liszt masterclass taken by Hans von Bülow, *The Man Liszt*, 1934

5   Imagine with your self what an unsightly matter it were to see a woman play upon a tabor or drum, or blow in a flute or trumpet, or any like instrument: and this because the boisterousness of them doth both cover and take away that sweet mildness which setteth so forth every deed that a woman doeth.

Baldassare Castiglione (1478–1529)
The Booke of the Courtyer, 1528, trans Sir Thomas Hoby, 1561

6   There's no music when a woman's in the concert.

Thomas Dekker (c 1570–1641)
The Honest Whore Pt 1, 1604, Act II

7   [Of Clara Schumann:] She is a large, very German-looking woman, with dark hair and superb neck and arms. At the last concert she was dressed in black velvet, low body and short sleeves, and when she struck powerful chords, those large white arms came down with a certain splendour.

Amy Fay (1844–1928)
Music Study in Germany, 1880

8   O! sir, I must not tell my age. They say women and music should never be dated.

Oliver Goldsmith (1730–74)
She Stoops to Conquer, 1773, Act III

9   . . . in those days young women didn't get the chances they now enjoy of displaying their attractions. The harp was a perfect godsend to girls with pretty wrists.

Harry Graham
Biffin on the Bassoon

10   Consort not with a female musician lest thou be taken in by her snares.

Ben Sira
The Book of Wisdom, c 190 BC

11   The legend relates that one afternoon while Adam was asleep, Eve, anticipating the Great God Pan, bored some holes in a hollow reed and began to do what is called 'pick out a tune'. Thereupon Adam spoke: 'Stop that horrible noise,' he roared, adding, after a pause, 'besides which, if anyone's going to make it, it's not you but me!'

Ethel Smyth (1858–1944)
Female Pipings in Eden, 1933

12   One day, when I was playing, I made too much movement with my hand in a rotatory sort of a passage where it was difficult to avoid it. 'Keep your hand still, Fräulein,' said Liszt, 'don't make omelette.' I couldn't help laughing, it hit me on the head so nicely.

Amy Fay (1844–1928)
Music Study in Germany, 1880

13   Most of our women pianists and violinists have physiques that can only be described as miserable, narrow-chested, shallow bodies, bad carriage, emaciated arms, underdeveloped muscles, feeble tissues; they look like the poor, mean, thin, parched, anaemic sounds they produce from their instruments – pale, wan changelings of tone. They can in the very nature of things do no better, but it is preposterous even for such people to expect to become great players, or even good second-raters.

Kaikhosru Shapurji Sorabji (1892–1988)
Around Music, 1932, 'Against Women Instrumentalists'

14   One can say that never had a person of her sex had such talents as she for the composition of music, and for the admirable manner in which she performed it at the Harpsichord and on the Organ.

Evrard Titon du Tillet (1677–1762)
On the merits of Elizabeth-Claude de la Guerre (1664–1729), quoted in Neuls-Bates, *Women in Music*, 1982

15   [Of Anne Boleyn:] Besides singing like a siren, accompanying herself on the lute, she harped better than King David and handled cleverly both flute and rebec.

Vicomte de Chateaubriand (1768–1848)
Quoted in Strickland, *Lives of the Queens of England*, 1840

16   I maintain at least sixty musicians, and in my youth I danced very well, composed ballets and music, and played and danced them myself.

Queen Elizabeth I (1533–1603)
Quoted in Chamberlin, *The Sayings of Queen Elizabeth*, 1923

183 TECHNIQUE

1   The most perfect technique is that which is not noticed at all.

Pablo Casals (1876–1973)
The Song of the Birds, Lloyd Webber (ed), 1985

2 I favour Czerny over Hanon. Hanon is like your multiplication tables. Don't knock Czerny, though: I've pulled a few women with Czerny.

Billy Joel (1949–)
Quoted in the *Independent*, 23 May 1990

3 The free arts and the beautiful science of composition will not tolerate technical chains. The mind and soul must be free.

Joseph Haydn (1732–1809)

4 There are limits to feats of skill, beyond which lie the realms of nonsense. Everything is quite difficult enough as it is, and what is simple actually comes hardest.

Hans Werner Henze (1926–)
Music and Politics, 1982, 'Instrumental Composition', 1963

5 Technique is to be able to lay open the basic sense of a great work of art, to make it clear.

Eugene Istomin (1925–)
Quoted in *Jacobson, Reverberations*, 1974

6 Instruments sound sweetest when they be touched softest.

John Lyly (c 1554–1606)
Euphues, 1580

7 It is much easier to play a thing quickly than to play it slowly.

Wolfgang Amadeus Mozart (1756–91)
Letter, 1778

184 INTERPRETATION

1 I have found only *one* absolute in music, and that is that there is no absolute. Everything in music is relative. Everything in music must be sifted through one's musical mind and personality. That's what music-making is all about.

Jorge Bolet (1914–90)

2 Never be carried away by temperament, for that dissipates strength.

Ferruccio Busoni (1866–1924)
Advice to Pianists

3   The art of interpretation is *not* to play what is written.
Pablo Casals (1876–1973)
The Song of the Birds, Lloyd Webber (ed), 1985

4   [Of rubato:] Play a piece lasting so many minutes through in strict time: then repeat it with any number of variations in speed, but let its total duration remain the same.
Frédéric Chopin (1810–49)

5   We do not play music as we write it.
François Couperin (1668–1733)
L'Art de toucher le clavecin, 1716

6   There is no feeling, perhaps, except the extremes of fear and grief, that does not find relief in music – that does not make a man sing or play the better.
George Eliot (1819–80)
The Mill on the Floss, 1860

7   The lack of expression is perhaps the greatest enormity of all. I should prefer music to say something other than it should, rather than it should say nothing at all.
Jean-Jacques Rousseau (1712–78)
Dictionnaire de musique, 1767

8   Whoever plays an instrument must be conversant with singing.
Georg Philipp Telemann (1681–1767)
Quoted in Young, *Handel*, 1947

9   Chopin's prescription for rubato playing, which is almost word for word Mozart's prescription for playing an accompanied melody, is that the right hand should take liberties with the time values, while the left hand remains rhythmically unaltered. This is exactly the effect you get when a good blues singer is accompanied by a good swing band. It is known to the modern world as *le style hot*.
Virgil Thomson (1896–1989)
In the *New York Herald Tribune*, 1940

10   Am I Too Loud?
Gerald Moore (1899–1987)
Title of autobiography, 1962

11   Poor accompanists are admittedly numerous enough, but there are very few good ones, for today everyone wants to be the soloist.
Leopold Mozart (1719–87)
Versuch einer gründlichen Violinschule, 1756

185 VIRTUOSITY

1   Whoever has not heard Liszt cannot even speak of piano playing.
Johannes Brahms (1833–97)
Quoted in Gal, *Johannes Brahms*, 1961

2   Clementi plays well where the right hand comes into use. His strongest passages are thirds. For the rest he does not possess a jot of feeling or taste, in short he is a mere technician.
Wolfgang Amadeus Mozart (1756–91)
Letter to his father, 12 January 1782, quoted in Gal, *The Musician's World*, 1965

3   That's no good. There's not enough for me to do here. I should be playing all the time.
Nicolò Paganini (1782–1840)
On the viola part written for him in *Harold in Italy*; Berlioz, *Memoirs*,

4   In order to get beyond the virtuoso level, one must first be a virtuoso: one arrives at something more, not something different.
Ferruccio Busoni (1866–1924)
Quoted in Stuckenschmidt, *Ferruccio Busoni*, 1967

5   One thing I can say, from my own experiences as an infant prodigy, is, that it was a great help having it impressed upon me from the beginning, that I could and should become a great man; however, no one ever appeared satisfied with my actual achievements.
Ferruccio Busoni (1866–1924)
Letter to Henri Petri, 1890

6   Kreisler plays as the thrush sings in Thomas Hardy's poem, hardly conscious of his own lovely significance.
Neville Cardus (1889–1975)
The Delights of Music, 1966

7   Throughout my career, nervousness and stage-fright have never left me before playing . . . at each of the thousands of concerts I have played at, I feel as bad as I did the very first time.
Pablo Casals (1876–1973)

8   The attraction of the virtuoso for the public is very like that of the circus for the crowd. There is always the hope that something dangerous may happen: M. Ysaÿe may play the violin with M. Colonne on his shoulders; or M. Pugno may conclude his piece by lifting the piano with his teeth.
Claude Debussy (1862–1918)
Monsieur Croche, antidilettante, 1921

9   We have been, let us say, to hear the
        latest Pole
      Transmit the Preludes, through his hair and
        fingertips.
    T.S. Eliot (1888–1965)
    Portrait of a Lady, 1917

10   You cannot imagine how it spoils one to have been a child prodigy.
Franz Liszt (1811–86)
Apologizing to a portrait painter who accused him of assuming airs

11   Paganini, the first time I saw and heard him, and the first moment
he struck a note, seemed literally to strike it; to give it a blow.
Leigh Hunt (1784–1859)
Autobiography, 1850

12   Everybody is talking of Paganini and his violin. The man seems to
be a miracle. The newspapers say that long streamy flakes of music fall
from his string, interspersed with luminous points of sound which
ascend the air and appear like stars. This eloquence is quite beyond me.
Thomas Babington Macaulay (1800–59)
Letter, 1831

13   [Of Paganini:] One must await him in an overcrowded opera house
among thousands of visitors and hear the strange rumours running from
row to row. And now, after a long pause, see the odd, sickly, wornout
man sliding through the orchestra, the face fleshless and bloodless in its
entanglement of dark locks and beard, the boldest of noses with an
expression of contemptuous scorn, eyes that shine like black jewels out
of bluish-white. And now, instantly, the hasty beginning of the ritornelli,
and then the tenderest and boldest song ever heard on the violin.
A.B. Marx (1795–1866)
In the *Allgemeine musikalische Zeitung*, 1829

14   If I don't practise for one day, I know it; if I don't practise for two
days, the critics know it; if I don't practise for three days, the audience
knows it.
Ignacy Jan Paderewski (1860–1941)
Quoted in Shapiro, *An Encyclopaedia of Quotations about Music*, 1978

15   Piano-playing is more difficult than statesmanship. It is harder to
wake emotions in ivory keys than it is in human beings.
Ignacy Jan Paderewski (1860–1941)

16   [Rachmaninov] was the only pianist I have ever seen who did not grimace. That is a great deal.
Igor Stravinsky (1882–1971)
Quoted in Craft, *Conversations with Igor Stravinsky*, 1958

17   I never met with any man that suffered his passions to hurry him away so much whilst he was playing on the violin as the famous Arcangelo Corelli, whose eyes still sometimes turn as red as fire.
François Raguenet (*c* 1660–1722)
Comparison between the French and Italian Music, 1709

18   It takes perhaps a thousand poor musicians to produce one virtuoso.
Ralph Vaughan Williams (1872–1958)
In *The New York Times*, 5 December 1954

19   Today music is only the art of performing difficult things, but what is merely difficult ceases to please in the long run.
Voltaire (1694–1778)
Candide, 1759

20   Competition is for horses, not artists.
Béla Bartók (1881–1945)
In the *Saturday Review*, 25 August 1962

186   ORCHESTRAS

1   There are no good or bad orchestras, only good and bad conductors.
Oral tradition

2   At a rehearsal I let the orchestra play as they like. At the concert I make them play as *I* like!
Thomas Beecham (1879–1961)
Quoted in Cardus, *Sir Thomas Beecham*, 1961

3   Have you ever thought about the 'Orchestra'? Each of its members is a poor disappointed devil. Collectively they are like a suppressed crowd of rebels, and, as an official 'body', they are bumptious and vain. Routine gives their playing the varnish of perfection and assurance. For the rest, they loathe their work, their job and, most of all, music.
Ferruccio Busoni (1866–1924)
Letters to his Wife, trans Ley, 1938

4 [When Rodzinski asked the New York Philharmonic if they had any suggestions for improving the peformance of a Mahler symphony:] Yep. Send for Bruno Walter.
Harry Glantz
Quoted in Kennedy, *Barbirolli, Conductor Laureate*, 1971

5 That noise or sound which musicians make while they are tuning their instruments, is nothing pleasant to hear, but yet is a cause why the music is sweeter afterwards.
Francis Bacon (1561–1626)
The Advancement of Learning, 1605

6 In the orchestra you must have air.
Georges Bizet (1838–75)
Quoted in Dean, *Bizet*, 1975

> 7 Organs and Regals thair did carpe
> With their gay goldin glittering strings,
> Thair was the Hautbois and the Harpe
> Playing maist sweit and pleasant springs;
> And some on Lutis did play and sing,
> Of instruments the onely king.
>
> Viols and Virginals were heir
> With Githornis mais jucundious,
> Trumpets and Timbrels maid gret beir,
> With instruments melodious;
> The Seister and the Sumphion
> With Clarche Pipe and Clarion.
>
> John Burel
> *The Queenis . . . Entry*, 1590

> 8 Play, orchestra play,
> Play something light and sweet and gay,
> For we must have music
> We must have music
> To drive our fears away.
>
> Noël Coward (1899–1973)
> *Tonight at Eight-Thirty*, 1935

9 They should ha' stuck to strings. Your brass-man is a rafting dog – well and good; your reed-man is a dab at stirring ye – well and good; your drum-man is a rare bowel-shaker – good again. But I don't care who hears me say it, nothing will spak to your heart wi' the sweetness o' the man of strings!
(Dewy)
Thomas Hardy (1840–1928)
Under the Greenwood Tree, 1872

10   [Cleopatra's] barge . . . kept stroke in rowing after the sound of the music of flutes, hautboys, citterns, viols, and such other instruments as they played upon.

Plutarch (*c* 46–*c* 120)
Life of Mark Antony, trans North, 1579

11   In pre-Bolshevik times, a Russian Grand Duke was shown the layout of the Imperial Orchestra.
   'These are the first violins,' explained the conductor, 'and these are the second violins.'
   'Second violins in the Imperial Orchestra?' exclaimed the Grand Duke. '*All* must be first!'

Recounted by Nicolas Slonimsky (1894–   )
A Thing or Two about Music, 1948

187   CHAMBER MUSIC

1   Chamber music is at once one of the most enjoyable and the most dignified of literatures. The musical amateur often makes it his hobby and considers it the mainspring of his musical existence . . . The professional musician turns to it for relaxation and for a kind of pleasure that no other field offers.

Homer Ulrich (1906–   )
Chamber Music, 1948

2   'E'en little things can yield a perfect pleasure, e'en little things can be supremely dear'–so run the lines of a Tuscan song beautifully set to music by Hugo Wolf. And of nothing is that so true as the 'little things' of chamber music. One finds in that field no necessary correlation between size and quality.

Homer Ulrich (1906–   )
Ibid

3   Most string quartets have a basement and an attic, and the lift is not working.

Neville Cardus (1889–1975)
The Delights of Music, 1966

4   The trombone and side-drums in the chamber music of Stravinsky will do well enough in a very smart house-party where all the conversation is carried on in an esoteric family slang and the guests are expected to enjoy booby-traps.

Donald Francis Tovey (1875–1940)
Musical Articles for the Encyclopaedia Britannica, 1944

> 5   Of instruments of strenges in acord
>   Herde I so playe a ravyshyng swetnesse
>   That God, that makere is of all and lord
>   Ne herde nevere beter, as I gesse.
>
>   Geoffrey Chaucer (*c* 1340–1400)
>   *The Parlement of Foules*, 1369–87

6   [Of quartets:] You listen to four sensible persons conversing, you profit from their discourse, and you get to know the peculiar properties of their several instruments.

Johann Wolfgang von Goethe (1749–1832)
Quoted in Barzun (ed), *Pleasures of Music*, 1952

7   The significance of chamber music is that in dealing with the intimate it can attain to the ineffable. Chamber music conceives itself as a world of sound that has external boundaries but no internal ones.

Hans Werner Henze (1926–   )
Music and Politics, 1982, 'Instrumental Composition', 1963

8   [Of his quartet, *From My Life*:] A work which in a sense is private, and therefore written for four instruments which should converse together in an intimate circle about the things which so deeply trouble me. Nothing more.

Bedřich Smetana (1824–84)
Quoted in Cardus, *The Delights of Music*, 1966

DANCE

Despite the frozen formality of serious concert audiences, it is a basic instinct of man *not* to keep still when listening to music. Dance is probably the most ancient practical manifestation of music, and has remained linked to it in an array of forms from magic ritual to the most complex contemporary choreography.

188 FORMS AND STYLES

1   We have piped unto you, and ye have not danced.
Bible, Authorized Version
St Matthew, Ch 11, v 17

2   A time to weep, and a time to laugh; a time to mourn, and a time to dance.
Bible, Authorized Version
Ecclesiastes, Ch 3, v 4

3   Dancing is a perpendicular expression of a horizontal desire.
Anonymous

4   On with the dance! let joy be unconfined . . .
George Gordon, Lord Byron (1788–1824)
Childe Harold's Pilgrimage, 1816, III xxii

5   Dance, dance, dance little lady,
Leave tomorrow behind.
Noël Coward (1899–1973)
This Year of Grace, 1928

6   Two things are always the same, the dance and war. One might say anything is the same but the dance and war are particularly the same because one can see them. That is what they are for.
Gertrude Stein (1874–1946)
Everybody's Autobiography, 1937

7   Dance, dance, for the figure is easy,
    The tune is catching and will not stop;
    Dance till the stars come down from the
       rafters;
    Dance, dance, dance till you drop.

W.H. Auden (1907–73)
Death's Echo

8   A dance is a measured pace, as a verse is a measured speech.

Francis Bacon (1561–1626)
Advancement of Learning, 1605

9   Dancing to song is a thing of great state and pleasure.

Francis Bacon (1561–1626)
Of Masques and Triumphs

10   Names of it can vary, but music that is inspiring to the head and heart, to dance by and cause you to pat your foot, it's there. Call it rock, call it jazz, call it what you may. If it makes you move, or moves you or grooves you, it'll be here.

Chuck Berry (1926–)
Late 1960s

11   At the still point of the turning world.
    Neither flesh nor fleshless;
    Neither from nor towards; at the still
    Point, there the dance is,
    But neither arrest nor movement.

T.S. Eliot (1888–1965)
Four Quartets, Burnt Norton, 1944

12   He that lives in hope danceth without musick.

George Herbert (1593–1633)
Outlandish Proverbs

13   Music . . . is an invisible dance, as dancing is silent music.

Jean Paul (1763–1825)
Levana, 1807

14   There is a definite limit to the length of time a composer can go on writing in one dance rhythm. This limit is obviously reached by Ravel toward the end of *La Valse* and toward the beginning of *Boléro*.

Constant Lambert (1905–51)
Music Ho!, 1934

15   That day, as other solemn days, they
        spent
In song and dance about the sacred hill –
Mystical dance, which yonder starry sphere
Of planets, and of fixed, in all her wheels
Resembles nearest . . .
And in their motions harmony divine
So smoothes her charming tones that God's own
    ear
Listens delighted.
John Milton (1608–74)
Paradise Lost, 1667, V

16 The dance is only incidentally an art; above all it is a cult.
Jacques Chailley (1910–)
40000 Years of Music, trans Meyers, 1964

17 Always those that dance must pay the music.
John Taylor (1580–1653)
Taylor's Feast, 1638

18   All night have the roses heard
The flute, violin, bassoon;
    All night has the casement jessamine stirred
To the dancers dancing in tune.
Alfred, Lord Tennyson (1809–92)
Maud, 1855

19 I have to tell you that I consider Isadora Duncan epoch-making in the sphere of dance – for she is the first artist who did not dance to the music, but incarnated music in her dance.
Serge Koussevitzky (1874–1951)
Quoted in Terry, *Isadora Duncan*, 1963

20   O body swayed to music, O brightening
      glance,
How can we know the dancer from the dance?
W.B. Yeats (1865–1939)
Among School Children, 1928

21   For nought can cheer the heart sae weel
As can a canty Highland reel.
Robert Fergusson (c 1637–1714)
An Elegy on Scotch Music

22 Ho! who comes here all along
With bagpiping and drumming?
O the Morris 'tis I see,
'Tis the Morris dance a-coming.

Text of a madrigal, 1594, set by Thomas Morley (1557?–1602)

23 *So rennet nun alles in vollem Galopp*
Und kurt sich im Saale sein Plätzchen;
Zum Drehen und Walzen und lustigen Hopp
Erkiest sich jeder ein Schätzchen.

And so they all race in full gallop
And pick their place in the hall;
To whirl and to waltz and to gaily hop
Every boy looks for a gal.

Johann Wolfgang von Goethe (1749–1832)
Hochzeitslied, trans Nettl

24 The dance we saw is more than strange. About 200 pairs were turning round to the accompaniment of very slow music … The posture of the women was agreeable and graceful, but the less said of the men, the better. They were repulsive, dirty, and common.

John Dean Paul (1802–68)
Observing the waltz at Tivoli

25 The young of all creatures cannot be quiet in their bodies or in their voices … the Gods, who, as we say, have been appointed to be our partners in the dance, have given the pleasurable sense of harmony and rhythm; and so they stir us into life, and we follow them and join hands with one another in dance and songs …

Plato (*c* 427–*c* 347 BC)
Laws

26 [Of Strauss the Elder:] Where he fiddles, all dance–dance they must … He himself dances, body and soul, while he plays–not with his feet but with his violin, which keeps bobbing up and down while the whole man marks the accent of every bar.

Ignaz Moscheles (1794–1870)
Journal, 1838

27 I was the best wiggler in the world.

Marc Bolan (1947–77)
Quoted in Green, *The Book of Rock Quotes*, 1982

28   The trouble with nude dancing is that not everything stops when the music stops.

Robert Helpmann (1909–86)
Comment on *Oh! Calcutta!*, quoted in Fraser, *Collins Concise Dictionary of Quotations*, 1983

29   Light quirks of music, broken and
         unev'n,
      Make the soul dance upon a jig to Heaven.

Alexander Pope (1688–1744)
Epistle to Lord Burlington, 1731

30   Away with the music of Broadway!
      Be off with your Irving Berlin!
      Oh, I'd give no quarter
      to Kern or Cole Porter
      and Gershwin keeps pounding on tin.
      How can I be civil
      when hearing this drivel?
      It's only for night-clubbing souses.
      Oh, give me the free 'n' easy
      waltz that is Viennesey
      And go tell the band
      if they want a hand
      the waltz must be Strauss's!
      . . .

      When I want a melody
      lilting through the house
      Then I want a melody
      By Strauss!

Ira Gershwin (1896–1983)
By Strauss, 1936

189   THE BALLET

1   The well-composed ballet should be a living painting of the drama, character, and customs of mankind; it must be acted, as moving in its effect as a declamation, so that it can speak through the eyes to the soul.

Arnold L. Haskell (1903–80)
Ballet, 1938

2   Ballet is the result of a collaboration in which musician, painter, and choreographer interpret a common subject, each one in his own medium; the closer the collaboration, the better the result.

Arnold L. Haskell (1903–80)
Ibid

3   My own personal reaction is that most ballets would be quite delightful if it were not for the dancing.

Quoted by Bateman in 'This England', selections from the *New Statesman*

4   I don't understand anything about the ballet. All I know is that during the intervals the ballerinas stink like horses.

Anton Chekhov (1860–1904)

5   A ballet is all very well in its proper place, as a pleasant after-dinner entertainment; but we don't want ballets to everything, and to proclaim the ballet as a form of great art, the art form of the future, in fact, is sheer bunkum. But the English public seems to have an insatiable appetite for ballets, and the demand for such works having speedily exhausted the slender stock of living composers' ideas, the scores of long-dead musicians are pressed into service.

Frederick Delius (1862–1934)
At the Crossroads, 1920

6   I am the enemy of ballet, which I look upon as false, absurd and outside the domain of art . . . I thank God that a cruel destiny did not inflict on me the career of a ballet dancer.

Isadora Duncan (1878–1927)
My Life, pub 1928

7   Ballet is not a musical form.

Arnold Schoenberg (1874–1951)
Quoted in Stravinsky, *Dialogues*, 1963

8   Little as I like ballets and little as, in my opinion, they deserve the aid of art that is lavished on them here, I do not deny that the Parisian ballet may afford agreeable amusement till one begins to weary of monotony of the mimic action and the sameness of the dances.

Louis Spohr (1784–1859)
Autobiography, 1864

9   The ballet is simply a lewd performance.

Leo Tolstoy (1828–1910)

FOLK AND POPULAR MUSIC

The lore associated with music of mass appeal and of countless varieties of human cultures is enormous, and grows apace with the ever more diverse popular musical movements of our time. What follows is but a distillation from this vast reservoir.

190   MUSIC OF THE PEOPLE

1   All music's folk music: leastways I never heard of no horse making it.
Attributed to Louis Armstrong (1900–71) and also to Big Bill Broonzy (1893–1958)

2   One should try everything once, except incest and folk-dancing.
Arnold Bax (1883–1953)
Farewell, My Youth

3   The negro mind, at work upon civilized music, produces the same kind of thing as the negro mind at work upon Christian theology. The product is not to be despised … If we could divest ourselves of prejudice, the songs that float down the Ohio river are one in feeling and character with the songs of the Hebrew captives by the waters of Babylon. We find the same tale of bereavement and separation, the same wild tenderness and passionate sweetness, like music in the night.
Rev H.R. Haweis (1838–1901)
Music and Morals, 1871

4   The national culture of music of every people rests on a healthy relationship between folk music and composed music.
   Only the music which has sprung from the ancient musical traditions of a people can reach the masses of that people.
Zoltán Kodály (1882–1967)

5   [Of folk music:] It is the free, direct speech of the soul.
Zoltán Kodály (1882–1967)
Quoted in *Nyugat*, 1918

6   The appalling popularity of music.
Constant Lambert (1905–51)
Title of chapter in *Music Ho!*, 1934

> 7   Then came the merry masquers in,
>   And carols roared with blythesome din;
>   If unmelodious was the song,
>   It was a hearty note, and strong.
>   Walter Scott (1771–1832)
>   *Marmion*, 1808

> 8   There's a barrel-organ carolling across a
>   golden street
>   In the city as the sun sinks low;
>   And the music's not immortal; but the world
>   has made it sweet
>   And fulfilled it with the sunset glow.
>   Alfred Noyes (1880–1958)
>   *The Barrel-Organ*

9   Come, sing me a bawdy song; make me merry.
(Falstaff)
William Shakespeare (1564–1616)
Henry IV Pt I, 1597–8, Act III, Sc III

10   As the custom prevails at present there is scarce a young man of any fashion . . . who does not make love with the town music.
Tatler, 1710

11   What kind of music is most necessary to men – scholarly or folk music?
Leo Tolstoy (1828–1910)
Remark to Fyodor Chaliapin, quoted in Bertensson and Leyda, *Sergei Rachmaninoff*, 1965

191 FOLK SONG AND MELODY

1   To handle folk tunes is one of the most difficult tasks; equally difficult, if not more so than to write a major original composition. If we keep in mind that borrowing a tune means being bound by its individual peculiarity, we shall understand one part of the difficulty. Another is created by the special character of folk tune. We must penetrate into it, feel it and bring out its sharp contours by the appropriate setting.
Béla Bartók (1881–1945)
1931

2   Folk music will have an immense, transforming influence on music in countries with little or no musical tradition.
Béla Bartók (1881–1945)

3   A genuine peasant melody of our land is a musical example of perfected art. I consider it quite as much of a masterpiece–in miniature–as a Bach fugue or Mozart sonata is a masterpiece in the larger forms.
Béla Bartók (1881–1945)
Quoted in Machlis, *Introduction to Contemporary Music*, 1963

4   I am inclined to think that a hunt for folksongs is better than a manhunt of the heroes who are so highly extolled.
Ludwig van Beethoven (1770–1827)

5 You discover her
     naked
   and taking her
   you will want to
   show her off to your friends.

   First you will clothe her
   for clothing is proof
   of possession.

   Do not overdress her
   lest she think you
   wish to disguise her
   or (worse) patronize her.

   And do not
   underdress her either:
   a peasant girl
   she has no need
   of foundation garments.

   But study her shape
   and set it
   sweetly against itself
   as your fancy directs:
   be rich or plain
   but never modest.

   And remember always
   that she is best naked:
   let this be an understanding
   between you.

   Keith Bosley (1937–   )
   The Possibility of Angels, 1969, 'Setting a Folk Song'

6 Compared with these, Italian trills are
     tame;
   The tickled ears no heartfelt raptures raise.

   Robert Burns (1759–96)
   The Cotter's Saturday Night, 1784–5

7 'Primitive' music is really not so primitive. It is ancient and therefore sophisticated.

Carlos Chavez (1899–1978)
Quoted in Machlis, *Introduction to Contemporary Music*, 1963

8   The fashion for popular airs has spread quickly throughout the musical world. From east to west the tiniest villages have been ransacked, and simple tunes, plucked from the mouths of hoary peasants, find themselves, to their consternation, trimmed with harmonic frills.

Claude Debussy (1862–1918)
Quoted in Lockspeiser, *Debussy*, 1963

9   The excellence of natural Andalusian melody is revealed by the fact that it is the only music continuously and abundantly used by foreign composers.

Manuel de Falla (1876–1946)
Cante Jondo, 1922

10   I don't especially value 'originality' in art, as I consider the communal development of folksongs is no whit inferior to the original achievement of a great outstanding 'original' genius. It is the *universal* that pulls me in all matters and I am more thrilled by these points that all people have in common than in the special achievements and specialness of individuals.

Percy Grainger (1887–1961)

11   Each folk song contains an entire man; his body, his soul, his surroundings, everything, everything. He who grows up among folk songs, grows into a complete man.

Leoš Janáček (1854–1928)
Quoted in Stedron (ed), *Leoš Janáček: Letters and Reminiscences*, 1955

12   Folk songs bind the nation, bind all nations and all people with one spirit, one happiness, one paradise.

Leoš Janáček (1854–1928)
Ibid

13   Folksongs must be dressed to be taken from the fields to the city. In urban attire, however, they are awkward and uncomfortable. Their apparel must be cut in a fashion that will not hinder their breathing. Whether for chorus or for piano, the accompaniment should always be of such a nature as to make up for the lost fields and village.

Zoltán Kodály (1882–1967)
Hungarian Folksongs, 1906, Foreword

14   To put it vulgarly, the whole trouble with a folk song is that once you have played it through there is nothing much you can do except play it over again and play it rather louder.

Constant Lambert (1905–51)
Music Ho!, 1934

15 Folk music is the ungarbled and ingenuous expression of the human mind and on that account it must reflect the essential and basic qualities of the human mind.

Cecil Sharp (1859–1924)
English Folk Song, 1907

16 If I may venture to give my own definition of a folk song, I should call it 'an individual flowering on a common stem'.

Ralph Vaughan Williams (1872–1958)
Quoted in Shapiro, *An Encyclopedia of Quotations about Music,* 1978

17 A truly creative musician is capable of producing, from his own imagination, melodies that are more authentic than folklore itself.

Heitor Villa-Lobos (1887–1959)

18 What is folklore? I am folklore.

Heitor Villa-Lobos (1887–1959)
Attributed

192 BALLADS

1 If a man were permitted to make all the ballads, he need not care who should make the laws of a nation.

Andrew Fletcher of Saltoun (1655–1716)
Letter to the Marquis of Montrose, and Others, 1703

2   Oh some are fond of fiddles, and a song
     well sung,
  And some are all for music for to lilt upon
    the tongue;
  But mouths were made for tankards, and for
    sucking at the bung,
  Says the old bold mate of Henry Morgan.

John Masefield (1878–1967)
Captain Stratton's Fancy

3 I love a ballad but even too well; if it be a doleful matter, merrily set down, or a very pleasant thing indeed, and sung lamentably.
(Clown)

William Shakespeare (1564–1616)
The Winter's Tale, 1611, Act IV, Sc IV

4 I had rather be a kitten and cry 'mew'
   Than one of those same metre ballad-mongers,
   I had rather hear a brazen canstick turned,
   Or a dry wheel grate on the axle-tree.
   (Hotspur)
   William Shakespeare (1564–1616)
   Henry IV Pt I, 1596, Act III, Sc I

5 He sings several tunes faster than you'll tell money. He utters them
as he had eaten ballads, and all men's ears grow to his tunes.
(Servant, of Autolycus)
William Shakespeare (1564–1616)
The Winter's Tale, 1611, Act IV, Sc IV

6 Let not the ballad-singer's shrilling
      strain
   Amid the swarm thy list'ning ear detain:
   Guard well thy pocket; for these sirens
      stand
   To aid the labours of the diving hand ...
   John Gay (1685–1732)
   Trivia, 1727

193 POPULAR SONG

1 [Of Cole Porter:] He was an aristocrat in everything he did and
everything he wrote. Everything had class.
Larry Adler (1914–)
Quoted in Eells, *The Life that Late He Led*, 1967

2 For even that vulgar and tavern music, which makes one man merry,
another mad, strikes in me a deep fit of devotion, and a profound
contemplation of the first Composer, there is something in it of divinity
more than the ear discovers.
Thomas Browne (1605–82)
Religio Medici, 1643

3 I cannot sing the old songs now!
   It is not that I deem them low;
   'Tis that I can't remember how
   They go.

   C.S. Calverley (1831–84)
   Changed

4 Extraordinary how potent cheap music is.

Noël Coward (1899–1973)
Private Lives, 1930

5 Irving just loves hits. He has no sophistication about it – he just loves hits.

Oscar Hammerstein II (1895–1960)
Quoted in Freedland, *Irving Berlin*, 1974

6 Compare the music of *The Beggar's Opera* with the music of a contemporary review. They differ as life in the garden of Eden differed from life in the artistic quarter of Gomorrah.

Aldous Huxley (1894–1963)
Along the Road, 1925, 'Popular Music'

7 Music-hall songs provide the dull with wit, just as proverbs provide them with wisdom.

W. Somerset Maugham (1874–1965)
A Writer's Notebook, 1949

8 And the tunes that mean so much to you
      alone –
   Common tunes that make you choke and blow
      your nose,
   Vulgar tunes that bring the laugh that brings
      the groan –
   I can rip your very heartstrings out with
      those.

   Rudyard Kipling (1865–1936)
   The Song of the Banjo

9 Every popular song has at least one line or sentence that is perfectly clear – the line that fits the music.

Ezra Pound (1885–1972)

10   So-called light music has its own value, not really belonging to music at all. Because, unlike serious work, it lacks musical content, it acts as a series of vials, often charmingly shaped and coloured, for the distillations of memory. The first few bars of it remove the stopper; we find ourselves re-living, not remembering, but magically recapturing, some exact moments of our past.
J.B. Priestley (1894–1984)
Margin Released, 1962

11   One never realizes the vulgarity of human beings so acutely as when listening to the mindless bawling of popular songs.
John Sullivan
But for the Grace of God

194   TWENTIETH-CENTURY STYLES

1   Syncopation is in the soul of every true American.
Irving Berlin (1888–1989)
Quoted in Whitcomb, *After the Ball*, 1972

2   Rock is a corruption of Rhythm and Blues which was a dilution of the blues, so that today's mass-marketed noise is a vulgarization of a vulgarization.
Benny Green (1927–   )
Notes for a Joe Turner record album, 1976

3   Rock has the ability to embarrass you several years later. It takes itself seriously whereas Pop never pretends to have any depth.
Jonathan Ross
Quoted in the *Guardian*, 10 September 1990

4   Punk rock: style of simple rock music played with great vigour but lacking polish.
Concise Oxford Dictionary, sixth edition

5   We're nothing like the Sex Pistols. We don't set out to shock people through being sick on-stage or through self-mutilation. I was never one for sticking a pin in me nose.
Mick Jones (The Clash) (1955–   )
Quoted in *Time*, 5 March 1979

6   The Clash, though hardly elegant instrumentalists, makes far better crafted music than the Pistols ever did. The sheets of sound they let loose have the cumulative effect of mugging.
Time, 5 March 1979

7   It don't mean a thing
If it ain't got that swing.
Duke Ellington (1899–1974) and Irving Mills (1884–1985)
Song, 1932

8   If it ain't got swing, it ain't worth playin'; if it ain't got gutbucket, it ain't worth doin'.
Bubber Miley (1903–32)
Quoted by Duke Ellington

9   Syncopations are no indication of light or trashy music, and to shy bricks at 'hateful ragtime' no longer passes for musical culture.
Scott Joplin (1868–1917)
The School of Ragtime, 1908

10   You know, I never did find out what ragtime was.
Irving Berlin (1888–1989)
Composer of 'Alexander's Ragtime Band', quoted in Palmer, *All You Need Is Love,* 1976

11   When Alexander takes his ragtime band to
France
He'll capture every Hun, and take them one by
one
Those ragtime tunes will put the Germans in a
trance;
They'll throw their guns away, Hip Hooray!
And start right in to dance.
Alfred Vryan, Cliff Hess and Edgar Leslie
Rag, c 1917

12   The Real American Folk Song is a Rag.
Ira Gershwin (1896–1983)
Title of song

13   I got a ragtime dog and a ragtime cat
A ragtime piano in my ragtime flat.
I'm wearing ragtime clothes from hat to shoes
I read a paper called the ragtime news.
I got ragtime habits and I talk that way
I sleep in ragtime and rag all day.
Got ragtime troubles with my ragtime wife
I'm certainly leading a ragtime life!

Jefferson and Roberts
Rag, 1899

14   Blues, Twentieth-Century Blues,
Are getting me down.

Noël Coward (1899–1973)
Cavalcade, 1931

15 The Blues, the most convenient harmonic progression ever discovered . . . the most hackneyed, overplayed, obvious musical effect in the world, and yet in some curious way at times the most compelling.

Benny Green (1927–)
This is Jazz, 1960

16 I told more truth in my blues than the average person tells in his church songs . . . sometimes I think the average person sings a church song just for the tune, not for the words, but the blues is sung not for the tune. It's sung for the words, mostly. A real blues singer sings a blues for the words.

Rev Rubin Lacy
Quoted in Green, *The Book of Rock Quotes*, 1982

17 No white man ever had the blues.

Huddie (Leadbelly) Ledbetter (1885–1949)
Quoted in Berendt, *The Jazz Book*, 1976

18 So when the people in them times, they'd be sad and feelin' bad, and they'd sing blues; they didn't know how to sing nothin' else, but that old feelin' came to 'em. That's what they'd call the blues, that old feelin' . . .

Huddie (Leadbelly) Ledbetter (1885–1949)

19 The blues is a feeling and when it hits you, it's the real news.

Huddie (Leadbelly) Ledbetter (1885–1949)

20 [Of rhythm and blues:] It's not a music. It's a disease.

Mitchel Miller of Columbia Records, *c* 1960
Quoted in Palmer, *All You Need Is Love*, 1976

21 The music was not particularly rhythmic, and it was almost never true blues.

Jerry Wexler of Atlantic Records, who invented the term 'rhythm and blues'
Quoted in Palmer, *All You Need Is Love*, 1976

22 The effect of rock 'n' roll on young people is to turn them into devil-worshippers; to stimulate self-expression through sex; to provoke lawlessness, impair nervous stability, and destroy the sanctity of marriage.

Rev Albert Carter
In 1956, quoted in Rogers, *Rock 'n' Roll*, 1982

23 Rock 'n' roll is a means of pulling down the white man to the level of the 'Negro'. It is part of a plot to undermine the morals of the youth of our nation. It is sexualistic, unmoralistic, and the best way to bring people of both races together.

Asa Carter, of the North Alabama White Citizens' Council
Quoted in *Melody Maker*, 1956

24 Poison put to sound—a brutalization of both life and art.

Pablo Casals (1876–1973)
On rock 'n' roll

25 Rock 'n' roll is instant coffee.

Bob Geldof (1953–)

26 It's only rock 'n' roll, but I like it.

The Rolling Stones
Song: *It's Only Rock 'n' Roll*

27 Rock music must give birth to orgasm and revolution.

Jerry Rubin
Do It!, 1970

28 Rock 'n' roll is the most brutal, ugly, vicious form of expression . . . sly, lewd—in plain fact, dirty.

Frank Sinatra (1915–)
In *The New York Times*, 1957

29   Rock 'n' roll isn't even music. It's a mistreating of instruments to get feelings over.

Mark Smith (The Fall)
Green, *The Book of Rock Quotes*, 1982

30   Reggae music is one of them stones that was refused by the builders.

Charlie Ace
Quoted in Johnson and Pines, *Reggae*, 1982

31   Reggae is a gift from Jah to the Jamaican people.

Harry J.
Quoted in *ibid*

32   Pop music is ultimately a show, a circus. You've got to hit the audience with it. Punch them in the stomach, and kick them on the floor.

Peter Townshend (1945–)
Quoted in Palmer, *Born Under a Bad Sign*, 1970

195   POPULAR LYRICS

1   You know my temperature's risin',
    The jukebox's blowin' a fuse,
    My heart's beatin' rhythm,
    My soul keeps a singin' the blues–
    Roll over Beethoven,
    Tell Tchaikovsky the news.

> Chuck Berry (1926–)
> *Roll over Beethoven*

2   She refused to begin the 'Beguine'
    Tho' they besought her to
    And with language profane and obscene
    She curs'd the man who taught her to
    She curs'd Cole Porter too!

> Noël Coward (1899–1973)
> *Nina*

3   Sex 'n' Drugs 'n' Rock 'n' Roll.

Ian Dury (1943–)
Title of song

4   O O O O that Shakespeherian Rag—
It's so elegant
So intelligent.

T.S. Eliot (1888–1965)
The Waste Land, 1922, misquoting from Gene Buck, Herman Ruby
and David Stamper, 'That Shakespearian Rag', 1912: 'That
Shakespearian Rag, most intelligent, very elegant . . .'

5   It is a pleasure to live at a time when light amusement is at last losing
its brutally cretin aspect, and such delicacies as your jingles prove that
songs can be both popular and intelligent.

Lorenz Hart (1895–1943)
Letter to Ira Gershwin

6   In modern songs, it is taken for granted that one is poor,
unsuccessful, and either sex-starved or unable to hold the affection of
such partner as one may have had the luck to pick up.

Constant Lambert (1905–51)
Music Ho!, 1934

7   Don't just move to the music, listen to what I'm saying.

Bob Marley (1945–81)
Quoted in Johnson and Pines, *Reggae*, 1982

8   The Tin Pantithesis of melody.

Cole Porter (1891–1964)
It's De-Lovely, 1936

196 MUSICALS

1   'The Rite of Spring' is an exciting piece of music, but I don't believe
that it has any future as a Broadway musical.

George Abbott (1887–   )
Dramatists' Guild Quarterly, spring 1974

2   A good musical comedy consists largely of disorderly conduct
occasionally interrupted by talk.

George Ade (1866–1944)

3 [Of a Romberg musical:] It's the kind of music you go into the theatre whistling.
George Gershwin (1898–1937)

4 I am trying to do something for the future of American music, which today has no class whatsoever and is mere barbaric mouthing.
Jerome Kern (1885–1945)
In *The New York Times*, 1920

5 Nothing is wrong when done to music.
Jerome Kern (1885–1945)

6 We are not an aria country. We are a song country.
Alan Jay Lerner (1918–86)
Quoted in Palmer, *All You Need Is Love*, 1976

197   STARS OF POPULAR MUSIC

1 Having played with other musicians, I don't even think The Beatles were that good.
George Harrison (1943–   )
Green, *The Book of Rock Quotes*, 1982

2 Q. How do you rate your music?
A. We're not good musicians. Just adequate.
Q. Then why are you so popular?
A. Maybe people like adequate music.
The Beatles

3 The Beatles are now my secret weapon.
Lord Home (1903–   ), then Sir Alec Douglas-Home, PM, in 1964, quoted in Green, *The Book of Rock Quotes*, 1982

4   Sexual intercourse began
In nineteen sixty-three
(Which was rather late for me)–
Between the end of the Chatterley ban
And the Beatles' first LP.
Philip Larkin (1922–86)
Annus Mirabilis, High Windows, 1974

5   We are more popular than Jesus now.
John Lennon (1940–80)
Interview in the *Evening Standard*, 1966

6   Nothing happened in the sixties except that we all dressed up.
John Lennon (1940–80)
Green, *The Book of Rock Quotes*, 1982

7   Pop music *is* the classical music of now.
Paul McCartney (1942–   )
Quoted in Palmer, *All You Need Is Love*, 1976

8   There are two things John and I always do when we're going to sit down and write a song. First of all we sit down. Then we think about writing a song.
Paul McCartney (1942–   )

9   I think the main point of the situation is that those pieces of plastic we did are still some of the finest pieces of plastic around.
Ringo Starr (1940–   )
Green, *The Book of Rock Quotes*, 1982

10   The closest Western civilization has come to unity since the Congress of Vienna in 1815 was the week that the *Sgt Pepper* album was released.
Langdon Winner
Ibid

11   Let's not forget James Brown picked cotton. James Brown shined shoes. And yet James Brown is still active. Because James Brown worked all the way to the top . . . I first started out tryin' to get a decent meal, a decent pair of shoes, So when I got to where I could do that, I thought I was on the top anyway.
James Brown (1928–   )
Los Angeles Weekly, 18 April 1984

12   We were all caught up in that game of wanting to be the next Elvis Presley, hopping from tinny band to tinny band.
David Bowie (1947–   )
February 1976

13   I don't think there's any point in doing anything artistically unless it astounds. The mums and dads thought I was weird, but I'm not an innovator. I'm really just a photostat machine.
David Bowie (1947–   )
July 1975

14 I've always done me little theatricality bit of throwing me arms about with the music. Some people think it's a bit too much. Like when I was on Ed Sullivan, they surrounded me with thousands of dancers to keep me hidden.

Joe Cocker (1944–)
Quoted in Stambler, *The Encyclopaedia of Rock, Pop and Soul*, 1975

15 What pop does is make me very rich.

Donovan (1946–)
Quoted in Palmer, *All You Need Is Love*, 1976

16 I don't care if my so-called work dies the minute I die. I don't want to be Shakespeare. I just want to do my gig.

Ian Dury (1943–)
Sounds, 16 December 1978

17 I like most music unless it's wrong.

Coleman Hawkins (1904–69)
Quoted in Dance, *The World of Swing*, 1974

18 When I was eleven, I wanted to be Mick Jagger so bad; when I was twelve I wanted to be John Lennon; when I was thirteen I wanted to be Peter Townshend. Now I just wanna be me. I want to revitalise the rock dream that was so essential to me.

Bob Geldof (1953–)
Trouser Press, December 1977

19 She showed me the air and taught me how to fill it.

Janis Joplin (1943–70)
On Bessie Smith, quoted by Albertson, *Bessie*, 1972

20 I'll never be satisfied. I'm not happy that we have the number one album, single, CD, video, that I sold out every show . . . and that I can buy a huge mansion if I want to. Next year I plan to do better. I want a bigger record, more shows. I want to be able to buy two houses instead of one.

Jon Bon Jovi (1962–)
Quoted in *Rolling Stone*

21 I came from a family where people didn't like rhythm and blues. Bing Crosby, 'Pennies From Heaven', Ella Fitzgerald was all I heard. And I knew there was something that could be louder than that, but I didn't know where to find it. And I found it was me.

Little Richard (1935–)
Quoted in Rogers, *Rock 'n' Roll*, 1982

22 I know of no music that is more lewd, feelable, hearable, seeable, touchable, that you can experience more intensely than this.

Wim Wenders (1945–) on Van Morrison (1945–)
Green, *The Book of Rock Quotes*, 1982

23 France, Edith Piaf is your great lady. She knows the secret of popular song (the secret Bernhardt knew so well) which is expressivity through banality, the secret of knowing what must be added where. This formula can apply only to 'popular' artists: they interpret mediocre works by completing them.

Ned Rorem (1923–)
Paris Diary, 1966

24 Elvis was as big as the whole country itself, as big as the whole dream. He just embodied the essence of it and he was in mortal combat with the thing. It was horrible and at the same time, it was fantastic. Nothing will ever take the place of that guy.

Bruce Springsteen (1949–)
Green, *The Book of Rock Quotes*, 1982

25 I was very lucky. The people were looking for something different and I came along just in time.

Elvis Presley (1935–77)
Farren, *Elvis in His Own Words*, 1977

26 I don't know anything about music – in my line you don't have to.

Elvis Presley (1935–77)
Attributed

27 The Nabob of Sob.

Johnnie Ray (1927–)
On himself; quoted in Palmer, *All You Need Is Love*, 1976

28 It was my idea to make my voice work in the same way as a trombone or violin – not sounding like them, but 'playing' the voice like those instruments.

Frank Sinatra (1917–)
Quoted in Shepherd, *Tin Pan Alley*, 1982

29 Rock groups ... are more concerned with doing things to an audience in a particular way than with creating a form which might puzzle the audience at first but ultimately yield a much greater satisfaction.

Chick Corea (1941–)
Quoted in Palmer, *All You Need Is Love*, 1976

30   Mick Jagger is the perfect pop star. There's nobody more perfect than Jagger. He's rude, he's ugly-attractive, he's brilliant. The Rolling Stones are the perfect pop group—they don't give a shit.

Elton John (1947–   )
Quoted in Green, *The Book of Rock Quotes*, 1982

31   I knew what I was looking at. It was sex. And I was just ahead of the pack.

Andrew Oldham
Manager of the Rolling Stones, quoted in Norman, *The Stones*, 1984

32   At her best and given her best material, Barbra Streisand, whose fan I happen to be, is probably the greatest singing-actress since Maria Callas.

Glenn Gould (1932–82)
Cobb, *Conversations with Glenn Gould*, 1984

33   I smash a guitar because I like them. I usually smash a guitar when it's at its best.

Peter Townshend (1945–   )
In 1965, quoted in Green, *The Book of Rock Quotes*, 1982

34   You just pick a chord, go twang and you've got music.

Sic Vicious (1958–79)
Quoted in the *Sun*, October 1976

35   I still like music; it gives me a lot to complain about.

Tom Waits (1949–   )

198   FILM MUSIC

1   Play it again, Sam.

A line not spoken by, but usually identified with, Humphrey Bogart in the film *Casablanca*, 1942

2   No music has ever saved a good picture, but a lot of good pictures have saved a lot of bad music.

Jerry Goldsmith (1929–   )
Quoted in Bazelon, *Knowing the Score*, 1975

3   A film musician is like a mortician—he can't bring the body back to life, but he's expected to make it look better.
Adolph Deutsch (1897–)
Quoted in Thomas, *Music for the Movies,* 1973

4   I believe that the film contains potentialities for the combination of all the arts such as Wagner never dreamt of. I would therefore urge those distinguished musicians who have entered into the world of the cinema . . . to realize their responsibility in helping to take the film out of the realm of hackwork and make it a subject worthy of a real composer.
Ralph Vaughan Williams (1872–1958)
Composing for the Films, 1945

5   The cinema is undoubtedly the most important of the mechanical stimuli offered to the composer of today. . . . Films have the emotional impact for the twentieth century that operas had for the nineteenth.
Constant Lambert (1905–51)
Music Ho!, 1934

6   The sound film opens up fascinating new possibilities of aesthetic and is bound to have a strong influence on the trend of music in this century. It offers the serious composer what has been lacking since the eighteenth century—a reasonable commercial outlet for his activities, comparable to the 'occasional' music which the greatest classical composers did not disdain to write. And in addition to its intrinsic interest as a new craft, writing for films will have the salutary effect of keeping composers in touch with a large audience and its human reactions.
Constant Lambert (1905–51)
1936

7   In the last resort film music should be judged solely as music—that is to say, by the ear alone, and the question of its value depends on whether it can stand up to this test.
Arthur Bliss (1891–1975)
Quoted in Manvell and Huntley, *The Technique of Film Music, 1957, rev Arnell and Day,* 1975

8   Film music is like a small lamp that you place below the screen to warm it.
Aaron Copland (1900–90)
Quoted in Shapiro, *An Encyclopedia of Quotations about Music,* 1978

9   For a long time the so-called symphonic composers were ostracized in film circles, and as a class rather looked down upon by film producers . . . Gradually the serious musicians managed to win their way into the studios by putting on false noses, that is by disguising their music in a style calculated to earn the approval of film producers and directors.

Darius Milhaud (1892–1974)
Notes without Music, trans Evans, 1952

10   One especially naive young man took one of his problems to Schoenberg, hopeful of a quick, concise solution. He had been assigned to write some music for an airplane sequence and was not sure how he should go about it. He posed the problem to Schoenberg, who thought for a moment and then said, 'Airplane music? Just like music for big bees, only louder.'

Oscar Levant (1906–72)
A Smattering of Ignorance, 1940

11   [Irving Thalberg, vainly persuading Schoenberg to write a filmscore:] 'Think of it!' he enthused. 'There's a terrific storm going on, the wheat field is swaying in the wind, and suddenly the earth begins to tremble. In the midst of the earthquake Oo-Lan gives birth to a baby. What an opportunity for music!'

  'With so much going on,' said Schoenberg mildly, 'what do you need music for?'

Oscar Levant (1906–72)
Ibid

12   *When is a concerto not a concerto?* The answer is: When a film forms all over it, and when it gets struck by the very dangerous moonshine of Hollywood.

Kaikhosru Shapurji Sorabji (1895–1988)
Mi Contra Fa, 1947

13   I believe that film music is capable of becoming, and to a certain extent already is, a fine art.

Ralph Vaughan Williams (1872–1958)
In *The Royal College of Music* magazine, 1944

14   In film the visual effect is of course predominant, and the music subserves the visual sequences, providing a subtle form of punctuation – lines can be seen to have been given the emphasis of italics, exclamation marks added to details of stage 'business', phases of the action broken into paragraphs, and the turning of a page at a crossfade or cut can be helped by music's power to summarize the immediate past or heighten expectation of what is to come.

William Walton (1902–83)
Quoted in Manvell and Huntley, *The Technique of Film Music*, 1957, rev Arnell and Day, 1975

15   A film is a composition and the musical composer is an integral part of the design.

H.G. Wells (1866–1946)
Letter to Arthur Bliss, 1934, concerning Bliss's music for *The Shape of Things to Come*

199   MILITARY MUSIC

1   O what is that sound which so thrills the
        ear
    Down in the valley, drumming, drumming?
    Only the scarlet soldiers, dear,
    The soldiers coming.

W.H. Auden (1907–73)
O What is the Sound

2   All the delusive seduction of martial music.

Fanny Burney (1752–1840)
Diary, 5–6 May 1802

3   'What are the bugles blowin' for?' said Files-on-Parade. 'To turn you out, to turn you out,' the Colour-Sergeant said.

Rudyard Kipling (1865–1936)
Danny Deever

4   See, the conquering hero comes!
    Sound the trumpets, beat the drums!

Thomas Morell (1703–84)
Joshua, 1748

5   They now to fight are gone,
Armour on armour shone,
Drum to drum did groan,
To hear was wonder.
That with the cries they make
The very earth did shake,
Trumpet to trumpet spake,
Thunder to thunder.

Michael Drayton (1562–1631)
Ballad of Agincourt

6   The best sort of music is what it should be – sacred; the next best, the military, has fallen to the lot of the devil.

Samuel Taylor Coleridge (1772–1834)
Table Talk, 1833

7   The double double double beat
     of the thundering Drum
Cries 'Hark! the foes come;
Charge, charge, 'tis too late to retreat.'

John Dryden (1631–1700)
A Song for St Cecilia's Day, 1687

8   How good bad music and bad reasons sound when one marches against an enemy.

Friedrich Nietzsche (1844–1900)

9   What passing bell for these who die as
     cattle?
Only the monstrous anger of the guns.
Only the stuttering rifles' rapid rattle
Can patter out their hasty orisons.
No mockeries for them from prayers or bells,
Nor any voice of mourning save the choirs,
The shrill, demented choirs from wailing
     shells;
And bugles calling for them from sad shires.

Wilfred Owen (1893–1918)
Anthem for Doomed Youth

10   But when our country's cause provokes
       to arms
    How martial music, every bosom warms!

Alexander Pope (1688–1744)
Ode on St Cecilia's Day, c 1708

11   I hate that drum's discordant sound,
    Parading round and round and round:
    To me it talks of ravaged plains,
    And burning towns, and ruined swains,
    And mangled limbs, and dying groans,
    And widows' tears, and orphans' moans;
    And all that misery's hand bestows,
    To fill the catalogue of human woes.

John Scott (1730–83)
Ode on Hearing the Drum

12   Make all our trumpets speak; give them
      all breath,
    Those clamorous harbingers of blood and
      death.
    (Macduff)

William Shakespeare (1564–1616)
Macbeth, 1605–6, Act V, Sc VI

13   Farewell the plumèd troops, and the big
      wars
    That make ambition virtue! O farewell!
    Farewell the neighing steed and the shrill
      trump,
    The spirit-stirring drum, th'ear-piercing
      fife,
    The royal banner, and all quality,
    Pride, pomp, and circumstance, of glorious
      war!
    (Othello)

William Shakespeare (1564–1616)
Othello, 1604, Act III, Sc III

14   The trumpets, sackbuts, psalteries, and
      fifes,
    Tabors and cymbals and the shouting Romans,
    Make the sun dance.

William Shakespeare (1564–1616)
Coriolanus, 1607–8, Act V, Sc IV

15   The song that nerves a nation's heart
     Is in itself a deed.

Alfred, Lord Tennyson (1809–92)
The Charge of the Heavy Brigade, 1885

16   . . . And with the clashing of their
     sword-blades make
     A rapturous music, till the morning break.

W.B. Yeats (1865–1939)
To Some I have Talked with by the Fire, 1893

AND ALL THAT JAZZ

Good jazz musicians, who can improvise at length and create spontaneously in concert with others, have been, arguably, the finest inventive practitioners of twentieth-century music. One must not wax too pompous though: they have also brought a much-needed dash of outrageous, dare-devil and joyous fun to that same century.

200 THE JAZZ WORLD

1   Today you play jazz, tomorrow you will betray your country.
Soviet poster of the Stalin era

2   The building of Socialism proceeds more lightly and more rhythmically to the accompaniment of jazz.
Polish government announcement, 1955
Quoted in Stearns, *The Story of Jazz*, 1956

3   Jazz is music by devils for the torture of imbeciles.
Henry van Dyke (1852–1933)
Quoted in Shapiro, *Encyclopedia of Quotations about Music*, 1978

4   Thus it came to pass that jazz multiplied all over the face of the earth and the wiggling of bottoms was tremendous.
Peter Clayton (1927–   ) and Peter Gammond (1925–   )
14 Miles on a Clear Night, 1966

5   Though popularly regarded as being a barbaric art, it is to its sophistication that jazz owes its real force. It is the first dance music to bridge the gap between highbrow and lowbrow successfully.
Constant Lambert (1905–51)
Music Ho!, 1934

6   If you have to ask what jazz is, you'll never know.
Louis Armstrong (1900–71)

7   The message my men have tried to deliver, no matter what personnel we had, was always jazz. When you get away from swinging, get away from the lines that were started by Dizzie Gillespie and Charlie Parker, then you are in danger of losing the essence of jazz.
Art Blakey (1919–90)

8   There's only two ways to sum up music: either it's good or it's bad. If it's good you don't mess about with it; you just enjoy it.
Louis Armstrong (1900–71)
Quoted in Shapiro, *An Encyclopedia of Quotations about Music*, 1978

9   Hot can be cool and cool can be hot, and each can be both. But hot or cool, man, jazz is jazz.
Louis Armstrong (1900–71)
Ibid

10   There'll probably be new names for it. There have been several names since I can remember back to the good ol' days in New Orleans, Louisiana, when Hot Music was called 'ragtime music', 'jazz music', 'gutbucket music', 'swing music', and now 'hot music'. So you see instead of dying out, it only gets new names.
Louis Armstrong (1900–71)
Quoted in Panaissie, *Le Jazz Hot*, 1934, Introduction

11   Jazz is about the only form of art existing today in which there is freedom of the individual without the loss of group contact.
Dave Brubeck (1920–   )
Quoted in Berendt, *The Jazz Book*, 1976

12   [Gershwin] is the prince who has taken Cinderella by the hand and openly proclaimed her a princess to the astonished world.
Walter Damrosch (1862–1950)
At the première of Gershwin's Concerto in F, quoted in Schwartz, *Gershwin*, 1973

13   I'll play it first and tell you what it is later.
Miles Davis (1926–   )
Quoted in Green, *The Book of Rock Quotes*, 1982

14   I don't write jazz, I write Negro folk music.
Duke Ellington (1899–1974)
Quoted in Jewell, *Duke*, 1977

15   [Of Ellington:] A Harlem Dionysus drunk on bad bootleg liquor.
Ernest Newman (1868–1959)
Quoted in *ibid*

16 *Leopold Stokowski:* You and I should go to Africa and hear that music.

   Duke Ellington: The only thing I could get in Africa that I haven't got now is fever.

Ibid

17 In the matter of jass [sic], New Orleans is particularly interested since it has been widely suggested that this particular form of musical vice had its birth in this city, that it came, in fact, from doubtful surroundings in our slums. We do not recognize the honour of parenthood.

The New Orleans Times Picayune, 1918

18 If I could find a white man who had the Negro sound and the Negro feel, I could make a million dollars.

Sam Phillips
Record producer, quoted in Hopkins, *Elvis*, 1974

19 Jazz may be thought of as a current that bubbled forth from a spring in the slums of New Orleans to become the main spring of the twentieth century.

Henry Pleasants (1910–   )

20 Drum on your drums, batter on your banjos, sob on the long cool winding saxophones. Go to it, O jazzmen.

Carl Sandburg (1878–1967)
Smoke and Steel, 1920

21 [Jazz:] The sound of surprise.

Whitney Balliett
The Sound of Surprise, 1960

22 Jazz . . . was illiterate, instinctual, impulsive, aleatoric, unscorable, unpredictable – therein lay its charm.

Anthony Burgess (1917–   )
Punch, 20 September 1967, 'The Weasels of Pop'

23 Jazz was borrowed from Central Africa by a gang of wealthy international Bolshevists from America, their aim being to strike at Christian civilization throughout the world.

Monseigneur Conefrey
In *The New York Times*, 1934

24   I don't like the word jazz that white folks dropped on us.
Miles Davis (1926–)
Quoted in *Down Beat*, 1970

25   We've all worked and fought under the banner of jazz for many
years, but the word itself has no meaning. There's a form of
condescension in it.
Duke Ellington (1899–1974)
Radio interview, 1968

26   Jazz is the result of the energy stored up in America.
George Gershwin (1898–1937)
Quoted in Morgenstern, *Composers on Music*, 1958

27   Jazz I regard as an American folk music; not the only one, but a very
powerful one which is probably in the blood and feeling of the American
people more than any other style of folk music.
George Gershwin (1898–1937)
The Relation of Jazz to American Music, 1933

28   All music is praise of the Lord, which some people cannot or will
not understand, the real jazz form of a spiritual soil, is truly the musical
psalms of the twentieth-century man's torment in the tigerish growl of
the trumpet. God's wrath and mercy are the demonic drumbeat and the
milk-smooth sound of the saxophone.
The Indian Express, 1963

29   You ain't heard nothin' yet.
Al Jolson (1886–1950)
The Jazz Singer (film), 1927

30   Jazz has always been a man telling the truth about himself.
Quincy Jones (1933–)
Quoted in Kendall, *The Tender Tyrant: Nadia Boulanger*, 1976

31   In his music [the Negro] gave voice to the character and quality of
his existence, to his rage and the infinite variations of joy, lust, languor,
growl, cramp, pinch, scream and despair of his orgasm. For jazz is
orgasm . . .
Norman Mailer (1923–)
The White Negro, 1957

32   The basic difference between classical music and jazz is that in the former the music is always greater than its performance – whereas the way jazz is performed is always more important than what is being played.
André Previn (1929–   )
In *The Times*, 1967

33   What I love about jazz is that it's 'blue' and you don't care.
Erik Satie (1866–1925)

34   Jazz is a symbol of the triumph of the human spirit, not of its degradation. It is a lily in spite of the swamp.
Archie Shepp (1937–   )
Quoted in Wilmer, *Jazz People*, 1977

35   Jazz will endure just as long as people hear it through their feet instead of their brains.
John Philip Sousa (1854–1932)

36   [Reply to question 'What is jazz?'] Madam, if you don't know by now, DON'T MESS WITH IT!
Fats Waller (1904–43)
Quoted in Stearns, *The Story of Jazz*, 1956

37   Jazz came to America 300 years ago in chains.
Paul Whiteman (1891–1967)
Jazz, 1926

---

201   BANDS

---

1   The jazz band can be used for artificial excitement and aphrodisiac purposes, but not for spreading eternal truths.
Arthur Bliss (1892–1975)
Music Policy, 1941

2   'Jazz', used mainly as an adjective descriptive of a band. The groups that play for dancing, when colored, seem infected with a virus that they try to instil as a stimulus to others. They shake and jump and writhe in ways to suggest a return to the medieval jumping mania.
Walter Kingsley
In the *New York Sun*, 1917

3   My band is my instrument.
Duke Ellington (1899–1974)
In *The New Yorker*, July 1944

4   Strike Up the Band!
Ira Gershwin (1896–1983)
Song title, 1927

5   This excruciating medley of brutal sounds is subordinated to a
barely perceptible rhythm. Listening to this screaming music for a
minute or two, one conjures up an orchestra of madmen, sexual
maniacs, led by a man-stallion beating time with an enormous phallus.
Maxim Gorky (1868–1936)
On an American dance band

202   PLAYERS

1   [Billie Holliday] doesn't need any horns. She sounds like one,
anyway.
Miles Davis (1926–   )
Quoted in Hentoff, *Jazz is*, 1978

2   Somehow I suspect that if Shakespeare were alive today, he might be
a jazz fan himself.
Duke Ellington (1899–1974)
Programme notes to *Such Sweet Thunder*, 1957

3   Bach and myself write with the individual performer in mind.
Duke Ellington (1899–1974)
Quoted in Jewell, *Duke*, 1977

4   A jazz musician is a juggler who uses harmonies instead of oranges.
Benny Green (1927–   )
The Reluctant Art, 1962

5   You can't write a good song about a whore-house unless you been in
one.
Woody Guthrie (1912–67)
Quoted in *Broadside*, 1964, 1

6 That note you hold, narrowing and rising,
       shakes
   Like New Orleans reflected on the water . . .

   On me your voice falls as they say love
       should,
   Like an enormous yes. My Crescent City
   Is where your speech alone is understood,

   And greeted as the natural noise of good,
   Scattering long-haired grief and scored pity.
   Philip Larkin (1922–86)
   For Sidney Bechet

7 [Of Fats Waller:] The black Horowitz.
Oscar Levant (1906–72)
Quoted in Palmer, *All You Need Is Love*, 1976

8 Jazz is to be played, sweet, soft, plenty rhythm.
Jelly Roll Morton (1895–1941)
Mister Jelly Roll, 1950

9 Music is your own experience, your thoughts, your wisdom. If you
don't live it, it won't come out of your horn.
Charlie Parker (1920–55)
Quoted in Stearns, *The Story of Jazz*, 1956

10 I was always in a panic.
Charlie Parker (1920–55)
Quoted in Williams, *The Jazz Tradition*, 1970

203 STYLES

1 [Ragtime:] White music–played black.
Joachim Berendt (1922–)
The Jazz Book, 1976

2   A wave of vulgar, filthy and suggestive music has inundated the land. The pabulum of theatre and summer hotel orchestra is coon music. Nothing but ragtime prevails and the cake-walk with its obscene posturings, its lewd gestures. It is artistically and morally depressing and should be suppressed by press and pulpit.
The Musical Courier, 1899

3   If there is a national American form of song it is the blues.
Russell Ames
The Story of American Folk Song, 1955

4   It's jam, but arranged.
Edward ('Eddie') Farley (1904–)
A definition of swing, 1936

5   Playing 'bop' is like playing Scrabble with all the vowels missing.
Duke Ellington (1899–1974)
Look, 1954

6   Bop is mad, wild, frantic, crazy–and not to be dug unless you've seen dark days, too.
Langston Hughes (1902–67)
Simple Takes a Wife, 1953

7   Bop is the shorthand of jazz, an epigram made by defying the platitude of conventional harmony; it performs a post-mortem on the dissected melody. The chastity of this music is significant. It shuns climaxes of feeling, and affirms nothing but disintegration.
Kenneth Tynan (1927–80)
In *The Observer*, 1955

8   [Of bop:] The complex response of over-sensitive men to a world they are afraid of would reject the natural expression of their emotions.
Colin Wilson (1931–)
Brandy of the Damned, 1964

9   One jazzer's jazz is another jazzer's junk.
Ian Whitcomb
After the Ball, 1972

VOICES

The human voice is the most refined, individual and intimate of all instruments of music. A well-trained one is in every sense unique and precious for it is, of course, a person.

204 SINGERS AND SONGS

1   Sing with your voices, and with your hearts, and with all your moral convictions, sing the new songs, not only with your tongue, but with your life.

St Augustine (354–430)

2   God's got his hand on you, son. Keep singing.

Johnny Cash (1932–   )
Quoting his mother, when he was seventeen years old

3   But the singer must still have one thing: the universal ground of all mood, the ability to apply imagination to the voice, the ability to sing with imagination.

Sören Kierkegaard (1813–55)
A Passing Comment on a Detail in 'Don Giovanni', 1845

4   I love not him, who o'er the wine cup's
        flow
     Talks but of war, and strife, and scenes of
        woe:
     But him who can the Muses' gift employ,
     To mingle love and song with festal joy.

Anacreon (late sixth century BC)
Trans Thomas Love Peacock

5   My spirit like a charmèd bark doth swim
     Upon the liquid waves of thy sweet singing.

Percy Bysshe Shelley (1792–1822)
Fragment: To One Singing

6   I celebrate myself, and sing myself.
Walt Whitman (1819–92)
Song of Myself

7   When I was young
    I had not given a penny for a song
    Did not the poet sing it with such airs
    That one believed he had a sword upstairs.
    W.B. Yeats (1865–1939)
    All Things Can Tempt Me

8   Long ago he was one of the singers,
    But now he is one of the dumbs.
    Edward Lear (1812–88)
    Nonsense Songs, 1870

9   I have a song to sing O!
    Sing me your song, O!
    W.S. Gilbert (1836–1911)
    The Yeomen of the Guard, 1888

10   Piping down the valleys wild,
     Piping songs of pleasant glee,
     On a cloud I saw a child,
     And he laughing said to me:

     'Pipe a song about a Lamb!'
     So I piped with merry cheer.
     'Piper, pipe that song again;'
     So I piped: he wept to hear.

     'Drop thy pipe, thy happy pipe;
     Sing thy songs of happy cheer!'
     So I sung the same again,
     While he wept with joy to hear.
     William Blake (1757–1827)
     Songs of Innocence, 1789

11   I'm Saddest when I Sing.
Thomas Haynes Bayly (1797–1839)
Title of poem

12 *Castrati:* These men, who sing so well but without warmth or expression are, in the theatre, the most disagreeable actors in the world. They lose their voice at an early age and become disgustingly fat . . . There are some letters, such as R, which they are quite unable to pronounce.

Jean-Jacques Rousseau (1712–78)
Dictionnaire de musique, 1767

13 A singer able to sing so much as sixteen bars of good music in a natural, well-poised and sympathetic voice, without effort, without affectation, without tricks, without exaggeration, without hiatuses, without hiccupping, without barking, without baa-ing—such a singer is a rare, a very rare, an excessively rare bird.

Hector Berlioz (1803–69)
A travers chant, 1862

14   To drop some golden orb of perfect song
        Into our deep, dear silence.
        Elizabeth Barrett Browning (1806–61)
        Sonnets from the Portuguese, 1850

15 A tenor is not a man but a disease.

Hans von Bülow (1830–94)
Attributed

16 The exercise of singing is delightful to nature and good to preserve the health of Man.

William Byrd (1543–1623)
Psalmes, Sonets and Songs, 1588

17   Since singing is so good a thing
        I wish all men would learne to sing.
        William Byrd (1543–1623)
        Ibid

18   I do not sing because I must,
        And pipe but as the linnets sing.
        Alfred, Lord Tennyson (1809–92)
        In Memoriam A.H.H., 1850

19 The tenor's voice is spoilt by
        affectation
    And for the bass, the beast can only bellow;
    In fact, he had no singing education,
    An ignorant, noteless, timeless, tuneless
        fellow.

    George Gordon, Lord Byron (1788–1824)
    Don Juan, 1818–22

20 Let the singing singers
    With vocal voices, most vociferous,
    In sweet vociferation, out-vociferise
    Ev'n sound itself.

    Henry Carey (*c* 1690–1743)
    Chrononhotonthologos, 1734

21 Let a man try the very uttermost to *speak* what he means, before
singing is had recourse to.

Thomas Carlyle (1795–1881)
Journal, 1843

22 He who sings scares away his woes.

Miguel de Cervantes (1547–1616)
Don Quixote, 1605, 1

23 Whilst thus I sing, I am a King,
    Altho' a poor blind boy.

    Colley Cibber (1671–1757)
    The Blind Boy

24 Swans sing before they die – 'twere no
        bad thing
    Should certain persons die before they sing.

    Samuel Taylor Coleridge (1772–1834)

25 Nor cold, nor stern, my soul! yet I
        detest
    Those scented rooms where to a gaudy throng,
    Heaves the proud harlot her distended breast
    In intricacies of laborious song.

    Samuel Taylor Coleridge (1772–1834)

26   Were there no women in the world, no women singers, I would never have become a composer. They have been my inspiration my whole life long.
Alexander Sergeievitch Dargomizhsky (1813–69)

27   Of things I'd rather keep in silence I must sing.
Countess of Dis, troubador (b *c* 1140)
Quoted in Neuls-Bates, *Women in Music*, 1982

28   So just, so small, yet in so sweet a
          note,
       It seem'd the music melted in the throat.
       John Dryden (1631–1700)
       The Flower and the Leaf

29   Be not drunk with wine, wherein is excess; but be filled with the Spirit; Speaking to yourselves in psalms and hymns and spiritual songs, singing and making melody in your heart to the Lord.
Bible, Authorized Version
Ephesians, Ch 5, vv 18–19

30   I see you have a singing face–a heavy, dull, sonata face.
George Farquhar (*c* 1677–1707)
The Inconstant, 1702, Act II, Sc I

31   A German singer! I should as soon expect to get pleasure from the neighing of my horse.
Frederick the Great (1712–86)

32   Singin' in the Rain
Arthur Freed (1894–   )
Song title, 1929

33   My voice is small but disagreeable.
George Gershwin (1898–1937)
Attributed

34   A wand'ring minstrel I,
       A thing of shreds and patches,
       Of ballads, songs and snatches,
       And dreamy lullaby!
       My catalogue is long,
       Through ev'ry passion ranging,
       And to your humour's changing
       I tune my supple song.
       W.S. Gilbert (1836–1911)
       The Mikado, 1885

35 A song will outlive all sermons in the memory.
Henry Giles (1809–82)

36 God in His Almighty Wisdom and Fairness has not always given the greatest voices to the persons with the greatest intellect or the best education, or to the most beautiful of His creatures.
Tyrone Guthrie (1900–71)
A Life in the Theatre, 1960

37 On wings of song.
Heinrich Heine (1797–1856)
Song title, 1832

38 The singing man keeps a shop in his throat.
George Herbert (1593–1633)
Jacula Prudentum, 1640

39 Let but thy voice engender with the
    string
And angels will be born, while thou dost
    sing.
Robert Herrick (1591–1674)
Upon her Voice

40 So smooth, so sweet, so silv'ry is thy
    voice,
As, could they hear, the damn'd would make no
    noise,
But listen to thee (walking in thy chamber)
Melting melodious words, to lutes of amber.
Robert Herrick (1591–1674)
Upon Julia's Voice

41 She gave him the gift of sweet song.
Homer (eighth century BC)
Odyssey

42 The fault, common to all singers, is that when their friends ask them to sing, they're never willing, but when they're *not* asked they will never leave off.
Horace (Quintus Horatius Flaccus, 65–8 BC)
Satires, 1, 3

43   A base barreltone voice.
James Joyce (1882–1941)
Ulysses, 1922

44   Tenors get women by the score.
James Joyce (1882–1941)
Ibid

45   The vocalists (they are hardly to be described as singers), who nowadays are given the courtesy title of counter-tenors, are simply falsetto male altos who have the wit to develop a bright clear tone as contrasted with the dark, hooting tone of the traditional English cathedral alto. The excruciating monotony of the tone of these personages is due to their incomprehensibly obstinate refusal ever to use more than a single resonator adjustment. Their emasculated bleatings would be rendered the more curious if not the more agreeable were they to use all three resonator adjustments, which they perfectly well could. As it is we are faced with the painful choice of the screech of a night-jar, or the hoot of a sort of supersonic owl. The most that can be said for this new kind of noise is that it is less disagreeable than the traditional kind.
Elster Kay
Bel Canto, 1963

46   I even think that *sentimentally* I am disposed to harmony. But *organically* I am incapable of a tune. I have been practising 'God Save the King' all my life; whistling and humming it over to myself in solitary corners; and am not yet arrived, they tell me, within many quavers of it.
Charles Lamb (1775–1834)
Essays of Elia, 1820–3

47   A vile beastly rottenheaded foolbegotten brazenthroated perni-cious piggish screaming, tearing, roaring, perplexing, splitmecrackle crashmewiggle insane ass of a woman is practising howling below-stairs with a brute of a singing-master so horribly, that my head is nearly off.
Edward Lear (1812–88)
Letter, 1859

48   Their lean and flashy songs
       Grate on their scrannel pipes of wretched
           straw.
       John Milton (1608–74)
       Lycidas, 1637

49 I like an aria to fit a singer as perfectly as a well-tailored suit of clothes.
Wolfgang Amadeus Mozart (1756–91)

50 Song is man's sweetest joy.
Musaeus (*c* 900 BC)
Quoted by Aristotle, *Politics*

51 I would much rather have written the best song of a nation than its noblest epic.
Edgar Allan Poe (1809–49)

52 But would you sing, and rival Orpheus'
       strain,
    The wond'ring forests soon should dance
       again;
    The moving mountains hear the powerful call,
    And headlong streams hang list'ning in their
       fall!
Alexander Pope (1688–1744)
Pastorals, 1709, 'Summer'

53 O come, let us sing unto the Lord; let us make a joyful noise to the rock of our salvation.
    Let us come before his presence with thanksgiving, and make a joyful noise unto him with psalms.
Bible, Authorized Version
Psalms, 95 vv 1–2

54 The good singer should be nothing but an able interpreter of the ideas of the master, the composer ... In short, the composer and the poet are the only true creators.
Gioachino Rossini (1792–1868)
Letter to F. Guidicini, 1851

55 If you have any soul worth expressing, it will show itself in your singing.
John Ruskin (1819–1900)
Sesame and Lilies, 1865

56 For my voice, I have lost it with hallowing and singing of anthems.
(Falstaff)
William Shakespeare (1564–1616)
Henry IV Pt II, 1597, Act I, Sc II

57 . . . an admirable musician. O, she will sing the savageness out of a bear!
(Othello)

William Shakespeare (1564–1616)
Othello, 1604, Act IV, Sc I

58 Warble, child, make passionate my sense of hearing.
(Armado)

William Shakespeare (1564–1616)
Love's Labour's Lost, 1590–4, Act III, Sc I

59 Now, good Cesario, but that piece of
      song,
    That old and antique song we heard last
      night;
    Methought it did relieve my passion much,
    More than light airs and recollected terms
    Of these most brisk and giddy-paced times:
    Come, but one verse.
    (Orsino)

William Shakespeare (1564–1616)
Twelfth Night, 1600–2, Act II, Sc IV

60 I cannot sing. I'll weep, and word it
      with thee,
    For notes of sorrows out of tune are worse
    Than priests and fanes that lie.
    (Guiderius)

William Shakespeare (1564–1616)
Cymbeline, 1609–10, Act IV, Sc II

61 First, rehearse your song by rote,
    To each word a warbling note.
    Hand in hand, with fairy grace,
    Will we sing and bless this place.
    (Titania)

William Shakespeare (1564–1616)
A Midsummer Night's Dream, 1595, Act V, Sc I

62   *Clown:*   By my troth, I take my young lord to be a very melancholy
man.

       Countess: By what observance, I pray you?

       Clown: Why, he will look upon his boot and sing, mend the ruff
and sing, ask questions and sing, pick his teeth and sing. I
know a man that had his trick of melancholy sold a goodly
manor for a song.

William Shakespeare (1564–1616)
All's Well that Ends Well, 1602–3, Act III, Sc II

63   My soul is an enchanted boat,
Which, like a sleeping swan, doth float
Upon the silver waves of thy sweet singing.

Percy Bysshe Shelley (1792–1822)
Prometheus Unbound, 1820, II v

64   I would rather be remembered by a song than by a victory.

Alexander Smith (1830–67)
Dreamthorp, 1863, 'Men of Letters'

65   And this shall be for music when no one
else is near,
The fine song for singing, the rare song to
hear!

Robert Louis Stevenson (1850–94)
Songs of Travel, 1896

66   Bright is the ring of words
When the right man rings them,
Fair the fall of songs
When the singer sings them.
Still they are carolled and said –
On wings they are carried –
After the singer is dead
And the maker buried.

Robert Louis Stevenson (1850–94)
Ibid

67   Cicala to cicala is dear, and ant to ant, and hawk to hawk, but to me
the muse and song.

Theocritus (*c* 310–250 BC)
Idylls, IX, trans Lang

68   Go, songs, for ended is our brief, sweet
       play;
    Go, children of swift joy and tardy sorrow:
    And some are sung, and that was yesterday,
    And some unsung, and that may be tomorrow.
Francis Thompson (1859–1907)
Envoy

69   The human voice is the oldest musical instrument and through the ages it remains what it was, unchanged; the most primitive and at the same time the most modern, because it is the most intimate form of human expression.
Ralph Vaughan Williams (1872–1958)
National Music, 1934

70   Do not commit your poems to pages alone. Sing them, I pray you.
Virgil (70–19 BC)
Aeneid, c 19 BC

71   Let us sing on our journey as far as we go; the way will be less tedious.
Virgil (70–19 BC)
Eclogues, c 37 BC

72   I can't sing. As a singist I am not a success. I am saddest when I sing. So are those who hear me. They are sadder even than I am.
Artemus Ward, pseudonym of Charles Farrar Browne (1834–67)

73   I hear America singing, the varied carols I hear.
Walt Whitman (1819–91)
Leaves of Grass, 1855

74   God guard me from the thoughts men think
    In the mind alone;
    He that sings a lasting song
    Thinks in the marrow-bone.
W.B. Yeats (1865–1939)
A Prayer for Old Age, 1935

205 THE NATURE OF SONG

1   They don't write songs like that any more.
Anonymous

2 Any good song must be of greater magnitude than either the words or music alone.

Ned Rorem (1923–)
Paris Diary, 1966

3 There exist labor songs, but no work songs. The songs of the craftsman are social; they are sung after work.

Hannah Arendt

4 Every high C accurately struck demolishes the theory that we are the irresponsible puppets of fate or chance.

W.H. Auden (1907–73)
In the *Partisan Review*, 1952, 'Some Reflections on Music and Opera'

5 Lose no opportunity to hear artistic singing. In so doing, the keyboard player will learn to think in terms of song. Indeed, it is a good practice to sing instrumental melodies in order to reach an understanding of their correct performance.

Carl Philipp Emanuel Bach (1714–88)
Essay on the True Art of Playing Keyboard Instruments, 1753–62

6 If a thing isn't worth saying, you sing it.

Pierre Augustin Caron de Beaumarchais (1732–99)
The Barber of Seville, 1775, Act I, Sc II

7 *Tout finit par des chansons.*
   Everything ends in songs.

Pierre Augustin Caron de Beaumarchais (1732–99)
Le Mariage de Figaro, 1784, last line

8 It is the best of all trades, to make songs, and the second best to sing them.

Hilaire Belloc (1870–1953)
On Everything–'On Song'

9 By the rivers of Babylon, there we sat down, yea, we wept, when we remembered Zion. We hanged our harps upon the willows in the midst thereof. For there they that carried us away captive required of us a song; and they that wasted us required of us mirth, saying, Sing us one of the songs of Zion. How shall we sing the Lord's song in a strange land?

Bible, Authorized Version
Psalm 137, vv 1–4

10   The morning stars sang together, and all the sons of God shouted for joy.

Bible, Authorized Version
Job 7, Ch 38, v 7

11   'Tis a sure sign that work goes on merrily, when folks sing at it.

Isaac Bickerstaffe (*c* 1735 – *c* 1812)
The Maid of the Mill, 1765, Act I, Sc I

12   Would you have your songs endure?
Build on the human heart.

Robert Browning (1812–89)
Sordello, 1840

13   Perhaps it may turn out a sang,
Perhaps turn out a sermon.

Robert Burns (1759–96)
Epistle to a Young Friend, 1786

14   Contented wi' little and cantie wi'
mair,
Whene'er I forgather wi' Sorrow and Care,
I gie them a skelp, as they're creeping
alang,
Wi' a cog o' gude swats and an auld Scottish
sang.

Robert Burns (1759–96)
Contented wi' Little, 1794

15   And deep things are song. It seems somehow the very central essence of us, song; as if all the rest were but wrappings and hulls.

Thomas Carlyle (1795–1881)
On Heroes, Hero-Worship, and the Heroic in History, 1841

16   I bought it for a song.

John Crowne (1640–*c* 1703)
Regulus, 1694, III

17   The high office of singing is to express what passes in the mind and soul.

H.C. Deacon (1822–90)
Grove's Dictionary of Music and Musicians, first edition

18   Why cause words to be sung by four or five voices so that they cannot be distinguished, when the Ancients aroused the strongest passions by means of a single voice supported by a lyre? We must renounce counterpoint and different kind of instruments and return to primitive simplicity.

Vincenzo Galilei (1520–91)
Dialogo della musica antica e della moderna, 1581

19   Singing is no more than a form of declamation.

Christoph Willibald von Gluck (1714–87)
Paride ed Elena, 1770, Preface

> 20   From grief too great to banish
>   Come songs, my lyric minions.
>
> Heinrich Heine (1797–1856)
> *Aus meinen grossen Schmerzen*

21   Song: the licensed medium for bawling in public things too silly or sacred to be uttered in ordinary speech.

Oliver Herford (1863–1935)

> 22   *Minuentur atrae*
>   *Carmine curae.*
>   Dark worries will be lessened by song.
>
> Horace (Quintus Horatius Flaccus, 65–8 BC)
> *Odes*, IV, 11

23   *Carmine di superi placantur carmine manes.*
     Both the gods above and in the underworld are placated by song.

Horace (Quintus Horatius Flaccus, 65–8 BC)
Epistles, II, 1

24   The question is whether a noble song is produced by nature or by art. I neither believe in mere labour being of avail without a rich vein of talent, nor in natural cleverness which is not educated.

Horace (Quintus Horatius Flaccus, 65–8 BC)
Ars Poetica

25   I remember when I was very young, this is very serious, I read an article by Fats Domino which has really influenced me. He said, 'You should never sing the lyrics out very clearly.'

Mick Jagger (1944–   )
Quoted in an interview in *Rolling Stone*, 1969

26   List to the heavy part the music bears,
      Woe weeps out her division, when she sings.

Ben Jonson (*c* 1573–1637)
Cynthia's Revels, Act I Sc II

27   There must be a strenuous attempt to replace music that comes from the fingers and the mechanical playing of instruments with music from the soul and based on singing.

Zoltán Kodály (1882–1967)
Fifty-five Two-part Exercises, 1954, Preface

28   There is delight in singing, tho' none hear beside the singer.

Walter Savage Landor (1775–1864)
To Robert Browning

29   Man was never meant to sing:
      And all his mimic organs e'er expressed
      Was but an imitative howl at best.

John Langhorne (1735–79)
The Country Justice, c 1766

30   Minnesingers traveled from town to town. They didn't really sing too good, which is the main reason they kept moving.

Art Linkletter
A Child's Garden of Misinformation

31 Blest pair of syrens, pledges of
        Heaven's joy
    Sphere-born harmonious sisters, Voice and
        Verse,
    Wed your divine sounds, and mix'd power
        employ
    Dead things with inbreath'd sense able to
        pierce;
    And to our high rais'd phantasy present
    That undisturbed song of pure content,
    Aye sung before the sapphire-colour'd throne
    To Him that sits thereon,
    With saintly shout, and solemn jubilee;
    Where the bright Seraphim, in burning row,
    Their loud up-lifted angel trumpets blow;
    And the Cherubick host, in thousand quires,
    Touch their immortal harps of golden wires,
    With those just Spirits that wear victorious
        palms,
    Hymns devout and holy psalms
    Singing everlastingly . . .
    John Milton (1608–74)
    At a Solemn Musick

32 And ever against eating cares,
        Lap me in soft Lydian airs,
        Married to immortal verse
        Such as the meeting soul may pierce
        In notes, with many a winding bout
        Of linked sweetness, long drawn out.
        John Milton (1608–74)
        L'Allegro, 1632

33 None knew whether
        The voice or lute was most divine,
        So wondrously they went together.
        Thomas Moore (1779–1852)
        Lalla Rookh, 1817, Prologue

34 The most despairing songs are the most beautiful, and I know some
immortal ones that are pure tears.
Alfred de Musset (1810–57)

35 A well-composed song or ballad strikes the mind, and softens the feelings, and produces greater effect than a moral work, which convinces our reason but does not warm our feelings or effect the slightest alteration of our habits.
Napoleon Bonaparte (1769–1821)

36 Let kings and the triumphs of kings yield before songs.
Ovid (43 BC–AD 18)
Amores

37 Songs have immunity from death.
Ovid (43 BC–AD 18)

38 *Etiam singulorum fatigatio quamlibet se rudi modulatione solatur.*
Even when alone, men comfort their weariness with song, however unskilled.
Quintilian (*c* 35–*c* 100)
De institutione oratoria

39 Speech is man's most confused and egocentric expression; the most orderly and magnanimous utterance is song.
Ned Rorem (1923–   )
The Final Diary, 1974

40 No song can reduplicate itself, each has its own rules.
Ned Rorem (1923–   )
The Later Diaries, 1983

41 [On Italian singing:] Of bestial howling, and entirely frantic vomiting-up of damned souls through their still carnal throats, I have heard more than, please God, I will ever endure the hearing of again, in one of His summers.
John Ruskin (1819–1900)

42 It is quite possible to lead a virtuous and happy life without books, or ink; but not without wishing to sing, when we are happy; not without meeting with continual occasions, when our song, if right, would be a kind service to others.
John Ruskin (1819–1900)

43 [Of Scotland:] Of all districts of the inhabited world, pre-eminently the singing country.
John Ruskin (1819–1900)
Quoted in Farmer, *A History of Music in Scotland*, 1947

44   Music began with singing.
Curt Sachs (1881–1959)

45   Everyone suddenly burst out singing;
     And I was filled with such delight
     As prisoned birds must find in freedom,
     Winging wildly across the white
     Orchards and dark green fields; on–on–
     And out of sight.

     Everyone's voice was suddenly lifted;
     And beauty came like the setting sun:
     My heart was shaken with tears; and horror
     Drifted away . . . O, but Everyone
     Was a bird; and the song was wordless; the
     Singing will never be done.
     Siegfried Sassoon (1886–1967)
     Picture Show, 1919

46   I can suck melancholy out of a song, as a weasel sucks eggs.
(Jaques)
William Shakespeare (1564–1616)
As You Like It, 1599, Act II, Sc V

47   Our sweetest songs are those that tell of saddest thought.
Percy Bysshe Shelley (1792–1822)
To A Skylark, 1819

48   No instrument is satisfactory except in so far as it approximates to
the sound of the human voice.
Stendhal (1783–1842)
Life of Rossini, 1824

49   Short-swallow-flights of song,
     That dip their wings in tears,
     And skim away.
     Alfred, Lord Tennyson (1809–92)
     In Memoriam, 1850

50   Of all of God's prerogatives, song is the fairest.
Theocritus (*c* 310–250 BC)
Idylls, c 270 BC

51 Singing is sweet, but be sure of this,
    Lips only sing when they cannot kiss.

James Thomson (1834–82)
Sunday up the River

52 Distinctness! The big notes will take care of themselves; the little notes, and their words, are the things to watch.

Richard Wagner (1813–83)
Notice to his singers at the Bayreuth Festival, 1876

53 Soft words, with nothing in them, make a song.

Edmund Waller (1605–87)
To Mr Creech, c 1635

54 I would rather spend my life trying to achieve one book of little songs that shall have a lasting fragrance, than pile up tome upon tome on the dusty shelves of the British Museum.

Peter Warlock (1894–1930)
Letter to Bernard van Dieren, 1920

55 I'm sure the programme will be delightful, after a few expurgations. French songs I cannot possibly allow. People always seem to think that they are improper, and either look shocked, which is vulgar, or laugh, which is worse. But German sounds a thoroughly respectable language, and, indeed I believe is so.
(Lady Bracknell)

Oscar Wilde (1854–1900)
The Importance of Being Earnest, 1895

56 The song of songs, which is Solomon's.

Bible, Authorized Version
Song of Solomon, Ch 1, v 1

206 WORD-SETTING

1 Nothing is capable of being well set to music that is not nonsense.

Joseph Addison (1672–1719)
In the *Spectator*, 21 March 1711

2 In harmony would you excel,
   Suit your words to your music well,
   music well, music well,
   Suit your words to your music well,
   suit your words to your music well.

   Jonathan Swift (1667–1745)
   From a burlesque cantata

3 A verse without music is a mill without water.

Anonymous troubadour
Quoted in Burke, *Musical Landscapes*, 1983

4 For music any words are good enough.

Aristophanes (c 448 – c 388 BC)
The Birds

5 A verbal art like poetry is reflective; it stops to think. Music is immediate; it goes on to become.

W.H. Auden (1907–73)
Quoted in Copland, *Music and Imagination*, 1952

6 Poetry appeals to me so much because it's eternal. As long as there are people, they can remember words and combinations of words. Nothing else can survive a holocaust but poetry and songs. No one can remember an entire novel. No one can describe a film, a piece of sculpture, a painting. But so long as there are human beings, songs and poetry can continue.

Jim Morrison (1943–71)
Quoted in *Rolling Stone*, 1969

7 Mediocrity seeks out melodies which flatter the ear. I do not chase such. I want music strictly to express the word. I want truth.

Alexander Sergeievitch Dargomizhsky (1813–69)

8 Between ourselves, your prosody was very bad; at least, you turn the French language into an accentuated language when it is, on the contrary, a language of fine shades.

Claude Debussy (1862–1918)
Open letter to Gluck, *Gil Blas*, 1903

9   Music should give to poetry what the brightness of colour and the happy combination of light and shade give to a well-executed and finely composed drawing—it should fill its characters with life without destroying their outline.

Christoph Willibald von Gluck (1714–87)
Alceste, 1767, Preface

10   When I compose a song, my concern is not to make music but, first and foremost, to do justice to the poet's intentions. I have tried to let the poem reveal itself, and indeed to raise it to a higher power.

Edvard Grieg (1843–1907)
Letter to Henry T. Finck

11   Let the word be master of the melody, not its slave.

Claudio Monteverdi (1567–1643)
Quoted in Morgenstern (ed), *Composers on Music*, 1958

12   You must have a care then when your matter signifieth ascending, high heaven and such like, you make your musicke ascend: and by the contrarie where your dittie speaketh of descending, lowenes, depth, hell and others such, you must make your musicke descend far as it will be thought a great absurdite to talke of heaven and point downwarde to the earth: so will it be counted great incongruitie if a musician upon the wordes 'hee ascended into heaven' shoulde cause his musicke [to] descend . . .

Thomas Morley (1557–1603)
A Plaine and Easie Introduction to Practicall Musicke, 1597

13   We must also take heed of seperating any part of a world from another by a rest, as some dunces have not slackt to do, yea one whose name is Johannes Dunstable [an ancient English author] hath not onlie devided the sentence, but in the verie middle of a word hath made two long rests . . . which is one of the greatest absurdities which I have seen committed in the dittying of music.

Thomas Morley (1557–1603)
Ibid

14   Verse is no doubt indispensable to music, but rhyme, for the sake of rhyme—is a curse.

Wolfgang Amadeus Mozart (1756–91)
Letter to his father, 13 October 1781

15   Proceeding from the conviction that human speech is strictly controlled by musical laws, he considers the task of musical art to be the reproduction in musical sounds not merely of the mood of a feeling, but chiefly of the mood of human speech.

Modest Mussorgksy (1839–81)
Statement prepared for Riemann's *Musik-Lexicon*, 1880

16   Melody and speech belong together. I reject the idea of a pure music.

Carl Orff (1895–1982)

17   If you can get the words, the Almighty sends you a tune.

Charles Pottipher, a Suffolk labourer
Quoted by Vaughan Williams, *Lecture*, 1912

18   The setting to music of a poem must be an act of love, never a marriage of convenience.

Francis Poulenc (1899–1963)
Quoted in Bernac, *Francis Poulenc*, 1977

19   Music is the exaltation of poetry. Both of them may excel apart, but surely they are most excellent when they are joined, because nothing is then wanting to either of their proportions; for thus they appear like wit and beauty in the same person.

Henry Purcell (1659–95)
Dioclesian, 1690, Preface

20   Let those which only warble long,
And gargle in their throats a song,
Content themselves with Ut, Re, Mi:
Let words, and sense, be set by thee.

Edmund Waller (1605–87)
To Mr Henry Lawes

21   If words are set to music, the music must be as independent an entity as the poem.

Peter Warlock (1894–1930)
In *The New Age*, 1917, 'Aphorisms'

22   Poetry is the true source of my music.

Hugo Wolf (1860–1903)

207 CHOIRS

1   I want you to sound like twenty-two women having babies *without* chloroform.

John Barbirolli (1899–1970) rehearsing the chorus of Vaughan Williams's *Sinfonia Antarctica*, quoted in Kennedy, *Barbirolli, Conductor Laureate*, 1971

2   [Remark to chorus:] You're singing about Angels and Archangels, not Gold Flake and Players.

John Barbirolli (1899–1970)
Ibid

3   Now, ladies and contraltos, if you will look to your parts, you'll see where the gentlemen and tenors come in.

Thomas Beecham (1879–1961)

4   There is not any music of instruments whatsoever comparable to that which is made of the voices of men, where the voices are good, and the same well sorted and ordered.

William Byrd (1543–1623)
Psalmes, Sonets and Songs, 1588

5   The lewd trebles squeak nothing but bawdy, and the basses roar blasphemy.

William Congreve (1670–1729)
The Way of the World, 1700, Act V, Sc V, referring to 'profane music-meetings'

6   The common singing-men in cathedral churches are a bad society, and yet a company of good fellows, that roar deep in the choir, deeper in the tavern.

John Earle (1601?–65)
Microcosmographic, 1628

7   Choristers bellow the tenor, as it were oxen; bark a counterpart, as it were a kennel of dogs; roar out a treble, as it were a sort of bulls; and grunt out a bass, as it were a number of hogs.

William Prynne (1600–69)
Histriomastix, 1632

208 ORATORIO

1 [On Gounod's *La Rédemption*:] If you will only take the precaution to go in long enough after it commences and to come out long before it is over, you will not find it wearisome.

George Bernard Shaw (1856–1950)
1882

2 I heard *Judith*, an oratorio, performed ... Some parts of it were exceedingly fine; but there are two things in all modern music which I could never reconcile to common sense. One is singing the same words ten times over; the other, singing different words by different persons, at one and the same time. And this in the most solemn addresses to God, whether by way of prayer or of thanksgiving. This can never be defended by all the musicians in Europe, till reason is quite out of date.

John Wesley (1703–91)
Journals, 29 February 1764

3 Oratorio (that profanation of the purposes of the cheerful playhouse).

Charles Lamb (1775–1834)
Essays of Elia, 1820–3

4 If I had the power I would insist on all oratorios being sung in the costume of the period – with a possible exception in the case of the *Creation*.

Ernest Newman (1868–1959)
In the *New York Post*, 1924

5 [Oratorios:] Unstaged operettas on scriptural themes, written in a style in which solemnity and triviality are blended in the right proportion for boring an atheist out of his senses.

George Bernard Shaw (1856–1950)
Quoted in Graf, *Composer and Critic*, 1947

6 Nothing can be more disgusting than an oratorio. How absurd, to see 500 people fiddling like madmen about the Israelites in the Red Sea!

Sydney Smith (1771–1845)

7 Four hours they sit in Exeter Hall, listening to one fugue after another, in perfect confidence that they have done a good deed for which they will be rewarded in heaven, where they will hear nothing but the most beautiful Italian arias. It was this earnest fervour in the English public that Mendelssohn understood so well.

Richard Wagner (1813–83)
Letter to Otto Wesendonck, 5 April 1855

8 [Handel's] oratorios thrive abundantly. For my part, they give me an idea of heaven, where everybody is to sing whether they have voices or not.

Horace Walpole (1717–97)
Letter, 1743

209 SOME SOLOISTS

See also 212 Divas and Heroes

1 She was a town-and-country soprano of the kind often used for augmenting the grief at a funeral.

George Ade (1866–1944)

2 An Italian diva had several times failed to appear on her cue during rehearsal. Eventually she tearfully appeared crying 'I cannot, I cannot.' I said to her, 'What cannot you, Madam?' She replied, 'I cannot make my entry; Mr Chaliapin *will* die too soon.' I said to her, 'Madam, you are grievously in error: no opera singer can die too soon to please me.'

Thomas Beecham (1879–1961)
Broadcast from Paris on his eightieth birthday

3 Who sent you to me – God?

Gioacomo Puccini (1858–1924)
On hearing Caruso at an audition

4 When a musician hath forgot his note,
 He makes as though a crumb stuck in his
 throat.

John Clarke
Paroemiologia, 1639

5   I think it's a duty for a singer while he is at his best to let everyone around the world hear him.
Placido Domingo (1941–)
In 1972, quoted in Jacobson, *Reverberations*, 1975

6   She was a singer who had to take any note above A with her eyebrows.
Montague Glass (1877–1934)

7   [To a singer who had threatened to jump on Handel's harpsichord:] Let me know when you will do that and I will advertise it. For I am sure more people will come to see you jump than to hear you sing.
George Frideric Handel (1685–1759)
Quoted in Lebrecht, *Discord*, 1982

8   Madam, I know you are a veritable devil, but I would have you know that I am Beelzebub, the head devil.
George Frideric Handel (1685–1759)
Remark to the singer Francesca Cuzzoni, 1723, quoted in Young, *Handel*, 1947

9   I would both sing thy praise and praise thy singing.
Hugh Holland (*d* 1633)
To Giles Farnaby

10   I can't stand to sing the same song the same way two nights in succession. If you can, then it ain't music, it's close order drill or exercise or yodelling or something, not music.
Billie Holliday (1915–59)
Lady Sings the Blues, 1956

11   [To a tenor whose singing he disliked:] You sang like a composer.
Jules Massenet (1842–1912)
Quoted in Harding, *Massenet*, 1970

12   Sing 'em muck – it's all they can understand.
Dame Nellie Melba (1861–1931)
Advice to Clara Butt, who was about to visit Australia

13   A mutual friend asked Melba if it were true that she had really given Clara Butt this dangerous advice. 'Of course not,' retorted Melba; 'in Clara's case, it wasn't necessary.'
Ivor Newton (1892–1981)
At the Piano, 1966

14 Orpheus with his lute made trees
And the mountain-tops that freeze
Bend themselves; that's more than you
With your disgusting voice can do.

J.B. Morton (1893–1979)
On a lady singing, 1932, 'Beachcomber'

15 A viable alternative to valium.

Mme Vera Galupe-Borszkh, alias Ira Siff on Dame Kiri te Kanawa, quoted in the
Independent, 10 May 1990

16 At Ranelagh I heard the famous Tenducci, a thing from Italy: it
looks for all the world like a man, though they say it is not. The voice, to
be sure, is neither man's nor woman's; but it is more melodious than
either, and it warbled so divinely, that, while I listened, I really thought
myself in paradise.

Tobias Smollett (1721–71)
Humphrey Clinker, 1771

17 After interrupting a rehearsal several times while a soprano soloist
went astray, Beecham asked in exasperation, 'Madam, have you looked
at this score before?' 'Indeed, Sir Thomas,' was the indignant reply. 'I
have eaten, drunk and slept with *Messiah* for weeks!' 'Then of course
you must have an immaculate conception of the role.'

OPERA

The real magic of this lavish form is when all its disparate ingredients – soloists, duets and ensembles, choruses, the orchestra, mime and choreography, lighting and design – combine to perfection. Then its expense, its supposed elitism, its absurdities and its anachronisms, dissolve into a rare and sublime celebration of unified perfection. At times, opera seems more ridiculous than sublime; and it has also generated a fine vintage of pithy observations.

210 OPERA OBSERVED

1   An opera may be allowed to be extravagantly lavish in its decorations, as its only design is to gratify the senses, and keep up an indolent attention in the audience.

Joseph Addison (1672–1719)
In the *Spectator*, 6 March 1711

2   One of the most magnificent and expenseful diversions the wit of man can invent.

John Evelyn (1620–1706)
Diary, 1645

3   'Bed', as the Italian proverb succinctly puts it, 'is the poor man's opera.'

Aldous Huxley (1894–1963)
Heaven and Hell, 1956
(*See also* 210.4 *below*)

4 From the first minute the listener is shocked by a deliberately discordant, confused stream of sounds. Fragments of melody, embryonic phrases appear, only to disappear again in the din, the grinding and the screaming. To follow this 'music' is difficult, to remember it impossible. So it goes on almost throughout the opera. Cries take the place of song. If by chance the composer lapses into simple, comprehensible melody, he is scared at such a misfortune and quickly plunges into confusion again ... All this is coarse, primitive and vulgar. The music quacks, grunts and growls, and suffocates itself in order to express the amatory scenes as naturalistically as possible. And 'love' is smeared all over the opera in this vulgar manner. The merchant's double bed occupies the central position on the stage. On it all problems are solved.

Pravda, 28 January 1936
On Shostakovich's *Lady Macbeth of Mtsensk*

5 Draughts are an admirable invention – just the thing to fill up the gaps whilst the long recitatives are being sung, as music itself is to relieve the pressure of a too great devotion to draughts.

Charles de Brosses (1709–77)
Letter from Rome, 1739

6 *Count:* Opera is an absurdity. Orders are delivered in song, politics discussed in duet. People dance around graves and dagger-blows are dealt in melody.
  Clairon: I could get used to people dying with an aria, but why are the words always worse than the music? Why must they owe their power of expression to it?
  Countess: It's different with Gluck ...

Clemens Krauss (1893–1954) and Richard Strauss (1864–1949)
Capriccio, 1942

7 The quality common to all the great operatic roles, eg, Don Giovanni, Norma, Lucia, Tristan, Isolde, Brünnhilde, is that each of them is a passionate and wilful state of being. In real life they would all be bores, even Don Giovanni.

W.H. Auden (1907–73)
The Dyer's Hand, 1962

8 Grand opera will never pay.

Thomas Beecham (1879–1961)
Quoted in Reid, *Thomas Beecham,* 1961

9   Opera has no business making money.
Rudolf Bing (1902–)
In *The New York Times*, 15 November 1959

10   Writing and performing an opera, creating any work of art in a world of violence and ease, hunger and obesity, could seem to be an act of private withdrawal. But art isn't about itself, it's about how men relate to the world and each other . . .
Edward Bond (1934–)
Note for *We Come to the River*, Covent Garden, 1976

11   The most expensive solution would be to blow up the opera houses.
Pierre Boulez (1925–)
Quoted in Wechsberg, *The Opera*, 1972

12   Music is in the opera what the verses are in the drama – a more stately expression, a stronger means of presenting thoughts and emotions.
Pierre Augustin Caron de Beaumarchais (1732–99)
Tarare, 1790 Preface

13   Opera is the most highly developed and complete form of art in music, and to sing in opera should be the aim of every vocalist. All vocal performance should be dramatized and opera should be the goal of every composer. And the utility of concerts should be to train audiences and all concerned for opera.
Thomas Beecham (1879–1961)

14   I want the classical operas produced as if they were modern, and vice versa.
Alban Berg (1885–1935)
In 1928, quoted in Barzun, *Pleasures of Music*, 1977

15   Opera today is a culinary opera.
Bertolt Brecht (1898–1956)
Notes to *The Rise and Fall of the City of Mahagonny*, 1929

16   [Of the Paris Opéra:] A stranger would take it for a railway station and, once inside, would mistake it for a Turkish bath.
    They continue to produce curious noises which the people who pay call music, but there is no need to believe them implicitly.
Claude Debussy (1862–1918)
Monsieur Croche, antidilettante, 1921

17   Whenever I go to an opera, I leave my sense and reason at the door with my half-guinea, and deliver myself up to my eyes and my ears.

Lord Chesterfield (1694–1773)
Letter to his son, 23 January 1752

18   They have been crucifying *Othello* into an opera (*Otello*, by Rossini): the music good but lugubrious; but as for the words, all the real scenes with Iago cut out, and the greatest nonsense inserted; the handkerchief turned into a *billet-doux*, and the first singer would not *black* his face, for some exquisite reasons assigned in the preface. Scenery, dresses, and music very good.

George Gordon, Lord Byron (1788–1824)
Letter from Venice to Samuel Rogers, 3 March 1818

19   At the theatre, we see and hear what has been said, thought and done by various people elsewhere; at the Opera we see and hear what was never said, thought or done anywhere but at the Opera.

William Hazlitt (1778–1830)
The Opera

20   An exotic and irrational entertainment.

Dr Samuel Johnson (1709–84)
On Italian opera

21   I have sat through an Italian opera, till, for sheer pain, and inexplicable anguish, I have rushed out into the noisiest places of the crowded streets, to solace myself with sounds which I was not obliged to follow, and get rid of the distracting torment of endless, fruitless, barren attention!

Charles Lamb (1775–1834)
Essays of Elia, 1820–3, 'A Chapter on Ears'

22   I love Italian opera–it's so reckless. Damn Wagner, and his bellowings at Fate and death. Damn Debussy, and his averted face. I like the Italians who run all on impulse, and don't care about their immortal souls, and don't worry about the ultimate.

D.H. Lawrence (1885–1930)
Letter to Louise Burrows, 1 April 1911

23   The opera house is an institution differing from other lunatic asylums only in the fact that its inmates have avoided official certification.

Ernest Newman (1868–1959)

24 Philip Glass's Akhnaten
Seems bound to dishearten
As the Pharaoh emotes
On very few notes.

Katie Mallet
Parrott (ed), *How to be Tremendously Tuned In to Opera, 1989*,
'Akhnaten'

25 The most rococo and degraded of all forms of art.
William Morris (1834–96)

26 In opera the text must be the obedient daughter of the music.
Wolfgang Amadeus Mozart (1756–91)

27 I sometimes wonder which would be nicer–an opera without an interval, or an interval without an opera.
Ernest Newman (1868–1959)
Heyworth (ed), *Berlioz, Romantic and Classic*, 1972

28 There was a time when I heard eleven operas in a fortnight . . . which left me bankrupt and half idiotic for a month.
J.B. Priestley (1894–1984)
All About Ourselves, 1923

29 Though opera is a noble craft
Most operatic plots are daft!

Ron Rubin
Parrott (ed), *How to be Tremendously Tuned In to Opera, 1989*

30 Who would endure the interminable harangues of the woeful Wotan without the superb music that goes with them? Would Orpheus weeping the loss of Eurydice move us as deeply if Gluck had not from the first few notes gripped our hearts? And without Mozart's music what should we think of the puppets in *The Magic Flute*?
Camille Saint-Saëns (1835–1921)
École buissonnière, 1913

31 Sleep is an excellent way of listening to an opera.
James Stephens (1882–1950)

32 [Overheard during the supper interval of *Der Rosenkavalier* at Glyndebourne in answer to the *query* 'Who's the composer?':] 'Mozart of course, dear. You can tell by the costumes.'

33 In opera everything is based upon the not-true!
Píotr Ilyich Tchaikovsky (1840–93)

34 'It ain't over till the fat lady sings.' Where does this saying, a favorite of sportscasters, come from? Well, what 'ain't over' is an opera, Wagner's *Siegfried*; and the 'fat lady' is 'Brünnhilde ... By 11.30 Siegfried makes it up to the mountaintop, right through the impenetrable fire. He finds Brünnhilde and removes the breastplate from the almost certainly amplitudinous body of the Wagnerian soprano who sleeps under it. As the musical comic Anna Russell describes it, 'He's never seen a woman before and doesn't know what she is.' What he says, with gargantuan understatement, is *'Das ist kein Mann.'* (*That is no man.*) Anyway, at about 11.40, Brünnhilde starts to sing. Vocally, she's fresh as a daisy. Siegfried, who's been singing non-stop since seven, must join in for a final love duet of Promethean difficulty, which ends, along with the opera, at 12.20.
Anthony Tommasini
The Boston Globe, 1990

35 The Opera is nothing but a public gathering place, where we assemble on certain days without precisely knowing why.
Voltaire (1694–1778)
Letter to Cideville, 1732

36 One goes to see a tragedy to be moved, to the opera one goes either for want of any other interest or to facilitate digestion.
Voltaire (1694–1778)

37 Music must be considered the true language of opera.
Christoph Martin Wieland (1733–1813)
Essay concerning German opera, 1775

38 There may be people who are serious enough to find this opera comic, just as there are people comical enough to take Brahms's symphonies seriously.
Hugo Wolf (1860–1903)
Reviewing *The Peasant a Rogue*, 1885

39 [Sir Isaac Newton] said he never was at more than one Opera. The first Act he heard with pleasure; the second stretched his patience; at the third he ran away.
Rev William Stukeley (1687–1765)
Diary, April 1720

211 COMPOSERS ON OPERA

1 Carve in your head in letters of brass: An Opera must draw tears, cause horror, bring death, by means of song.

Vincenzo Bellini (1801–35)
Letter to his librettist, 1834

2 A modern opera needs just as nice singing as *Trouvatore!*

Alban Berg (1885–1935)
Quoted in Reich, *The Life and Work of Alban Berg*, 1963

3 I have thought it necessary to reduce music to its true function, which is that of seconding poetry in the expression of sentiments and dramatic situations of a story, neither interrupting the action nor detracting from its vividness by useless and superfluous ornament.

Christoph Willibald von Gluck (1714–87)
Alceste, 1767, Preface

4 On the stage, it is not always the best word for vocalizing that we require; we need the everyday word, its melodic turn, torn from life, misery congealed, despair in sharp relief. Real life is needed in opera.

Leoš Janáček (1854–1928)
Quoted in *The Slavonic Review*, 1922–3

5 Life, wherever it is shown; truth, however bitter; speaking out boldly, frankly, point-blank to men—that is my aim ... I am a realist in the highest sense—that is, my business is to portray the soul of man in all its profundity.

Modest Mussorgsky (1835–81)
Quoted in Shapiro, *An Encyclopedia of Quotations about Music*, 1978

6 Superfluous detail has no place in opera. Everything should be drawn in bold strokes, as clearly and vividly as is practically possible for voice and orchestra. The voices should take first place, and the orchestra second.

Alexander Borodin (1833–87)
Quoted in Dianin, *Borodin*, 1963

7 Opera to me comes before everything else.

Wolfgang Amadeus Mozart (1756–91)
Letter, 1782

8 When Verdi was asked by a journalist if he, like Wagner, had a theory about the theatre, Verdi replied, 'Yes. The theatre should be full.'

9 How wonderful opera would be if there were no singers.
Gioachino Rossini (1792–1868)

212 DIVAS AND HEROES
See also 209 Some Soloists

1 I loathe Divas, they are curse of true music and musicians.
Hector Berlioz (1803–69)

2 Nobody knows the Traubels I've seen.
Rudolf Bing (1902–   )
General manager of the Metropolitan Opera, after a dispute with the Wagnerian soprano Helen Traubel

3 One God, one Farinelli!
Lady Bingley
Shouted at the opera, 1734, quoted in Young, *Handel*, 1947

4 The prima-donna, though a little old,
   and haggard with a dissipated life,
   And subject, when the house is thin, by cold,
   has some good notes.
George Gordon, Lord Byron (1788–1824)
Don Juan, 1819–24

5 [Stopping singing during a rehearsal of Ethel Smyth's *The Wreckers*:] Is this the place where I'm supposed to be drowned by the waves or by the orchestra?
John Coates (1865–1941)
Quoted in Reid, *Thomas Beecham*, 1961

6 When in doubt, sing loud.
Robert Merrill (1919–   )
In the *Saturday Evening Post*, 26 October 1957

7   My own objection to the prima donna is that, as a rule, she represents merely tone and technique without intelligence.
Ernest Newman (1868–1959)
A Musical Motley, 1919

> 8   [Of Francesca Cuzzoni:]
> Little *Siren* of the stage,
> Charmer of an idle age,
> Empty warbler, breathing lyre,
> Wanton gale of fond desire,
> Bane of every manly art,
> Sweet enfeebler of the heart,
> O, too pleasing in thy strain,
> Hence to southern climes again;
> Tuneful mischief, vocal spell,
> To this island bid farewell;
> Leave us as we ought to be,
> Leave the *Britons* rough and free.
> Ambrose Philips (1674–1749)
> *To Signora Cuzzoni,* 25 May 1724

9   Within forty-eight hours of his arrival in Paris Chaliapine received between eighty and ninety letters from women.
Arnold Bennett (1867–1931)
Journals, 30 May 1907

10   You are quite right to prefer dogs – they are more entertaining than concert artists and cows, more prepossessing than great prima donnas.
Claude Debussy (1862–1918)
Letter to Jacques Durand

11   People applaud a prima donna as they do the feats of the strong man at a fair. The sensations are painfully disagreeable, hard to endure, but one is so glad when it is all over that one cannot help rejoicing.
Jean-Jacques Rousseau (1712–78)
La Nouvelle Héloïse, 1761

12   An English lord who was enamoured of the prima donna, Henrietta Sontag, was nicknamed Lord Montag because he followed her with the same inevitability as Monday (*Montag*) follows Sunday (*Sontag*). Madame Sontag was also the subject of the worst possible musical joke, published in the *Musical Standard* of 1870:

We hang on every note Madame Sontag sings –
This proves the lady's great power of execution.
Recounted by Nicolas Slonimsky (1894–   )
A Thing or Two About Music, 1948

13 In my productions the principals are of the least importance.
Franco Zeffirelli (1923–)
Quoted in Jacobson, *Reverberations*, 1975

14 [On the swan-boat failing to appear for his exit in *Lohengrin*
Act III:] What time's the next swan?
Leo Slezak (1873–1946)

213 LIBRETTI

1 The writer must be convinced that opera offers possibilities that are
excluded from drama, and that these very possibilities are worth more
than everything of which drama is capable.
W.H. Auden (1907–73)
Quoted in Henze, *Music and Politics*, 1982

2 It is certainly not chance which made two men like us meet at the
same period in history.
Hugo von Hofmannsthal (1874–1929)
Letter to Richard Strauss, 20 January 1913, quoted in Gal, *The Musician's World*, 1965

3 *Olivier: Prima le parole–dopo la musica!*
    Flamand: Prima la musica–dopo le parole!

The Poet and the Musician in Strauss's *Capriccio* argue the eternal
question of opera: Which comes first, the words or the music?
Clemens Krauss (1893–1954) and Richard Strauss (1864–1949)
Capriccio, 1942

4 No good opera plot can be sensible, for people do not sing when they
are feeling sensible.
W.H. Auden (1907–73)
Quoted in *Time*, 1961

5 I have seen to it that nothing is sung that is necessary for the
comprehension of the play, because usually the words that are sung are
only poorly understood by the audience.
Pierre Corneille (1606–84)
Andromède, 1650, Preface

6   A writer of operatic librettos, if he wishes to be modern, must not have read the Greek and Latin classic authors, nor should he do so in the future. After all, the old Greeks and Romans never read modern writers . . .

For the finale of his opera he should write a magnificent scene with more elaborate effects, so that the audience will not walk out before the work is half over. He should conclude with the customary chorus in praise of the sun, the moon, or the impresario.

Benedetto Marcello (1686–1739)
Il teatro alla moda, 1720

7   An opera is sure of success when the plot is well worked out, the words written solely for the music and not shoved in here and there to suit some miserable rhyme . . .

Wolfgang Amadeus Mozart (1756–91)
Letter to his father, 13 October 1781

8   In the end it all depends on a libretto. A libretto, a libretto and the opera is made!

Giuseppe Verdi (1813–1901)
Letter, 1865

9   If the action demanded it, I would immediately abandon rhythm, rhyme, and stanza. I would use blank verse in order to say clearly and forthrightly all that the action demands.

Giuseppe Verdi (1813–1901)
Letter to librettist, 1870

10   I read with reluctance the librettos that are sent me. It is impossible, or almost impossible for someone else to divine what I want.

Giuseppe Verdi (1815–1901)
Letter, 1853

214   THEATRE MUSIC

1   There is too much music in our music for the theatre.

Pierre Augustin Caron de Beaumarchais (1732–99)
Tarare, 1790, Preface

2   Music in the theatre is a powerful, an almost immorally potent weapon.

Marc Blitzstein (1905–64)
Quoted in Ewen, *American Composers*, 1982

> 3   But never shall a truly British age
>   Bear a vile race of eunuchs on stage:
>   The boasted works called national in vain,
>   If one Italian voice pollute the strain.
>
> Charles Churchill (1731–64)
> *The Rosciad*, 1761

4   Music in the theatre throws a man off his guard, makes way for an ill Impression, and is most Commodiously planted to do mischief.

Jeremy Collier (1650–1726)
A Short View of the Immorality and Profaneness of the English Stage, 1698

5   Theatre music must make its point and communicate its emotion at the same moment the action develops. It cannot wait to be understood until after the curtain comes down.

Gian Carlo Menotti (1911–)
Quoted in Ewen, *American Composers*, 1982

6   The theatre is not the place for the musician. When the curtain is up the music interrupts the actor, and when it is down the music interrupts the audience.

Arthur Sullivan (1842–1900)

7   I believe that the musical theatre is the highest, the most expressive and the most imaginative form of theatre, and that a composer who has a talent and a passion for the theatre can express himself completely in this branch of musical creativeness.

Kurt Weill (1900–50)
Quoted in Ewen, *American Composers*, 1982

CONDUCTING AND TEMPO

Mr Harold C. Schonberg in his book *The Great Conductors* begins with a definition of the *genus*: 'He is of commanding presence, infinite dignity, fabulous memory, vast experience, high temperament and serene wisdom. He has been tempered in the crucible but he is still molten and he glows with a fierce inner light. He is many things: musician, administrator, executive, minister, psychologist, technician, philosopher and dispenser of wrath . . . above all, he is a leader of men . . .'

215   THE ART OF CONDUCTING

1   The English people may not understand music, but they absolutely love the noise it makes.
Thomas Beecham (1879–1961)

2   James Agate, meeting a friend, a member of the BBC orchestra: 'Who conducted this afternoon?'
    Alec Whittaker, First Oboe: 'Sorry, James, I forgot to look.'
Jacques Barzun (1907–)
Pleasures of Music, 1952

3   For a fine performance only two things are necessary: the maximum of virility coupled with the maximum of delicacy.
Thomas Beecham (1879–1961)
Quoted in Atkins and Newman, *Beecham Stories,* 1978

4   You must have the score in your head, not your head in the score.
Hans von Bülow (1830–94)
Remark to Richard Strauss, quoted in Schonberg, *The Great Conductors,* 1967

5   [Of Weingartner:] He is seldom disturbed from a calm physical balance; his laundry-bill probably disappoints those who attend to the weekly linen of most of the other conductors.
Neville Cardus (1889–1965)
In the *Manchester Guardian,* 1939

6 People no longer speak of Beethoven's but of Karajan's or Furtwängler's *Fifth Symphony*.

Jacques Chailley (1910–)
40000 Years of Music, trans Myers, 1964

7 This birdman, this scarecrow – it's the conductor.

Jean Cocteau (1889–1963)

8 Some conductors display their mastery by playing everything faster than it should be, but with Damrosch, it took the form of beginning everything slower than anybody else and then getting progressively slower.

Oscar Levant (1906–72)
On Walter Damrosch, *A Smattering of Ignorance,* 1940

9 [Of Beecham:] A pompous little duckarsed bandmaster who stood against everything creative in the art of his time.
('G.P.')

John Fowles (1926–)
The Collector, 1963

10 It is the most wonderful of all sensations that any man can conceive. It really oughtn't to be allowed.

Eugene Goossens (1893–1962)
Quoted in Nicholas, *Are They the Same at Home,* 1927

11 The conductor is nothing more than the driver of the coach engaged by the composer. He should stop at every request or quicken the pace according to the fare's orders. Otherwise the composer is entitled to get out and complete the journey on foot.

Charles Gounod (1818–93)
Quoted in Harding, *Gounod,* 1973

12 As one member of the Philharmonic Symphony expressed himself after a rehearsal, 'Two hours with Klemperer is like two hours in church.'

Oscar Levant (1906–72)
A Smattering of Ignorance, 1940

13 At that time Lennie [Bernstein] was in an agitated embryonic state. His conducting had a masturbatory, oppressive and febrile zeal, even for the most tranquil passages. (Today he uses music as an accompaniment to his conducting.)

Oscar Levant (1906–72)
Memoirs of an Amnesiac, 1960

14   A conductor should reconcile himself to the realization that regardless of his approach or temperament the eventual result is the same – the orchestra will hate him.

Oscar Levant (1906–72)
A Smattering of Ignorance, 1940

15   Signor Costa does not beat time, he threshes it.

Felix Mendelssohn (1809–47)
Attributed

16   Oh! to be a conductor, to weld a hundred men into one singing giant, to build up the most gorgeous arabesques of sound, to wave a hand and make the clamouring strings sink to a mutter, to wave again, and hear the brass crashing out in triumph, to throw up a finger, then another and another, and to know that with every one the orchestra would bound forward into a still more ecstatic surge and sweep, to fling oneself forward, and for a moment or so keep everything still, frozen, in the hollow of one's hand, and then to set them all singing and soaring in one final sweep, with the cymbals clashing at every flicker of one's eyelid, to sound the grand Amen.

J.B. Priestley (1894–1984)
Quoted in Schonberg, *The Great Conductors*, 1967

17   Beethoven was wont to give the signs of expression to his orchestra by all manner of extraordinary motions of his body. Whenever a *sforzando* occurred, he flung his arms wide, previously crossed upon his breast. At a *piano*, he bent down, and all the lower in proportion to the softness of tone he wished to achieve. Then when a crescendo came, he would raise himself again by degrees, and upon the commencement of the *forte*, would spring bolt upright. To increase the *forte* yet more, he would sometimes shout at the orchestra, without being aware of it.

Louis Spohr (1784–1859)
Autobiography, pub 1865

18   You conductors who are so proud of your power! When a new man faces the orchestra – from the way he walks up the steps to the podium and opens his score – before he even picks up his baton – we know whether he is the master or we.

Franz Strauss (1822–1905)
Quoted in Schonberg, *The Great Conductors*, 1967

19 Bear in mind that you are not making music for your own pleasure, but for the pleasure of your audience.

You must not perspire while conducting; only the public must get warm.

Direct *Salome* and *Elektra* as if they had been written by Mendelssohn: Elfin music.

Never encourage the brass, except with a curt glance, in order to give an important entrance cue.

Richard Strauss (1864–1949)
From *10 Golden Rules inscribed in the Album of a Young Conductor*, *c* 1925

20 'Great' conductors, like 'great' actors, soon become unable to play anything but themselves.

Igor Stravinsky (1882–1971)
Themes and Conclusions, 1972

---

216 CONDUCTORS TALKING

---

1 Just play the notes as they are rotten.

Ernest Ansermet (1883–1969)
Attributed remark to an orchestra, quoted in Hopkins, *Music All Around Me*, 1967

2 You're not bank clerks on a Sunday outing, you're souls sizzling in hell.

John Barbirolli (1889–1970)
Remark to chorus, quoted in Kennedy, *Barbirolli, Conductor Laureate*, 1971

3 You know why conductors live so long? Because we perspire so much.

John Barbirolli (1889–1970)

4 Today, conducting is a question of ego: a lot of people believe they are actually playing the music.

Daniel Barenboim (1942–   )
In 1968, quoted in Jacobson, *Reverberations*, 1975

5   I struggled against English snobbery for thirty years ... Until 1935 music was monopolized by such old humbugs as Mengelberg and Toscanini. They gave third-rate performances ... Toscanini was a good conductor of Italian opera. But the Germans and the French never accepted him as an interpreter of their music. In this country he was accepted with slavish snobbery as a brilliant conductor of everything in sight. The same thing applied to Mengelberg ... I have struggled against this prejudice and nonsense for half a century. All these damned foreign importations! Take Richter. He could conduct five works, no more.

Thomas Beecham (1879–1961)
To his biographer, Charles Reid

6   After a succession of effusive tributes, telegrams and letters from composers, conductors and musicians congratulating him on his seventieth birthday, Sir Thomas asked innocently, 'What! Nothing from Mozart?'

7   [Of Karajan:] A kind of musical Malcolm Sargent.

Thomas Beecham (1879–1961)
Quoted in Atkins and Newman, *Beecham Stories*, 1978

8   I am not a fascist. I hate Tchaikovsky and I will not conduct him. But if the audience wants him, it can have him.

Pierre Boulez (1925–)
Quoted in Peyser, *Boulez*, 1976

9   I have always maintained that I am an executant and not, and have no right to be, a critic of any kind, even to the extent of having preferences and favourites. I consider it is my job to make the best of whatever is put before me once I have agreed to conduct the work. I am often asked which is my favourite Beethoven or Brahms symphony, and I can only answer that my favourite is the one that I am at the moment performing, or studying, the one that is uppermost in my mind.

Adrian Boult (1889–1983)
My Own Trumpet, 1973

10   If I tell the Berliners to step forward, they do it. If I tell the Viennese to step forward, they do it. But then they ask why!

Herbert von Karajan (1908–89)
On his preference for Berlin audiences, *Sunday Times*, 30 January 1983

11   *Friend:*   What a number of distinguished conductors have died
this year [1954] – Clemens Krauss, Wilhelm Furtwän-
gler . . .

    Klemperer: *Ja*, it's been a good year, hasn't it?

Quoted in Gattey, *Peacocks on the Podium*, 1982

12   In my day, Furtwängler and Bruno Walter and Kleiber and I *hated*
each other. It was more healthy.

Otto Klemperer (1885 – 1973)
Quoted in Harewood, *The Tongs and the Bones*, 1981

13   [Of conducting:] The important thing is that one should let the
orchestra breathe.

Otto Klemperer (1885 – 1973)
In 1973, quoted in Green, *Dictionary of Contemporary Quotations*, 1982

14   [On rehearsing Gershwin's concerto:] 'Mr Gershwin wanted it this
way' I had explained. 'Thata poor boy . . . he was asick,' said Toscanini.

Oscar Levant (1906 – 72)
Memoirs of an Amnesiac, 1960

15   We are steersmen, not oarsmen.

Franz Liszt (1811 – 86)
Letter on conducting, 1853

16   I never use a score when conducting my orchestra . . . Does a lion
tamer enter a cage with a book on how to tame a lion?

Dimitri Mitropoulos (1896 – 1960)
22 January 1951

17   The leader of the Vienna Philharmonic once called over to me at a
rehearsal when, my baton not being at hand, I was about to take another:
'Not that one, Doctor – that one has no rhythm.'

Richard Strauss (1864 – 1949)
Recollections and Reflections, 1949

18   Conductors must give unmistakeable and suggestive signals to the
orchestra – not choreography to the audience.

George Szell (1897 – 1970)
Quoted in *Newsweek*, 28 January 1963

19   I am a pig.

Arturo Toscanini (1867 – 1957)
Remark to John Barbirolli, 1940

20 [During a stormy rehearsal:] After I die I am coming back to earth as the doorkeeper of a *bordello*. And I won't let a one of you in.
Arturo Toscanini (1867–1957)
Quoted in Lebrecht, *Discord*, 1982

217 TEMPO

1 The metronome has no value . . . for I myself have never believed that my blood and a mechanical instrument go well together.
Johannes Brahms (1833–97)
Letter to George Henschel, 1880

2 Every composer has his own basic tempo which decrees that speed in his music is not the same as speed in any other composer.
Neville Cardus (1889–1975)
In the *Manchester Guardian*, 1936

3 We were none of us musical, though Miss Jenkyns beat time, out of time, by way of appearing to be so.
Mrs Gaskell (1810–65)
Cranford, 1853

4 If a man does not keep pace with his companions, perhaps it is because he hears a *different drummer*. Let him step to the music which he hears, however measured or far away.
Henry David Thoreau (1817–62)
Walden, 1854

> 5 There was a young lady of Rio
> Who tried to play Hummel's Grand Trio
> But her pace was so scanty
> She took it *Andante*
> Instead of *Allegro con brio*!
>
> Text set for an examination in a three-part vocal counterpoint by Tovey at Edinburgh University

LIFE, FAITH AND THE HEREAFTER

While some composers, Haydn and Bruckner for example, repeatedly proclaimed their faith, others, like Brahms and Delius, would have echoed Tennyson's *In Memoriam*: 'There lives more faith in honest doubt/Believe me, than in half the creeds.' Perhaps one should seek composers' true feelings on the subjects of this section in their notes rather than their words or lives. But then, as Shelley asked, what *is* life?

218 MUSICIANS ON LIFE AND POLITICS

1 My own idea . . . of which I have been fully conscious since I found myself as a composer – is the brotherhood of peoples, brotherhood despite all wars and conflicts. I try – to the best of my ability – to serve this idea in my music.
Béla Bartók (1881–1945)
Letter to Octavian Beu, 1931

2 Music is not an acquired culture . . . it is an active part of natural life.
Isaac Stern (1920–)
Quoted in *Celebrity Register*, 1973

3 The only thing to do, if you want to contribute to culture, or politics, or music, or whatever, is to utilize your own persona rather than just music. The best way to do this is to diversify and become a nuisance everywhere.
David Bowie (1947–)
March 1976

4 Oh society! What can be more appalling, duller, more intolerable.
Píotr Ilyich Tchaikovsky (1840–93)
Letter of 26 February 1881 to his brother Modest, quoted in Gal, *The Musician's World*, 1965

5 Is there a high social role of music here in our decadent bourgeois society? Yes, there is, if we embrace partisanship in our art, and place it at the service of those who are partisans in the glorious struggle of mankind for the new world of true freedom, which socialism and communism will secure to all.
Alan Bush (1900–)
In *The Modern Quarterly*, 1945

6 The decision of the Central Committee of February 10, 1948, has separated the rotten threads from the healthy ones in the creative work of composers. No matter how painful it is for many composers, myself included, I agree to the resolution of the Central Committee, which establishes the condition for making the whole organism of Soviet music healthy.

Sergei Prokofiev (1891–1953)
On Soviet music, quoted in Barzun, *Pleasures of Music,* 1952

7 Lenin spoke of the spirit of the people and of the Party in art, of the spiritual majesty of art, of its mighty educative power, of its role in the fight for the new man. He called on artists to be in the thick of life, to relate their creative work to the needs of the times.

Dmitri Shostakovich (1906–75)
On joining the Soviet Communist Party, 1961

8 Time, time – that is our greatest master! Alas, like Ugolino, time devours its own children . . .

Hector Berlioz (1803–69)
Letter to Princess Carolyne Sayn-Wittgenstein, 12 August 1856, quoted in Lockspeiser, *The Literary Clef,* 1958

9 When the pattern of one's life is broken up, everything disintegrates; one's homophony becomes polyphony, one's harmony becomes counterpoint – all becomes chaotic. Then gradually it settles down, a few dominant themes emerge, then two, then one. And then one begins again. And again the same thing happens. And so on. Until the end.

Cecil Gray (1895–1951)
Notebooks, Pauline Gray (ed), 1989

10 Lenny Bernstein once said (it must have been at least eight years ago), 'The trouble with you and me, Ned, is that we want everyone in the world to personally love us, and of course that's impossible: you just don't *meet* everyone in the world.'

Ned Rorem (1923–   )
Paris Diary, 1966

11 Prince, what you are, you are by the accident of birth; what I am, I am of myself. There are and there will be thousands of princes. There is only one Beethoven.

Ludwig van Beethoven (1770–1827)
Letter to Prince Lichnowsky, 1806

12   As a revolutionary I'm very Leninistic. I'm all for the efficiency of the revolution, by going to the important organizations to change the sense of them and to convince them by my existence.

Pierre Boulez (1925–)
In 1969, quoted in Jacobson, *Reverberations*, 1975

13   Music – that wonderful universal language – should be a source of communication among men. Again I implore my fellow musicians throughout the world to put the purity of their art at the service of mankind in order to unite all races. Let each of us contribute as much as he can until this ideal is attained in all its glory.

Pablo Casals (1876–1973)

14   The bourgeois capitalistic world is tonal; that of love (unhappiness, despair) atonal.

Hans Werner Henze (1926–)
Speaking of his *Boulevard Solitude*, in *Music and Politics*, 1982, 'German Music in the 1940s and 1950s'

15   Party allegiance cannot be expressed in music.

Zoltán Kodály (1882–1967)
Lecture, 1946

16   Courage is the mainspring of our best qualities; where it is lacking they wither, and without courage one is not even sufficiently prudent. One must, of course, consider, reflect, calculate, weigh the 'pros and cons'. But after that one must make up one's mind and act, without paying undue attention to the direction of the wind or to any passing clouds . . .

Franz Liszt (1811–86)
Letter to Richard Pohl, 7 November 1868, quoted by Gal, *The Musician's World*, 1965

17   Art and life are not two different things.

Felix Mendelssohn (1809–47)
Letter

18   What do you think of Mussolini? I hope he will prove to be the man we need. Good luck to him if he will cleanse and give a little peace to our country!

Giacomo Puccini (1858–1924)
Letter to G. Adami, 30 October 1922

19   Sing, if you're glad to be gay,
Sing, if you're happy that way.

Tom Robinson (1950–)

20 Supposing times were normal—normal as they were before 1914—then the music of our time would be in a different situation.
Arnold Schoenberg (1874–1951)
In 1936, quoted in Rosen, *Schoenberg*, 1976

21 Without music we shall surely perish of drink, morphia, and all sorts of artificial exaggerations of the cruder delights of the senses.
George Bernard Shaw (1856–1950)
Fortnightly Review, 1894, 'The Religion of the Pianoforte'

22 Success is never luck, but a mysterious power of the successful.
Giuseppe Verdi (1813–1901)

---

219 POLITICIANS ON MUSIC

1 Am I to understand that an overweight Italian singing in his own language is part of my heritage?
Terence Dicks (1937–)
English Conservative Member of Parliament

2 Pop music is rock music without the sex or the soul.
Mark Fisher (1944–)
English Labour Member of Parliament, quoted in the *Guardian,* 10 September 1990

3 I only know two tunes. One of them is 'Yankee Doodle', and the other isn't.
Attributed to Ulysses Simpson Grant (1822–85), US president

4 I know nothing more beautiful than the 'Appassionata', I could hear it every day. It is marvellous, unearthly music. Every time I hear these notes, I think with pride and perhaps childlike *Naïveté,* that it is wonderful what man can accomplish. But I cannot listen to music often, it affects my nerves. I want to say amiable stupidities and stroke the heads of the people who can create such beauty in a filthy hell.
Vladimir Ilyich Lenin (1870–1924)
Quoted by Maxim Gorky, *Days With Lenin,* 1933

5   It is hard for the normal person to understand what the word 'dodecaphony' means, but apparently it means the same as the word 'cacophony'. Well, we flatly reject this cacophonous music. Our people cannot use this garbage as a tool of their ideology.

Nikita Khrushchev (1894–1971)

6   The composer must learn to master all musical resources for the complete musical expression of the ideas and passions motivating Soviet heroes.

Josef Stalin (1879–1953)
Quoted by Cooper, *Russian Opera*, 1951

7   A careless song, with a little nonsense in it now and then, does not misbecome a monarch.

Horace Walpole (1717–97)
Letter to Horace Mann, 1774

8   The people do not need music which they cannot understand.

Andrei A. Zhdanov (1896–1948)
Speech, 1947

220 MUSIC IN SOCIETY

1   As the music is, so are the people of the country.

Turkish proverb

2   To you it is commanded, O peoples, nations, and languages, That at what time ye hear the sound of the cornet, flute, harp, sackbut, psaltery, dulcimer, and all kinds of musick, ye fall down and worship the golden image that Nebuchadnezzar the king hath set up: And who so falleth not down and worshippeth shall the same hour be cast into the middle of a burning fiery furnace.

Bible, Authorized Version
Daniel, Ch 3, vv 4–7

3   I believe that an artist *should* be part of his community, *should* work for it, and be used *by* it. Over the last hundred years this has become rarer and rarer and the artist and community have both suffered as a result.

Benjamin Britten (1913–76)
Speech on acceptance of the freedom of Aldeburgh, 1962

4   If you love music, hear it; go to operas, concerts, and pay fiddlers to play to you; but I insist upon your neither piping nor fiddling yourself. It puts a gentleman in a very frivolous, contemptible light . . . and takes up a great deal of time, which might be much better employed.
Lord Chesterfield (1694–1773)
Letters to his Son

5   A *great* fondness for music is a mark of great weakness, great vacuity of mind: not of hardness of heart; not of vice; not of downright folly; but of a want of capacity, or inclination, for sober thought.
William Cobbett (1763–1835)
Advice to Young men and (Incidentally) to Young Women, in the Middle and Higher Ranks of Life, 1829

6   Music is almost as dangerous as gunpowder; and it maybe requires looking after no less than the press, or the mint. 'Tis possible a public regulation might not be amiss.
Jeremy Collier (1650–1726)
A Short View of the Immorality and Profaneness of the English Stage, 1698

7   If you would know if a people are well governed, and if its laws are good or bad, examine the music it practises.
Confucius (551–479 BC)
Analects

8   We *are* rock against racism.
Noel Davies
Quoted in Green, *The Book of Rock Quotes,* 1982

9   Tchaikovsky thought of committing suicide for fear of being discovered as a homosexual, but today, if you are a composer and *not* homosexual, you might as well put a bullet through your head.
Serge Diaghilev (1872–1929)
Quoted in Duke, *Listen Here!,* 1963

10   It cannot be emphasized too strongly that art, as such, does not 'pay' . . . at least, not in the beginning – and that the art that has to pay its own way is apt to become vitiated and cheap.
Antonin Dvořák (1841–1904)
Music in America, 1895

11   Beethoven and Liszt have contributed to the advent of long hair.
Louis Moreau Gottschalk (1829–69)

12 Music should either be done in a church or in someone's home.
Gustav Holst (1874–1934)
Quoted in Imogen Holst, *Holst*, 1974

13 Lots of people who complained about us receiving the MBE received theirs for heroism in the war–for killing people. We received ours for entertaining other people. I'd say we deserve ours more.
John Lennon (1940–80)
Beatles Illustrated Lyrics, 1969

14 *Génie oblige!*
Franz Liszt (1811–86)
Obituary of Paganini, 1840

15 Music must be supported by the king and the princes, for the maintenance of the arts is their duty no less than the maintenance of the laws.
Martin Luther (1483–1546)
Table Talk, pub 1566

16 Music quickens time, she quickens us to the finest enjoyment of time; she quickens–and in so far she has moral value. Art has moral value, in so far as it quickens. But what if it does the opposite? What if it dulls us, sends us to sleep, works against action and progress? Music can do that too; she is an old hand at using opiates. But the opiate, my dear sirs, is a gift of the devil; it makes for lethargy, inertia, slavish inaction, stagnation. There is something suspicious about music, gentlemen. I insist that she is, by her nature, equivocal. I shall not be going too far in saying at once that she is politically suspect.
(Settembrini)
Thomas Mann (1875–1955)
The Magic Mountain, 1924

17 If the king loves music, there is little wrong in the land.
Mencius (372–289 BC)
Discourses

18 Music is a beautiful opiate, if you don't take it too seriously.
Henry Miller (1891–1980)
The Air-Conditioned Nightmare, 1945, 'With Edgar Varèse in the Gobi Desert'

19 Who shall silence all the airs and madrigals that whisper softness in chambers?
John Milton (1608–74)
Areopagitica, 1644

20   Without music a State cannot exist. All the disorders, all the wars which we see in the world, only occur because of the neglect to learn music. Does not war result from a lack of union among men? . . . And were all men to learn music, would not this be the means of agreeing together, and of seeing universal peace reign throughout the world?

Molière (1622–73)
Le Bourgeois gentilhomme, 1670

21   Whistle While You Work.

Larry Morey
Title of song in Walt Disney's *Snow White*, 1937

22   Let kings and the triumphs of kings yield before songs.

Ovid (43 BC–AD 17)
Amores

23   Musical innovation is full of danger to the State, for when modes of music change, the laws of the State always change with them.

Plato (428–347 BC)
The Republic

24   If any person has sung or composed against another person a song such as was causing slander or insult to another, he shall be clubbed to death.

Roman Twelve Tables, 449 BC

25   Music is essentially useless, as life is: but both lend utility to their conditions.

George Santayana (1863–1952)
The Life of Reason: Reason in Art

26   It is 'music with her silver sound' because musicians have no gold for sounding.
(Peter)

William Shakespeare (1564–1616)
Romeo and Juliet, 1595–6, Act IV, Sc V

27   Slavedrivers know well enough that when the slave is singing a hymn to liberty he is consoling himself for his slavery and not thinking about breaking his chain.

Miguel de Unamuno (1864–1936)
Essays and Soliloquies, trans 1925

28 New arts shall bloom of loftier mould
   And mightier music thrill the skies,
   And every life a song shall be
   When all the earth is paradise.

John Addington Symonds (1840–93)
From *A Vista* (set by John Ireland in *These Things Shall Be*)

221 THE PROFESSION OF MUSIC

1 There should be a single Art Exchange in the world, to which the artist would simply send his works and be given in return as much as he needs. As it is, one has to be half a merchant on top of everything else, and how badly one goes about it!

Ludwig van Beethoven (1770–1827)
Letter, 1801

2 The secret of longevity is staying out of the business for long periods of time . . . they'll eat you alive and spit the bones out. If you hang around long enough, they'll get you. But if you're not there they can't get you.

Jeff Beck (1944–)
Los Angeles Times, 25 August 1985

3 Now, I daresay that a good thing will make its way without being pushed. But I do not expect to live a century, and, in the meantime, as I cannot afford to give you my art, I should like you to recognize my right to a decent livelihood on the strength of it. The fact that you allow this commercialized life to continue proves that you do not object to it, so you cannot logically object to this advertisement. After all, a few good things are advertised. Mr Pears did not wait for posterity to enjoy his very nice soap.

Rutland Boughton (1878–1960)
Self-advertisement, 1911

4 Do not take up music unless you would rather die than not do so.

Nadia Boulanger (1887–1974)
Quoted in Kendall, *The Tender Tyrant: Nadia Boulanger*, 1976

5   Men of our profession hang between the church and the playhouse, as Mahomet's tomb does between the two load-stones, and must equally incline to both, because by both we are equally supported.
Tom Brown (1663–1704)
Letters from the Dead to the Living, 1704, 'John Blow'

6   Had I learned to fiddle, I should have done nothing else.
Dr Samuel Johnson (1709–84)
Quoted in Boswell, *Life,* 1791

222   MUSIC FOR THE MASSES

1   A composer should fit his music to the genius of the people, and consider that the delicacy of hearing, and taste of harmony, has been formed upon those sounds which every country abounds with. In short, that music is of a relative nature, and what is harmony to one ear, may be dissonance to another.
Joseph Addison (1672–1719)
In the *Spectator,* 1710

> 2   We have to sing, you see, here in the
>   darkness
>   All men have to sing–poor broken things,
>   We have to sing here in the darkness in the
>   roaring flood.
>   Sherwood Anderson (1876–1941)
>   *Songs of Industrial America*

3   Only that art can live which is an active manifestation of the life of the people. It must be a necessary and essential portion of that life, and not a luxury.
Ernest Bloch (1880–1959)
Man and Music, 1917

4   The Ritter Gluck confessed that the groundtone of the noblest passage, in one of his noblest operas, was the voice of the populace he had heard in Vienna, crying to the Kaiser: Bread! Bread!
Thomas Carlyle (1795–1881)
The French Revolution, 1837

5 Music must be made popular, not by debasing the art, but by elevating the people.

Henry Cleveland
National Music, 1840

6 I have taken the decision that in my work I will embody all the difficulties and all the problems of contemporary bourgeois music, and that I will, however, try to transform these into something usable, into something that the masses can understand.

Hans Werner Henze (1926–)
Music and Politics, 1982, 'Art and the Revolution', 1971

7 The masses, their senses still sound and unadulterated, must be introduced to musical culture.

Zoltán Kodály (1882–1967)
What is Hungarian in Music?, 1939

8 A real musical culture should not be a museum culture based mainly on music of past ages; nor should it be, like most commercial music, a drug. It should be the active embodiment in sound of the life of a community – of the everyday demands of people's work and play and of their deepest spiritual needs.

Wilfrid Mellers (1914–)
Quoted in Kendall, *The Tender Tyrant: Nadia Boulanger,* 1976

223 THE FOOD OF LOVE

1 Love me little, love me long,
Is the burden of my song.

Anonymous
Love me Little, Love me Long, c 1570

2 Music is the imagination of love in *sound.* It is what man imagines of his life, and his life is love.

W.J. Turner (1889–1946)
Orpheus, or The Music of the Future, 1926

3   The Owl and the Pussy-cat went to sea
In a beautiful pea-green boat.
They took some honey, and plenty of money,
Wrapped up in a five-pound note.
The Owl looked up to the Stars above
And sang to a small guitar,
'Oh lovely Pussy! O Pussy, my love,
What a beautiful Pussy you are.'

Edward Lear (1812–88)
Nonsense Songs, 1871

4   Objectivity in music is rubbish . . . Have you ever had an objective love affair? And what is music but love?

Lili Kraus (1905–)
In *The New York Times*, 1 August 1976

5   It is impossible to write atonal love music. A certain yearning, yes, but not the fulfilment.

Cecil Gray (1895–1951)
Notebooks, Pauline Gray (ed), 1989

6   If Music and sweet Poetry agree,
As they must needs (the Sister and the
Brother)
Then must the love be great, 'twixt thee and
me,
Because thou lov'st the one, and I the other.

Richard Barnfield (1574–1627)
Sonnet

7   Which of the two powers, love or music, is able to lift man to the sublimest heights? It is a great question, but it seems to me that one might answer it thus: love cannot express the idea of music, while music may give an idea of love. Why separate the one from the other? They are the two wings of the soul.

Hector Berlioz (1803–69)
Memoirs

8   Amongst other good qualities an amorous fellow is endowed with, he must learn to sing and dance, play upon some instrument or other, as without all doubt he will, if he be truly touched with this loadstone of love. For as Erasmus hath it, *Musicam docet amro et Poesin*, love will make them musicians, and to compose ditties . . .

Robert Burton (1577–1640)
Anatomy of Melancholy, 1621

9   O, my Luve's like a red, red rose
     That's newly sprung in June;
     O my Luve's like the melodie
     That's sweetly play'd in tune.

Robert Burns (1759–96)
A Red, Red Rose, 1794

10   Music arose with its voluptuous swell,
     Soft eyes look'd love to eyes which spake
        again,
     And all went merry as a marriage bell.

George Gordon, Lord Byron (1788–1824)
Childe Harold's Pilgrimage, 1816, III

11   I conclude that musical notes and rhythms were first acquired by
the male or female progenitors of mankind for the sake of charming the
opposite sex.

Charles Darwin (1809–82)
The Descent of Man, 1871

12   How sweet the answer Echo makes
     To music at night,
     When roused by lute or horn, she wakes
     And far away o'er lawns and lakes
     Goes answering light!

     Yet Love hath echoes truer far
     And far more sweet
     Than e'er, beneath the moonlight's star,
     Of horn or lute or soft guitar
     The songs repeat.

Thomas Moore (1779–1852)
Echoes

13   A love song is just a caress set to music.

Sigmund Romberg (1887–1951)

14   The sly whoresons
     Have got a speeding trick to lay down ladies.
     A French song and a fiddle has no fellow.
     (Lovell)

William Shakespeare (1564–1616)
Henry VIII, 1613, Act I, Sc III

15 I am advised to give her music o' mornings; they say it will penetrate.
(Cloten)

William Shakespeare (1564–1616)
Cymbeline, 1609–10, Act II, Sc III

16 If music be the food of love, play on;
Give me excess of it, that, surfeiting,
The appetite may sicken and so die.
That strain again! It had a dying fall:
O! it came o'er my ear like the sweet sound
That breathes upon a bank of violets,
Stealing and giving odour!
(Duke Orsino)

William Shakespeare (1564–1616)
Twelfth Night, 1660–2, Act I, Sc I

17 Give me some music; moody food
Of us that trade in love.
(Cleopatra)

William Shakespeare (1564–1616)
Antony and Cleopatra, 1606–7, Act II, Sc V

18 And when love speaks the voice of all
the gods
Makes heaven drowsy with the harmony.
(Biron)

William Shakespeare (1564–1616)
Love's Labour's Lost, 1590–4, Act IV, Sc III

19 How silver-sweet sound lovers' tongues
by night,
Like softest music to attending ears.
(Romeo)

William Shakespeare (1564–1616)
Romeo and Juliet, 1595–6, Act II, Sc II

20 No, Music, thou art not the 'food of
love',
Unless love feeds upon its own sweet self,
Till it becomes all Music murmurs of.

Percy Bysshe Shelley (1792–1822)
Fragment: To Music

21
                              Take
This slave of Music, for the sake
Of him who is the slave of thee;
And teach it all the harmony
In which thou canst, and only thou;
Make the delighted spirit glow,
Till joy denies itself again
And, too intense, is turned to pain.
(Ariel to Miranda)

Percy Bysshe Shelley (1792–1822)
To a Lady, with a guitar

22   Doubt you to whom my Muse these notes
        intendeth,
     Which now my breast o'ercharged to music
        lendeth?
     To you, to you, all song of praise is due;
     Only in you my song begins and endeth.

Philip Sidney (1554–86)
First song/Astrophel and Stella, 1591

23   For a day and a night Love sang to us,
        played with us,
     Folded us round from the dark and the light;
     And our hearts were fulfilled with the music
        he made with us,
     Made with our hands and our lips while he
        stayed with us,
     Stayed in mid passage his pinions from flight
     For a day and a night.

Algernon Charles Swinburne (1837–1909)
At Parting

24   Oh, how peacefully then shall my bones
        rest,
     If your reed shall make music of my loves!

Virgil (70–19 BC)
Eclogues, 37 BC

224 THE LOVE OF FOOD

1   Music with dinner is an insult both to the cook and violinist.
Gilbert Keith Chesterton (1874–1936)
Quoted in *The New York Times*, 16 November 1967

2   A concert of music in a banquet of wine is as a signet of carbuncle set
in gold. As a signet of an emerald set in a work of gold, so is the melody of
music with pleasant wine.
Apocrypha
Ecclesiasticus, Ch 32, vv 5–6

3   A society fop greeted Rossini at a reception. Noticing that Rossini
did not recognize him, he said, 'Don't you remember me? I sat next to
you when they served a gigantic macaroni pie at a dinner in your honour
in Milan.' 'Indeed I remember the macaroni very well,' replied Rossini,
'but I do not remember you.'
Recounted by Nicolas Slonimsky (1894–   )
A Thing or Two about Music, 1948

4   After a dinner which he particularly enjoyed, the hostess turned to
him and said: 'Maestro, you have conferred a great honour upon us by
accepting our invitation to dine. When will you come to dinner again?'
   Rossini, smacking his lips over the delicious food, replied:
   'Right away, Madam!'
Recounted by Nicolas Slonimsky (1894–   )
Ibid

225 SAINT CECILIA

1   In a garden shady this holy lady
    With reverent cadence and subtle psalm,
    Like a black swan as death came on
    Poured forth her song in perfect calm:
    And by ocean's margin this innocent virgin
    Constructed an organ to enlarge her prayer,
    And notes tremendous from her great engine
    Thundered out on the Roman air.
W.H. Auden (1907–73)
Anthem for St Cecilia's Day (set by Britten as *Hymn to St Cecilia*, 1942)

2   Blessed Cecilia, appear in visions
     To all musicians, appear and inspire:
     Translated Daughter, come down and startle
     Composing mortals with immortal fire.

     W.H. Auden (1907–73)
     Ibid

3   Soul of the world, inspired by thee
     The jarring seeds of matter did agree.
     Thou didst the scattered atoms bind,
     Which, by the laws of true proportion joined,
     Made up of various parts one perfect harmony.

     Nicolas Brady (1659–1726)
     Ode for St Cecilia's Day (set to music by Purcell)

4   Orpheus could lead the savage race;
     And trees unrooted left their place
     Sequacious of the lyre;
     But bright Cecilia raised the wonder higher:
     When to her organ vocal breath was given,
     An angel heard and straight appeared,
     Mistaking earth for heaven.

     John Dryden (1631–1700)
     A Song for St Cecilia's Day, 1687

5   At last divine Cecilia came,
     Inventress of the vocal frame;
     The sweet enthusiast from her sacred store
     Enlarged the former narrow bounds,
     With Nature's mother-wit, and arts unknown
       before.
     –Let old Timotheus yield the prize
     On both divide the crown;
     He raised a mortal to the skies
     She drew an angel down!

     John Dryden (1631–1700)
     Alexander's Feast, or The Power of Music

6   Of Orpheus now no more let poets tell,
     To bright Cecilia greater pow'r is giv'n;
     His numbers rais'd a shade from Hell,
     Hers lift the soul to Heav'n.

     Alexander Pope (1688–1744)
     Ode for Music, on St Cecilia's Day, c 1708

226 CHURCH MUSIC

1   There are many hymns I like as one likes old song hits, because, for me, they have sentimental associations; but the only hymns I find poetically tolerable are either versified dogma or biblical ballads.
W.H. Auden (1907–73)

2   God is gone up with a shout, the LORD with the sound of a trumpet. Sing praises to God, sing praises; sing praises unto our King, sing praises.
Bible, Authorized Version
Psalm 47, vv 5–6

3   I will sing of mercy and judgement:
    unto theee, O Lord, I will sing.
Bible, Authorized Version
Psalm 101, v 1

4   Make a joyful noise unto the LORD, all ye lands. Serve the LORD with gladness: come before his presence with singing.
Bible, Authorized Version
Psalm 100, vv 1–2

5   Merrily sang the monks in Ely,
    When Cnut, King, rowed thereby;
    Row, my knights, near the land,
    And hear we these monks' song.
King Canute (944?–1035)
Song of the Monks of Ely

6   And six little Singing-boys–dear
        little souls!
    In nice clean faces, and nice white stoles.
Rev R.H. Barham (1788–1845)
The Jackdaw of Rheims

7   They have so much of it in England that the monks attend to nothing else. A set of creatures who ought to be lamenting their sins fancy they can please God by gurgling in their throats. Boys are kept in the English Benedictine colleges solely and simply to sing hymns to the Virgin.
Desiderius Erasmus (1466–1536)
After visiting England at the invitation of Thomas More

8 How greatly did I weep in thy hymns and canticles, deeply moved by the voices of thy sweet-speaking church!

St Augustine (354–430)
Confessions

9 I am inclined to approve of the custom of singing in church, in order that by indulging the ears, weaker spirits may be inspired with feelings of devotion. Yet when I find the singing itself more moving than the truth which it conveys, I confess that this is a grievous sin, and at these times I would prefer not to hear the singer.

St Augustine (354–430)
Ibid

10 I have always kept one end in view, namely, with all good will to conduct a well-regulated church music to the honour of God.

Johann Sebastian Bach (1685–1750)
Letter to the Mühlhausen Council, 1708

11 I would earnestly entreat those who sing ill, not to sing at all, at least in the church.

James Beattie (1735–1803)
On the Improvement of Psalmody in Scotland, 1778

12 Sing on with hymns uproarious,
Ye humble and aloof.

John Betjeman (1906–84)
Hymn, 1932

13 The music of the church must be expressive . . . The passions of opera are cold in comparison to those of our church music.

Jacques Bonnet (d 1724)
Histoire de la musique, 1705

14 Whosoever is harmonically composed delights in harmony; which makes me much distrust the symmetry of those heads which declaim against all church music.

Thomas Browne (1605–82)
Religio Medici, 1642

15 The better the voice is, the meeter it is to honour and serve God therewith; and the voice of man is chiefly to be employed to that end.

William Byrd (1543–1623)
Psalmes, Sonets and Songs, 1588

16   Song is the daughter of prayer, and prayer is the companion of religion.

Vicomte de Chateaubriand (1768–1848)
Genius of Christianity, 1802

17   He was a rationalist, but he had to confess that he liked the ringing of church bells.

Anton Chekhov (1860–1904)
Note Book, trans 1921

18   In quires and places where they sing.

The Book of Common Prayer, 1662

19   [Of his translation of the Litany:] In mine opinion the song, that shall be made thereunto, would not be full of notes, but, as nearly as may be, for every syllable a note, so that it may be sung distinctly and devoutly.

Archbishop Cranmer (1489–1556)
Letter to Henry VIII, quoted in Phillips, *The Singing Church*, 1968

20   Modern church music is so constructed that the congregation cannot hear one distinct word.

Desiderius Erasmus (1466–1536)
In the early sixteenth century, quoted in Lee, *Music of the People*, 1970

21   Let all the world in ev'ry corner sing
     My God and King.
     The Church with psalms must shout,
     No door can keep them out:
     But above all, the heart
     Must bear the longest part.

George Herbert (1593–1633)
The Temple, 1633, 'Antiphon'

22   Just as the body of Christ was born of the Holy Spirit from the integrity of the Virgin Mary, just so is the song of praise according to the heavenly music radiated by the Holy Spirit in the Church. The body is truly the garment of the soul, which has a living voice, for that reason it is fitting that the body simultaneously with the soul repeatedly sing praises to God through the voice.

Hildegard of Bingen (1098–1179)
Letter, 1178, quoted in Neuls-Bates, *Women in Music*, 1982

23   We do not mean to prohibit the use of harmony occasionally on festive days . . . We approve such harmony as follows the melody at the intervals, for example, of the octave, fifth, and fourth, and such harmony as may be supported by the simple chant of the church; but we prescribe this condition, that the integrity of the chant itself remain undamaged, and that no well-established piece of music is altered as under this authority.

Pope John XXII (1244–1334)
Edict, 1325

24   He is verye often drunke and by means there of he hathe by unorderlye playing on the organs putt the quire out of time and disordered them.

From the archives of Lincoln Cathedral relating to Thomas Kingston, organist, 1599–1616

25   We have decided to follow the example of the prophets and the fathers of the church and write German hymns for the German people.

Martin Luther (1483–1546)
Table Talk, pub 1566

> 26   The playing of the merry organ,
>   Sweet singing in the choir.
>
> Anonymous carol
> *The Holly and the Ivy*

27   Our wisest mortals have decided that music should give zest to divine worship, so that those whom pious devotion to religious practice has led to the temple might remain there to delight in voices blending in harmony. If men take great pains to compose beautiful music for profane songs, they should devote at least as much thought to sacred song, nay, even more than to more worldly matters.

Giovanni Pierluigi da Palestrina (*c* 1525–94)
Dedication to Cardinal Carpi of his *First Book of Motets*, 1563

> 28   Some to church repair,
>   Not for the doctrine, but the music there.
>
> Alexander Pope (1688–1744)
> *Essay on Criticism*, 1711

29   That music itself is lawful, useful, and commendable, no man, no Christian dares deny, since the Scriptures, Fathers, and generally all Christians, all pagan authors extant, do with one consent aver it.

William Prynne (1600–69)
Histriomastix, 1632

30   Take a psalm, and bring hither the timbrel, the pleasant harp with the psaltery. Blow the trumpet in the new moon, in the time appointed, on our solemn feast day.

Bible, Authorized Version
Psalm 81, vv 2–3

31   Karolles, wrastling, or summer games,
Whosoever haunteth any swich shames
In cherche, other in cherchyerd,
Of sacrilege he may be aferd:
Of enterludes of singing,
Or tabor bete or other pypinge –
Whyle the prest stondeth at masse.

Richard Rolle (early fourteenth century)
Quoted in Lee, *Music of the People*, 1970

32   Once, for example, [Brother Vita of Lucca] sang so enchantingly that a nun who heard him threw herself from her window, in order to follow him. But she could not do this, for she broke her leg in the fall.

Fra Salimbene (1221–c 1290)
Chronicle, trans Bernini

33   I pant for music which is divine;
My heart in its thirst is a dying flower;
Pour forth the sound like enchanted wine,
Loosen the notes in a silver shower;
Like a herbless plain, for the gentle rain,
I gasp, I faint, till they wake again.

Percy Bysshe Shelley (1792–1822)
Music

34   Glorious the song, when God's the theme.

Cristopher Smart (1722–71)
Song to David, 1763

35   Among all the arts, music alone can be purely religious.

Madame de Staël, born Anne Louise Germaine Necker (1766–1817)
Corinne, 1807

36   The Church knew what the Psalmist knew: Music praises God. Music is well or better able to praise Him than the building of the church and all its decoration; it is the Church's greatest ornament.

Igor Stravinsky (1882–1971)
Conversations with Stravinsky, 1958

37   [On editing *The English Hymnal*:] Two years of close association with some of the best (as well as some of the worst) tunes in the world was a better musical education than any amount of sonatas and fugues.
Ralph Vaughan Williams (1872–1958)
Quoted in Machlis, *Introduction to Contemporary Music*, 1963

38   The most High has a decided taste for vocal music, provided it be lugubrious and gloomy enough.
Voltaire (1694–1778)
Dictionnaire philosophique, 1764

39   [George Herbert] would say that 'his time spent in prayer, and cathedral music, elevated his soul, and was his Heaven upon Earth'.
Izaak Walton (1593–1683)
Life of Herbert, 1670

40   The illusive and fascinating effect of musical sound in a Cathedral unfortunately serves to blunt criticism and casts a veil over defects otherwise unbearable. No coat of varnish can do for a picture what the exquisitely reverberating qualities can do for music. And then the organ. What a multitude of sins does that cover!
Samuel Sebastian Wesley (1810–76)
A few Words on Cathedral Music, 1849

41   Where through the long-drawn aisle and
            fretted vault
        The pealing anthem swells the note of praise.
        Thomas Gray (1716–71)
        Elegy Written in a Country Churchyard, 1750

227 RELIGIOUS MOVEMENTS AND MUSIC

1   Music religious hearts inspires,
        It wakes the soul, and lifts it high,
        And wings it with sublime desires,
        And fits it to bespeak the Deity.
        Joseph Addison (1672–1719)
        A Song for St Cecilia's Day

2   I consider music as a very innocent diversion, and perfectly compatible with the profession of a clergyman.

Jane Austen (1755–1817)
Pride and Prejudice, 1813

3   In truth we know by experience that song has great force and vigour to move and inflame the hearts of men to invoke and praise God with a more vehement and ardent zeal.

Jean Calvin (1509–64)
The Geneva Psalter, 1543

4   The music of the Gospel leads us home.

F.W. Faber (1814–63)
Oratory Hymns, 'The Pilgrims of the Night'

5   I do not see any good reason why the devil should have all the good tunes.

Rowland Hill (1744–1833)
Sermons

6   Music defiles the service of religion.

John of Salisbury (c 1160)
Quoted in *The Oxford History of Music*, 1929

7   Music is no different from opium. Music affects the human mind in a way that makes people think of nothing but music and sensual matters. Opium produces one kind of sensitivity and lack of energy, music another kind. A young person who spends most of his time with music is distracted from the serious and important affairs of life; he can get used to it in the same way as he can to drugs. Music is a treason to the country, a treason to our youth, and we should cut out all this music and replace it with something instructive.

Ayatollah Khomeini (1900–89)
Ramadan speech, 23 July 1979, quoted in Lebrecht, *Discord*, 1982

8   Except for theology, there is no art that can be placed in comparison with music.

Martin Luther (1483–1546)
Letters, 1530–41

9   I am not of the opinion that all the arts shall be crushed to earth and perish through the Gospel, as some bigoted persons pretend, but would willingly see them all, and especially music, servants of Him who gave and created them.

Martin Luther (1483–1546)
Wittenberg Gesangbuch, 1524, Foreword

10   King David and King Solomon
      Led merry, merry lives,
      With many, many lady friends
      And many, many wives;
      But when old age crept over them,
      With many, many qualms,
      King Solomon wrote the Proverbs
      And King David wrote the Psalms.

James Ball Naylor
David and Solomon

11   That which is always accompanied with effeminate lust-provoking music is doubtless inexpedient and unlawful unto Christians.

William Prynne (1600–69)
Histriomastix, 1632

12   You can sometimes see a man, with his mouth wide open, stop making a sound, as if to imitate silence; at other times he simulates the agony of a dying man or the delirium of the sick; his whole body is agitated; his shoulders shake, his lips are contorted—and these ridiculous antics are what they call religion! These lascivious gestures and harlot's tones are more suited to the theatre than to the church . . .

Aelred de Rievaulx (1109–66)
Speculum caritatis, c 1150

13   I am highly susceptible to the force of all truly religious music, especially to the music of my own church, the church of Shelley, Michelangelo, and Beethoven.

George Bernard Shaw (1856–1950)

14   Listed into the cause of sin,
      Why should a good be evil?
      Music, alas! too long has been
      Pressed to obey the Devil.
      Drunken, or lewd, or light, the lay
      Flower to the soul's undoing;
      Widened and strewed with flowers the way
      Down to eternal ruin.

Charles Wesley (1707–89)
The True Use of Music, 1749

228 COMPOSERS AND RELIGION

1   The end and goal of thorough bass is nothing but the honour of God.
Johann Sebastian Bach (1685–1750)

2   The Bible tells us with wonderful consistency the exact opposite of
the truth of this world: for it is not that God has made man in his own
image and likeness, but that man made God after his image.
Béla Bartók (1881–1945)
Letter to Stefi Geyer, 1907

3   If I ever crossed myself, it would signify 'In the name of Nature, Art
and Science'.
Béla Bartók (1881–1945)
Ibid

4   When I open my eyes I must sigh, for what I see is contrary to my
religion, and I must despise the world which does not know that music is
a higher revelation than all wisdom and philosophy.
Ludwig van Beethoven (1770–1827)
Quoted by Bettina von Arnim in a letter to Goethe, 1810

5   There is nothing higher than to approach the Godhead more nearly
than other mortals and by means of that contact to spread the rays of the
Godhead through the human race.
Ludwig van Beethoven (1770–1827)
Letter to Archduke Rudolph, 1823

6   Music is edifying, for from time to time it sets the soul in operation.
John Cage (1912–   )
Silence, 1961

7   You'll never convince me that music will be any good until it gets rid
of the Jesus element. It has paralysed music all along.
Frederick Delius (1862–1934)
Quoted in Fenby, *Delius as I knew him*, 1936

8   I always said God was against art and I still believe it.
Edward Elgar (1857–1934)
Quoted in Moore, *Edward Elgar: A Creative Life*, 1984

9   In whatever we begin we must keep our integrity, directing our acts
to both centres. Let us thank the earth. Let us praise heaven.
Paul Hindemith (1895–1963)
Mathis der Maler, 1935

10   In every creature a spark of God.
Leoš Janáček (1854–1928)
Epigraph for the score of his last opera, *From the House of the Dead*, 1928

11   I was born out of due time in the sense that by temperament and
talent I should have been more suited for the life of a small Bach, living
in anonymity and composing regularly for an established service and for
God.
Igor Stravinsky (1882–1971)
Dialogues and a Diary, 1963

---

229   LIFE AND DEATH

---

1   Ah, make the most of what we yet may
          spend,
      Before we too into the Dust descend;
      Dust into Dust, and under Dust, to lie,
      Sans Wine, sans Song, sans Singer, and – sans
          End!

   The Rubáiyát of Omar Khayyám, trans Edward Fitzgerald (1809–93)

2   O, whar shill we go w'en de great day
          comes;
      Wid de blowin' er de trumpits en de bangin'
          er de drums?

   Joel Chandler Harris (1848–1908)
   Uncle Remus: His Songs and Sayings

3   Thaw evr'y breast
    Melt evr'y eye with woe
    Here's dissolution
    By the hand of Death!
    To dirt, to water turned
    The fairest Snow
    O the King's Trumpeter
    Has lost his Breath.

Epitaph for Valentine Snow (d 1770) for whom Handel
wrote the trumpet obbligati in *Messiah*, quoted in Spiegl,
A Small Book of Grave Humour, 1971

4   This city is a cemetery dotted with memorial stones. I live only in the
past. Everywhere I find reminders of friends or enemies who are no
more: here I met Balzac for the last time: there I walked with Paganini:
in another spot I accompanied the Duchesse d'Abrantes, a silly good
woman: this is the house where Madame de Girardin lived, a clever
woman who thought me a lunatic: this is the pavement where I talked to
Adolphe Nourrit: that empty house over there is Rachel's: and so on,
and so on. They are all dead. So many people dead! Why aren't we dead
yet?

Hector Berlioz (1803–69)
To Princes Carolyne von Sayn-Wittgenstein, Paris, 22 January 1859

5   Behold, I shew you a mystery. We shall not all sleep, but we shall all
be changed, in a moment, in the twinkling of an eye, at the last trump: for
the trumpet shall sound, and the dead shall be raised incorruptible, and
we shall be changed.

Bible, Authorized Version
I Corinthians, Ch 15, vv 51–2

6   Everyone has to have some experience to assure himself life is worth
living.

Johannes Brahms (1833–97)

7   I will be patient and proud, and
    soberly acquiesce.
  Give me the keys. I feel for the common
    chord again,
  Sliding by semitones, till I sink to the
    minor – yes,
  And I blunt it into a ninth, and I stand on
    alien ground,
  Surveying awhile the heights I rolled from
    into the deep;
  Which, hark, I have dared and done, for my
    resting-place is found,
  The C major of this life; so, now I will try
    to sleep.

Robert Browning (1812–89)
Abt Vogler, 1864

8   And all the trumpets sounded for him on the other side.

John Bunyan (1628–88)
The Pilgrim's Progress, 1678–84

9   [Of the beginning of Mozart's Piano Concerto No 23 in A major:]
If any of us were to die and then wake hearing it we should know at
once that (after all) we had got to the right place.

Neville Cardus (1888–1975)
In the *Manchester Guardian,* 1938

10   [Of music:] Nothing among the utterances allowed to man is felt to
be so divine. It brings us near to the Infinite.

Thomas Carlyle (1795–1881)
The Opera

11   One's work should be a salute to life.

Pablo Casals (1876–1973)

12   Since I am coming to that holy room,
  Where, with thy quire of Saints for evermore,
  I shall be made thy Music, as I come
  I tune the instrument here at the door,
  And what must I do then, think here before.

John Donne (1571?–1631)
Hymn to God my God in My Sickness

13   In that house they shall swell, where there shall be . . . no noise nor silence, but one equal music.
John Donne (1571?–1631)
Sermon

14   As from the power of sacred lays
     The spheres began to move,
     And sung the great Creator's praise
     To all the Blest above;
     So, when the last and dreadful hour
     This crumbling pageant shall devour,
     The Trumpet shall be heard on high,
     The dead shall live, the living die,
     And Music shall untune the sky.
     John Dryden (1631–1700)
     A Song for St Cecilia's Day, 1687

15   We're not interested in writing for posterity. We just want it to sound good right now!
Duke Ellington (1899–1974)
Quoted in Jewell, *Duke,* 1977

16   It has been said that my *Requiem* does not express the fear of death and someone has called it a lullaby of death. But it is thus that I see death: as a happy deliverance, an aspiration towards happiness above . . .
Gabriel Fauré (1845–1924)
Quoted in *Comoedia,* 1954

17   When I am no longer here you will hear it said of my works: 'After all, that was nothing much to write home about!' You must not let that hurt or depress you. It is the way of the world . . . There is always a moment of oblivion. But all that is of no importance. I did what I could . . . now . . . let God judge!
Gabriel Fauré (1845–1924)
Last words to his sons, quoted in Fauré-Fremiet, *Gabriel Fauré,* 1957

18   Now I'll have *eine kleine Pause.*
Kathleen Ferrier (1912–53)
Shortly before her death, quoted in Moore, *Am I Too Loud?,* 1962

19   If you wait a little I shall be able to tell you from personal experience.
Christoph Willibald von Gluck (1714–87)
To Salieri as to whether a bass or tenor should sing Christ in *The Last Judgement,* quoted in Cooper, *Gluck,* 1935

20   Music of God, so powerful and so sweet,
       Why do you seek me out here in the dust?
       Johann Wolfgang von Goethe (1749–1832)
       Faust, 1808, Pt I, Sc I, trans MacDonald

21   And at the end I see: the great harmony is death. To effect it, we
must die. In life it has no place.
Paul Hindemith (1895–1963)
Die Harmonie der Welt, 1957

22   A few can touch the magic string,
       And noisy Fame is proud to win them:–
       Alas for those that never sing,
       But die with all their music in them!
       Oliver Wendell Holmes (1809–94)
       The Voiceless

23   Take a music-bath once or twice a week for a few seasons, and you
will find that it is to the soul what the water-bath is to the body.
Oliver Wendell Holmes (1809–94)
Over the teacups

24   There is music in heaven because in music there is no self-will.
Music goes on certain laws and rules. Man did not make these rules of
music, he has only found them out. And if he be self-willed and break
them, there is an end to his music instantly; all he brings out is discord
and ugly sounds.
Charles Kingsley (1819–75)
From a Christian sermon

25   Your music – dear me, it is a sort of luggage van to the kingdom of
heaven.
Franz von Lenbach (1836–1904)
Remark to Wagner

26   Dante? Bah! Beatrice? Bah! The Dantes create the Beatrices, and
the real ones die at eighteen.
Franz Liszt (1811–86)

27   What is life but a series of preludes to that unknown song whose
first solemn note is sounded by death?
Alphonse de Lamartine (1790–1869)
Preface to *Les Préludes*, paraphrased by Liszt

28 He is dead, the sweet musician!
  He the sweetest of all singers!
  He has gone from us for ever,
  He has moved a little nearer
  To the Master of all music,
  To the Master of all singing!
  O my brother, Chibiabos!

  Henry Wadsworth Longfellow (1807–82)
  Hiawatha's Lamentation

29 But wheesht!–Whatna music is this,
  While the win's haud their breath?
  –*The Moon has a wunnerfu' finger*
  For the back-lill o' Death!

  Hugh MacDiarmid (1892–1978)
  Prelude to Moon Music, 1925
  [back-lill=thumb on bagpipe chanter]

30 When music sounds, all that I was I am
  Ere to the haunt of brooking dust I came.

  Walter de la Mare (1873–1956)
  Music

31 God hath men who enter Paradise through their flutes and drums.

Mohammed (*c* 570–632)

32 As death, strictly speaking, is the true goal of our lives, I have for some years past been making myself so familiar with this truest and best friend of man that its aspect has not only ceased to appal me, but I find it very soothing and comforting! And I thank my God that He has vouchsafed me the happiness of an opportunity (you will understand me) to recognize it as the *key* to our true bliss. I never lie down to sleep without reflecting that (young as I am) I may perhaps not see another day–yet none of those who know me can say that I am morose or melancholy in society–and I thank my Creator every day for this happiness and wish from the bottom of my heart that all my fellow men might share it.

Wolfgang Amadeus Mozart (1756–91)
Letter to his father, 1 April 1787

33 Yet beauty who indulged the swan
  At death completes her with a song
  And Paradise till we are there
  Is in these measured lengths of air.

  Peter Porter (1929–)
  Three Poems for Music

34   And I heard a voice from heaven, as the voice of many waters, and as the voice of a great thunder: and I heard the voice of harpers harping with their harps:

   And they sung as it were a new song . . . and no man could learn that song but the hundred and forty-four thousand, which were redeemed from the earth.

Bible, Authorized Version
Revelation, Ch 14, vv 2–3

> 35   Art is long, and Time is fleeting,
>   And our hearts, though stout and brave,
>   Still, like muffled drums, are beating
>   Funeral marches to the grave.
>
> Henry Wadsworth Longfellow (1807–82)
> *A Psalm of Life*

36   Whether to the right, whether to the left, whether forwards or backwards, up hill or down dale—a man has to go ahead, without questioning what lies before him or what behind.

Arnold Schoenberg (1874–1951)
Last words of *Die Jakobsleiter*, 1915–22

> 37   Cause the musicians play me that sad
>   note
>   I named my knell, whilst I sit meditating
>   On that celestial harmony I go to.
>   (Queen Katherine)
>
> William Shakespeare (1564–1616)
> *Henry VIII*, 1613, Act IV, Sc II

> 38   Sing again, with your dear voice
>   revealing
>   A Tone
>   Of some world far from ours,
>   Where music and moonlight and feeling
>   Are one.
>
> Percy Bysshe Shelley (1792–1822)
> *To Jane: The Keen Stars were Twinkling*

39   [After a week in intensive care, 1982:] It was all very quiet. Didn't see a soul, not even Ben Britten's. There was a fanfare, but it wasn't one of mine. Bliss, I suppose.

William Walton (1902–83)
Quoted in *The Observer*, 1983

40   [On Schubert's premature death:] A man is not taken away before he has said all he has to say.

Hugo Wolf (1860–1903)
Quoted in Rolland, *Essays on Music*, 1948, 'Hugo Wolf'

CRITICS AND LISTENERS

All musicians and listeners should be critics in the best sense, that is – to paraphrase Matthew Arnold – endeavouring to learn and propogate the best that is known or thought in the musical world. Professional critics (those who brush the clothes of their betters, as Bacon put it) do come in for some stick though. Thanks to technology we in the developed world have more music around us at the flick of a switch than ever before: wise and critical listening is thus ever more needful, lest we be deluged by 'muzak'.

230   THE ART OF LISTENING

1   The musick is not in the instrument, nor in the ear. Only the stroke or motion of the instrument causing a corresponding motion or undulation in the air, and this striking on the ear, and thence the auditory nerves, doth by the law or word of the Creator, raise those delightful sensations in the Soul, we call sounds. The instruments and their furniture, we see, are mere matter, wood, metal, or string, the work of the craftsman; which neither feel, nor hear, nor of themselves move nor send forth any sound. And the ear, though it seems to hear, and is the work of the Divine artificer, is still but an instrument; and though of finer texture and materials than the former, is in itself altogether as insensible. But by the co-operation of both these instruments, natural and artificial, God works in us to hear all we hear and enjoy as musick.

Thomas Bisse DD (d 1731)
Sermon, 7 September 1726

2   To know whether you are enjoying a piece of music or not you must see whether you find yourself looking at the advertisements of Pears' soap at the end of the programme.

Samuel Butler (1835–1902)
Note-Books, pub 1912

3   Music has always been interwoven with my life – so much that I can hardly imagine the one without the other. I am not sure that this is altogether a good thing, but it is too late now to change. With the passing of time I have learned to wean myself away from certain musical influences, and especially not to think of music as a refuge in times of trouble. On the contrary, it is just at those times that I avoid it. I no longer want to hear music except when I am serene and, if possible, happy. But to coddle one's melancholy by feeding it with the accumulated sadness of the Nocturnes – none of that!

Julian Green (1900–)
Journal, 1938

4   The suspended cadences in the adagios of Corelli's 'church' sonatas were ceremonious promises of love, full of renunciation; the allegros in Bach, Vivaldi and Bach-Vivaldi represented sexual excitement. In the closing chorus of the *St Matthew Passion* we, the chosen children, sat down in actual tears after the long evening of lamentation.

Hans Werner Henze (1926–)
Music and Politics, 1982, 'German Music in the 1940s and 1950s'

5   I wonder who is the sadder in this world of hunger, he who sings or he who listens?

Edmondo de Amicis (1848–1908)
Mendicant Melody, trans Brooks, 1905

> 6   Come, follow me into the realm of music.
> Here is the gate
> Which separates the earthly from the eternal.
> It is not like stepping into a strange
>   country
> As we once did. We soon learn to know
>   everything there
> And nothing surprises us any more. Here
> Our wonderment will have no end, and yet
> From the very beginning we feel at home.

At first you hear nothing, because everything
   sounds.
But now you begin to distinguish between
   them. Listen.
Each star has its rhythm and each world its
   beat.
The heart of each separate living thing
Beats differently, according to its needs,
And all the beats are in harmony.

Your inner ear grows sharper. Do you hear
The deep notes and the high notes?
They are immeasurable in space and infinite
   as to number.
Like ribbons, undreamt-of scales lead from
   one world to another,
Steadfast and eternally moved.

Hugh MacDiarmid (1892–1978)
In Memoriam James Joyce, 1955, 'Plaited like the Generations of Man',
after a description of music by Busoni in a letter to his wife, 3 March 1910

7   A musical experience needs three human beings at least. It requires
a composer, a performer, and a listener; and unless these three take part
together there is no musical experience . . . Music demands more from
the listener than simply the possession of a tape-machine or a transistor
radio. It demands some preparation, some effort, a journey to a special
place, saving up for a ticket, some homework on the programme
perhaps, some clarification of the ears and sharpening of the instincts. It
demands as much effort on the listener's part as the other two corners of
the triangle, this holy triangle of composer, performer and listener.

Benjamin Britten (1913–76)
On receiving the First Aspen Award, 31 July 1964

8   Composers tend to assume that everyone loves music. Surprisingly
enough, everyone doesn't.

Aaron Copland (1900–90)
In *The New York Times* magazine, 1964

9   True music is for the ear alone; a fine voice is the most universal thing that can be figured . . . Accordingly he always used to shut his eyes while hearing music; thereby to concentrate his whole being on the single pure enjoyment of the ear.

Johann Wolfgang von Goethe (1749–1832)
Wilhelm Meister, 1795–6

10   The other arts persuade us, but music takes us by surprise.

Eduard Hanslick (1825–1904)
The Beautiful in Music, 1854

11   Great art presupposes the alert mind of the educated listener.

Arnold Schoenberg (1874–1951)
Memories and Commentaries, 1960

12   Only the developing composer can compose for the developing listener.

Arnold Schoenberg (1874–1951)
Quoted in Walker, *Anatomy of Musical Criticism*, 1966

13   He has Van Gogh's ear for music.

Orson Welles (1915–85)
Attributed (also to others)

14   Face the music.

Anonymous (nineteenth century)

15   We can face the music together.

Howard Dietz (1896–1983)
Dancing in the Dark, popular song, 1931

16   What I love best about music is the women who listen to it.

Jules de Goncourt (1830–70)

17 Composers do not often hear the music that is being played; it only serves as an impulse for something quite different—for the creation of music that only lives in their imagination. It is a sort of schizophrenia— we are listening to something and at the same time creating something else.

Witold Lutoslawski (1913–)
Quoted in Stucky, *Lutoslawski and his Music*, 1981

18 *Lorenzo:* Come, ho, and wake Diana with a hymn;
             With sweetest touches pierce your mistress' ear,
             And draw her home with music.
   Jessica: I am never merry when I hear sweet music.
   Lorenzo: The reason is, your spirits are attentive . . .

William Shakespeare (1564–1616)
The Merchant of Venice, 1597–8, Act V, Sc I

19 *All:*   The music, ho!
   Cleopatra: Let it alone; let's to billiards.

William Shakespeare (1564–1616)
Antony and Cleopatra, 1606–7, Act II, Sc V

20 *Berinthia:*   Your lordship, I suppose, is fond of music?
   Lord Foppington: Oh, passionately, on Tuesdays and Saturdays for
                     then there is always the best of company, and one
                     is not expected to undergo the fatigue of
                     listening.

Richard Brinsley Sheridan (1751–1816)
A Trip to Scarborough, Act II, Sc I

21 Listen to music religiously, as if it were the last strain you might hear.

Henry David Thoreau (1817–62)

22 If one hears bad music, it is one's duty to drown it by one's conversation.

Oscar Wilde (1854–1900)
The Picture of Dorian Gray, 1891

231 CRITICS

1   When an impecunious music critic died in Vienna, his colleagues made a round of local musicians to raise money for the funeral.
'How much is my share?' asked one of them.
'Thirty kronen,' was the reply.
'Here's sixty kronen,' said the musician.
'Bury two music critics.'

Recounted by Nicolas Slonimsky (1894–)
A Thing or Two about Music, 1948

2   How seldom do we meet with a proper amount of sympathy, knowledge, honesty and courage in a critic – four qualities they ought, in any event, to possess to some extent. It is sad indeed for the world of music that criticism, in many respects so useful, should often be the occupation of persons in no way endowed with these qualities.

Carl Philipp Emanuel Bach (1714–88)
Autobiography, 1773

3   6 December 1950. President Truman, infuriated by the disparaging review by Paul Hume in the *Washington Post* of a song recital by Truman's daughter Margaret, dispatches a letter to him written in longhand on White House stationery, as follows: 'Mr Hume: I have just read your lousy review of Margaret's concert. I've come to the conclusion that you are an eight-ulcer man on four-ulcer pay . . . Some day I hope to meet you. When that happens, you'll need a new nose, a lot of beefsteak for black eyes, and perhaps a supporter below.'

Nicolas Slonimsky (1894–)
Music Since 1900, 1949

4   Successes are made by the public, not by the critics.

Hugo von Hofmannsthal (1874–1929)
Letter to Richard Strauss, 23 July 1911

5 ,Can you remember any tunes from this comic-opera, this so-called original novelty? Can you call it dramatic in any sense whatsoever? Story and music are 'staged simultaneously', but in reality each is quite independent of the other. One of two things can be done – either write new music to the libretto, or write a new libretto to the music – this so-called music, filled with menacing obscurities, desperate screams and dagger stabs. It is true that one sometimes laughed, but this was at the absurdity of the story, nothing more. The Overture, with its instability of key sense and wavering harmony gave proof of the composer's genius – to induce deafness.

Leoš Janáček (1854–1928)
Reviewing *The Bridegrooms* by Karel Kovařovic (1862–1920), *Hudební Listy*, 1887, trans Erik Chisholm.
  Kovařovic later became director of the National Theatre in Prague, where for a time he rejected Janáček's *Jenůfa*

6 That the affirmative gestures of the reprise in some of Beethoven's greatest symphonies assume the force of crushing repression, of an authoritarian 'That's how it is' … that is the tribute Beethoven was forced to pay to the ideological character whose spell extends even to the most sublime music ever to mean freedom by continued un-freedom.

T.W. Adorno (1903–69)
Introduction to the Sociology of Music, 1959

7 The critic – the honest and intelligent critic – writes only when he has ideas, when he intends to clear an issue, fight a system, give praise or blame. He has an incentive for his view, for praising or condemning. The unfortunate journalist, obliged to write on anything that happens, only desires to reach the end of a task that has been forced upon him.

Hector Berlioz (1803–69)
The section in his *Memoirs* describing his new vocation is headed 'Calamity – I become a critic!'

8 [Of critics:] Poor devils! Where do they come from? At what age are they sent to the slaughter house? What is done with their bones? Where do such animals pasture in the daytime? Do they have females, and young? How many of them handled the brush before being reduced to the broom?

Hector Berlioz (1803–69)
Les Grotesques de la musique, 1859

9 Musical criticism, even of the very best, seems to attract little public attention and has practically no influence.

Havergal Brian (1876–1972)
In *Musical Opinion*, 1931

10   With him [Hanslick] one cannot fight. One can only approach him with petitions.

Anton Bruckner (1824–96)
Letter to J.A. Vergeiner

11   Musical discussions are conducted in Berlin with more heat and animosity than elsewhere. Of course, as there are more theorists than practitioners in this city, there are more critics too.

Charles Burney (1726–1814)
Present State of Music in Germany, 1773

12   Regrettably, one can pay little regard either to the factual or to the evaluatory content of musical criticism in Britain today, with one or perhaps three exceptions. No doubt the very bad conditions of employment are responsible for the fact that only musicians who are in the very most deplorable material circumstances, amateurs who are not dependent upon the work for their existence, or professional journalists, who from mere chance have reported concerts instead of football matches, gravitate to this department.

Alan Bush (1900–   )
Letter, 2 August 1961, author's collection

13   Criticism could be an art if it were practised under the necessary conditions of free judgment. But it is now no more than a trade. It must be said in passing that the so-called artists have contributed a great deal to this state of affairs.

Claude Debussy (1862–1918)
Letter to Varèse, 12 February 1911

14   If they will criticize, they shall do it out of their own *fond*; but let them first be assured that their ears are nice; for there is neither writing nor judgment on this subject without that good quality.

John Dryden (1631–1700)
Albion and Albanius, Preface

15   The worst of musical criticism in this country is that there is so much of it.

Edward Elgar (1857–1934)
Quoted in Cumberland, *Set Down in Malice,* 1919

16   You know, the critics never change; I'm still getting the same notices I used to get as a child. They tell me I play very well for my age.

Mischa Elman (1891–1967)
In his seventies, quoted in Hopkins, *Music all around me,* 1967

17   You make as good music as a wheelbarrow.
Thomas Fuller (1608–61)
Gnomologia, pub 1732

18   I have hitherto nearly always fared badly with the so-called critics. Where there was sympathy there was no comprehension, and for so-called comprehension without sympathy I do not give a penny.
Edvard Grieg (1843–1907)
Letter to Henry T. Finck, 1900

19   When I wish to annihilate, then I do annihilate.
Eduard Hanslick (1825–1904)
Attributed

20   The essence of music is revelation; it does not admit of exact reckoning, and the true criticism of music remains an empirical art.
Heinrich Heine (1797–1856)
Letters on the French Stage, 1837

21   The critical faculty is as important, as necessary, as divine, as the imaginative one: it is impossible to overrate the real critic.
Gustav Holst (1874–1934)
Quoted in Imogen Holst, *Holst*, 1974

22   A sympathetic critic's disapproval is the most interesting and stimulating experience I know.
Gustav Holst (1874–1934)
Quoted in *ibid*

23   Music remains the only art, the last sanctuary, wherein originality may reveal itself in the face of fools and not pierce their mental opacity.
James G. Huneker (1860–1920)
Iconoclasts, 1905

24   The average English critic is a don *manqué*, hopelessly parochial when not teutonophile, over whose desk must surely hang the motto (presumably in Gothic lettering) 'Above all no enthusiasm'.
Constant Lambert (1905–51)
Quoted in *Opera*, 1950

25   What you said hurt me very much. I cried all the way to the bank.
Liberace (1919–87)
Reacting to his critics

26   Keep on good terms with the critics! Visit the gentlemen now and then! Consider that you cannot behave with the 'dignity of man' in a kennel, but that you have only to take care that the watchdogs leave you alone.

Gustav Mahler (1860–1911)
Letter to Bruno Walter, 1897

27   If the artist gravely writes,
        To sleep it will beguile.
        If the artist gaily writes,
        It is a vulgar style.

        If the artist writes at length,
        How sad his hearers' lot!
        If the artist briefly writes,
        No man will care one jot.

        If an artist simply writes,
        A fool he's said to be.
        If an artist deeply writes,
        He's mad; 'tis plain to see.

        In whatsoever way he writes
        He can't please every man;
        Therefore let an artist write
        How he likes and can.

        Mendelssohn's response to the sneers of the press, 1826,
        quoted and trans by George Grove, *Dictionary of Music and
        Musicians*, 1878–89

28   The lot of critics is to be remembered by what they failed to understand.

George Moore (1852–1933)
Impressions and Opinions, 1891

29   I pay no attention whatever to anybody's praise or blame …
I simply follow my own feelings.

Wolfgang Amadeus Mozart (1756–91)
Letter to his father, 1781

30   [Of criticism:] The most useless occupation in the world.

Giacomo Puccini (1858–1924)
Attributed

31   Critics love mediocrity.

Giacomo Puccini (1858–1924)

32   I am sitting in the smallest room of my house. I have your review before me. In a moment it will be behind me.
Max Reger (1873–1916)
To a critic

33   *Monsieur et cher ami: Vous n'êtes qu'un cul, mais un cul sans musique.*
Erik Satie (1866–1925)
Postcard to a critic

34   Last year, I gave several lectures on 'Intelligence and Musicality in Animals'. Today, I shall speak to you about 'Intelligence and Musicality in Critics'. The subject is very similar.
Erik Satie (1866–1925)
Lecture, 'In Praise of Critics', 1918

35   A review, however favourable, can be ridiculous at the same time if the critic lacks average intelligence, as is not seldom the case.
Franz Schubert (1797–1828)
Letter, 1825

36   Pay no attention to what the critics say; there has never been a statue set up in honour of a critic.
Jean Sibelius (1865–1957)

37   There was a review by Irving Kolodin which noted that Korngold's Violin Concerto had more corn than gold; and there was a remark of an anonymous critic that a performance of Chopin's *Minute* Waltz gave the listeners a bad quarter of an hour.
Recounted by Nicolas Slonimsky (1894–   )
A Thing or Two about Music, 1948

38   I had another dream the other day about music critics. They were small and rodent-like with padlocked ears, as if they had stepped out of a painting by Goya.
Igor Stravinsky (1882–1971)
Quoted in *Evening Standard*, London, 29 October 1969

39   Nobody is ever patently right about music.
Virgil Thomson (1896–1989)
Quoted in Barzun (ed), *Pleasures of Music*, 1952

40   The general and musical culture shown in Hanslick's writings represents one of the unlovelier forms of parasitism; that which, having the wealth to collect *objets d'art* and the birth and education to talk amusingly, does not itself attempt a stroke of artistic work, does not dream of revising a first impression, experiences the fine arts entirely as the pleasures of a gentleman, and then pronounces judgment as if the expression of its opinion were a benefit and a duty to society.

Donald Francis Tovey (1875–1940)
Essays in Musical Analysis, 1935

41   [Of critics:] Misbegotten abortions.

Ralph Vaughan Williams (1872–1958)
Letter to Holst, 1930

42   You cannot have critics with standards; you can only have *music* with standards which critics may observe.

Alan Walker (1930–)
An Anatomy of Musical Criticism, 1968

43   I have become so used to being slated by those critics, that I felt there must be something wrong when the worms turned on some praise.

William Walton (1902–83)
Letter to Dario and Dorle Soria on the favourable reception of his opera *The Bear,* 1967

---

232   AUDIENCES

---

1   He who pays the piper calls the tune.

English proverb

2   Give the piper a penny to play, and twopence to leave off.

Thomas Fuller (1608–61)
Gnomologia, pub 1732

3   Why in the name of heaven and all its angels must the searching fire of enthusiasm always come out through the hands and feet? Why must there be clapping and stamping?

Hugo Wolf (1860–1903)
Quoted in Barzun, *Pleasures of Music,* 1952

4 [To test the acoustics at his new Bayreuth theatre] soldiers from the local garrison were brought in to squat on the floor and Wagner was moved to describe them as the ideal audience on three counts:
1 They were all in their places before the music began
2 They did not talk or fidget while it was being played
3 When it was over they made no pretence of having understood anything of what they had seen or heard and so refrained from airing their opinions about it.

Robert Hartford
Bayreuth: The Early Years, 1980

5 Walking with a friend one day Kreisler passed a large fish-shop where on the front slab, arranged in a row, lay a fine catch of codfish, with their mouths wide open and glassy eyes staring. Kreisler suddenly stopped, looked at them, and clutching his friend violently by the arm exclaimed: 'Heavens, they remind me – I should have been playing at a concert!'

Fritz Kreisler (1875–1962)
Quoted in Shore, *The Orchestra Speaks*, 1938

6 [On a Beethoven chamber concert in Paris:] Five-sixths, or nine-tenths, of the audience were of course women. It seemed to me that they went there for a pleasure that ought to be called voluptuous. You could see them shiver under the ecstacy. But when some particularly expressive sweetness drew an involuntary cry from persons in the audience, such cries were always masculine. The artificiality, and insecurity of this idle world, on which musicians and painters live, strikes me more and more.

Arnold Bennett (1867–1931)
Journals, 14 May 1907

7 In olden times the feeling for nobility was always maintained in the art of music, and all its elements skilfully retained the orderly beauty appropriate to them. Today, however, people take up music in a haphazard and irrational manner. The musicians of our day set as the goal of their art success with their audiences.

Athenaeus (*c* AD 200)
The Deipnosophists

8 Convicts are the best audiences I ever played for.

Johnny Cash (1932–)
Attributed

9   Naldi, a good fellow, remarked to me once at a concert, that I did not seem much interested with a piece of Rossini's which had just been performed. I said, it sounded to me like nonsense verses. But I could scarcely contain myself when a thing of Beethoven's followed.

Samuel Taylor Coleridge (1772–1834)
Table Talk, 1830

10   People don't very much like things that are beautiful – they are so far from their nasty little minds.

Claude Debussy (1862–1918)
Letter to Pierre Louÿs, 1900

11   Everything that Liszt says is so striking. For instance, in one place where V was playing the melody rather feebly, Liszt suddenly took his seat at the piano and said 'When *I* play, I always play for the people in the gallery (by the gallery he meant the cock-loft, where the rabble always sit, and where the places cost next to nothing), so that those persons who pay only five groschens for their seat also hear something.'

Amy Fay (1844–1928)
Music Study in Germany, 1880

12   Audiences have kept me alive.

Judy Garland (1922–69)
Quoted in Palmer, *All You Need is Love*, 1976

13   Let's Ban Applause!

Glenn Gould (1932–82)
Title of essay

14   The Public doesn't *want* to be asked to work: it doesn't seek to understand: it wants to *feel*, and to *feel immediately*.

Charles Gounod (1818–93)
Letter to Mme Charles Rhone, 1862

15   When people hear good music, it makes them homesick for something they never had, and never will have.

Edgar Watson Howe (1853–1937)
Country Town Sayings

16   Will people in the cheaper seats clap your hands? All the rest of you, if you'll just rattle your jewellery . . .

John Lennon (1940–80)
At the Royal Command Performance, 1963

17   The indifference of the public is what's depressing. Enthusiasm, or vehement protest, shows that your work really lives.

Darius Milhaud (1892–1974)
On the protests about his music for *Protée*, 1920, quoted in Harding, *The Ox on the Roof,* 1972

18   'This *must* be music,' said he, 'of the *spears*,
     For I'm curst if each note of it doesn't run through one!'

Thomas Moore (1779–1852)
The Fudge Family, 1818.

19   A great deal of noise . . . is always appropriate at the end of an act. The more noise the better, and the shorter the better, so that the audience has no time to cool down with their applause.

Wolfgang Amadeus Mozart (1756–91)
Letter, 1781

20   The excellence of music is to be measured by pleasure. But the pleasure must not be that of chance persons; the fairest music is that which delights the best and best-educated, and especially that which delights the one man who is pre-eminent in virtue and education.

Plato (*c* 427–347 BC)
Laws

21   The andante had just ended on a phrase filled with a tenderness to which I had entirely surrendered. There followed, before the next movement, a short interval during which the performers laid down their instruments and the audience exchanged impressions. A duke, in order to show that he knew what he was talking about, declared: 'It's a difficult thing, to play well.' Other more agreeable people chatted for a moment with me. But what were their words, which like every human and external word left me so indifferent, compared with the heavenly phrase of music with which I had just been communing? I was truly like an angel, who, fallen from the inebriating bliss of paradise, subsides into the most humdrum reality. And, just as certain creatures are the last surviving testimony to a form of life which nature has discarded, I wondered whether music might not be the unique example of what might have been – if the invention of language, the formation of words, the analysis of ideas had not intervened – the means of communication between souls.

Marcel Proust (1871–1922)
The Captive, trans Scott Moncrieff and Kilmartin

22   It is often by seeing and hearing musical works (operas and other good musical compositions), rather than by rules, that taste is formed.
Jean Philippe Rameau (1683–1764)
Le Nouveau Système de musique théorique, 1726

23   The current state of music presents a variety of solutions in search of a problem, the problem being to find somebody left to listen.
Ned Rorem (1923–   )
Music from Inside Out, 1967

24   What most people relish is hardly music; it is rather a drowsy reverie relieved by nervous thrills.
George Santayana (1863–1952)
Life of Reason, 1905–6

25   I know two kinds of audience only—one coughing and one not coughing.
Artur Schnabel (1882–1951)
My Life and Music, 1961

26   The throwing of oranges seems to have been a more or less recognized means of expressing disappointment in the eighteenth century. Pergolesi was once hit full in the face with one at the first performance of one of his operas.
Percy A. Scholes (1877–1958)
The Oxford Companion to Music, 1955, 'Applause'

27   [Applause:] The custom of showing one's pleasure at beautiful music by immediately following it with an ugly noise.
Percy A. Scholes (1877–1958)
Ibid

28   At every one of those concerts in England you will find rows of weary people who are there, not because they really like classical music, but because they think they ought to like it.
George Bernard Shaw (1856–1950)
Man and Superman, 1902, Act III

29   The only reality in music is the state of mind which it induces in the listener.
Stendhal (1783–1842)
Life of Rossini, 1824

30 A painter paints his pictures on canvas. But musicians paint their pictures on silence. We provide the music, and you provide the silence.
Leopold Stokowski (1882–1977)
Addressing a Carnegie Hall audience

31 I never understood the need for a 'live' audience. My music, because of its extreme quietude, would be happiest with a dead one.
Igor Stravinsky (1882–1971)
Quoted in *London Magazine*, 1967

32 Men profess to be lovers of music, but for the most part they give no evidence in their opinions and lives that they have heard it. It would not leave them narrow-minded and bigoted.
Henry David Thoreau (1817–62)
Journal, 5 August 1851

33 I have seen all sorts of audiences – at theatres, operas, concerts, lectures, sermons, funerals – but none which was twin to the Wagner audience of Bayreuth for fixed and reverential attention. Absolute attention and petrified retention to the end of the act of the attitude assumed at the beginning of it. You detect no movement in the solid mass of heads and shoulders. You seem to sit with the dead in the gloom of a tomb. You know that they are being stirred to their profoundest depths; that there are times when they want to rise and wave handkerchiefs and shout their approbation, and times when tears are running down their faces, and it would be a relief to free their pent emotions in sobs and screams; yet you hear not one utterance till the curtain swings together and the closing strains have slowly faded out and died; then the dead rise with one impulse and shake the building with their applause.
Mark Twain (1835–1910)
At the Shrine of Wagner, 1891

34 My experimenting is done before I make the music. Afterwards, it is the listener who must experiment.
Edgar Varèse (1885–1965)
Quoted in Yates, *Twentieth Century Music*, 1968

35 I do not mean to blame the public, but I accept their criticism and scorn only so long as I do not have to be grateful for their applause.
Giuseppe Verdi (1813–1901)
To T. Ricordi, 1840, after the catastrophic première of *Un Giorno di Regno*

36   Of the ladies that sparkle at a musical performance, a very small
number has any quick sensibility of harmonious sounds. But every one
that goes has the pleasure of being supposed to be pleased with a refined
amusement, and of hoping to be numbered among the votaresses of
harmony.

Dr Samuel Johnson (1709–84)
In *The Idler*, 1758

37   During this terzetto, the Reverend Mr Portpipe fell asleep, and
accompanied the performance with rather a deeper bass than was
generally deemed harmonious.

Thomas Love Peacock (1785–1866)
Melincourt, 1817

233   CONCERTS

1   It is not unjust to define amateur concerts by saying that the music
performed at them seems to have been composed to make those who
render it happy, and drive those who listen to despair.

Adolphe Adam (1803–56)
Souvenirs d'un musicien, 1857

2   It has always been a terrible thing for me that if you compose
something there is no means of hearing it other than at a concert. This is
like relating the most precious secrets of one's soul to police officials . . .

Mily Alexeyevich Balakirev (1837–1910)
Letter to Stassov, 1863

3   The music-hall singer attends a series
Of masses and fugues and 'ops'
By Bach, interwoven
With Spohr and Beethoven,
At Classical Monday Pops.

W.S. Gilbert (1836–1911)
The Mikado, 1885

4   At concerts I feel demeaned, like a vaudevillian.

Glenn Gould (1932–82)
Page (ed), *The Glenn Gould Reader*, 1984

5   Beware of the person who says he never goes to concerts because the people, the hall, etc prevent him from enjoying the music: he is first cousin to the numerous family of those who 'have no time for reading', the truth being that music bores him—though he dares not say so.

Edward Sackville-West (1901–65)

6   If you feel like singing along, don't.

James Taylor (1948–   )
Green, *The Book of Rock Quotes*, 1982

7   If one plays good music people don't listen, and if one plays bad music people don't talk.

Oscar Wilde (1854–1900)
The Picture of Dorian Gray, 1891

234 TECHNOLOGY

1   Put another nickel in,
    In the nickelodeon,
    All I want is loving you
    And music, music, music!

Stephen Weiss and Bernie Baum
Music, Music, Music, 1950

2   [Of the gramophone:] Should we not fear this domestication of sound, this magic that anyone can bring from a disk at will? Will it not bring to waste the mysterious force of an art which one might have thought indestructible?

Claude Debussy (1862–1918)
In *La Revue S.I.M.*, 1913

3   I can only say that I am astonished and somewhat terrified at the result of this evening's experiment. Astonished at the wonderful form you have developed and terrified at the thought that so much hideous and bad music will be put on record for ever.

Arthur Sullivan (1842–1900)
Letter to Thomas Alva Edison, 1888

4   When lovely woman stoops to folly and
    Paces about her room again, alone,
    She smoothes her hair with automatic hand,
    And puts a record on the gramophone.

T.S. Eliot (1888–1965)
The Waste Land, 1922

5   Sometimes he bent over the whirring, pulsating mechanism as over a spray of lilac, wrapt in a cloud of sweet sound.

Thomas Mann (1875–1955)
The Magic Mountain, 1924

6   I've never had a gramophone; I never had a picture of myself in my life.

Maggie Teyte (1888–1976)
BBC broadcast, 1959

7   The composer, in my estimation, has been helped a great deal by the mechanical reproduction of music. Music is written to be heard, and any instrument that tends to help it to be heard more frequently and by greater numbers is advantageous to the person who writes it . . . The radio and the phonograph are harmful to the extent that they bastardize music and give currency to a lot of cheap things. They are not harmful to the composer.

George Gershwin (1898–1937)

8   In an unguarded moment some months ago, I predicted that the public concert as we know it today would no longer exist a century hence, that its functions would have been entirely taken over by electronic media. It had not occurred to me that this statement represented a particularly radical pronouncement. Indeed, I regarded it almost as self-evident truth and, in any case, as defining only one of the peripheral effects occasioned by developments in the electronic age. But never has a statement of mine been so widely quoted – or so hotly disputed.

Glenn Gould (1932–82)
Page (ed), *The Glenn Gould Reader,* 1984, 'The Prospects of Recording'

9   Since the advent of the gramophone, and more particularly the wireless, music of a sort is everywhere and at every time; in the heavens, the lower parts of the earth, the mountains, the forest and every tree therein. It is a Psalmist's nightmare.

Constant Lambert (1905–51)
Music Ho!, 1934

10 . . . Canned music.
John Philip Sousa (1854–1932)
Article in *Appleton* magazine, 1906

11 Sir Arthur Bliss, Master of the Queen's Music, once described the
BBC's pop programme as 'aural hashish', but it's not *that* good.
Richard Neville
Playpower, 1970

12 *Threefold Function of Broadcast Music:*
1 Inexorably to continue and expand the principle of great music as an
  ultimate value, indeed a justification of life.
2 Faithfully to enrich leisure hours with entertainment.
3 Physically and mentally to stimulate tired bodies and worn nerves.
NB It betrays its trust if it debases the spiritual value of music, acts as a
narcotic or drug, or bores by sheer inanity.
Arthur Bliss (1891–1975)
Music Policy, 1941

13 If I had my life to live over again I should devote it to the
establishment of some arrangement of headphones and microphones or
the like whereby the noises used by musical maniacs should be audible
to themselves only. In Germany it is against the law to play the piano
with the window open. But of what use is that to the people in the house?
It should be made a felony to play a musical instrument in any other than
a completely soundproof room. The same should apply to loud speakers
on pain of confiscation.
George Bernard Shaw (1856–1950)
London Music in 1888–9, 1935, Preface

14 The song of today is machine-made, machine-played, machine-
heard.
Isaac Goldberg
Tin Pan Alley, 1930

15 Technology has the capability to create a climate of anonymity and
to allow the artist the time and the freedom to prepare his conception of
a work to the best of his ability. It has the capability of replacing those
awful and degrading and humanly damaging uncertainties which the
concert brings with it.
Glenn Gould (1932–82)
Page (ed), *The Glenn Gould Reader*, 1984

16   The synthesizer world opens the door to musical infinity.
John McLaughlin (1942–   )
Quoted in *Time*, 1975

17   To me, the music industry has got about as much meaning as a comic book.
Van Morrison (1945–   )
Green, *The Book of Rock Quotes*, 1982

18   As I went under the new telegraph-wire, I heard it vibrating like a harp high overhead. It was as the sound of a far-off glorious life, a supernal life, which came down to us, and vibrated the lattice-work of this life of ours.
Henry David Thoreau (1817–62)
Journal, 1851

19   What we want is an instrument that will give us a continuous sound at any pitch. The composer and the electrician will have to labour together to get it.
Edgar Varèse (1883–1965)
1922

235   ENVOI

1   When it sounds good, it *is* good.
Duke Ellington (1899–1974)

2   Of all noises I think music the least disagreeable.
Dr Samuel Johnson (1709–84)

3   Musick is the thing of the world that I love most.
Samuel Pepys (1633–1703)
Diary, 30 July 1666

4   To me the greatest objective is when the composer disappears, the performer disappears, and there remains only the work.
Nadia Boulanger (1887–1979)
Quoted in Kendall, *The Tender Tyrant: Nadia Boulanger*, 1976

5   Music, indeed! Give me a mother singing to her clean and fat and rosy baby.

William Cobbett (1762–1835)
Advice to Young Men, 1830

6   Give me books, fruit, French wine and fine weather and a little music out of doors, played by somebody I do not know.

John Keats (1795–1821)
To Fanny Keats, 1819

7   Music and women I cannot but give way to, whatever my business is.

Samuel Pepys (1633–1703)
Diary, 9 March 1666

8   Musicians will have their little jokes. When one of them invited a friend to lunch, he sent a card reading: 'The pleasure of your company is requested for luncheon, key of G.' The guest interpreted the invitation correctly and came at one sharp.

Recounted by Nicolas Slonimsky (1894–   )
A Thing or Two about Music, 1948

> 9   There was a young lady named Cager
> Who, as a result of a wager
>   Consented to fart
>   The whole oboe part
> Of Mozart's Quartet in F major.
>
> Quoted in *The Lure of the Limerick*, Baring-Gould (ed), 1969

10   Sheshell ebb music wayriver she flows.

James Joyce (1882–1941)
Finnegan's Wake, 1939

INDEX OF TOPICS AND KEY WORDS

This index is arranged alphabetically, both for the key words and for the entries following each key word.

If the key word sought is the same as a topic title (shown in bold print), the topic title should be consulted first.

For entries other than topic titles, the reference consists of two numbers, the first of which indicates the topic and the second the quotation itself. For example, the first entry is 'abstract (absolute) music: 13.2'. This refers to the 2nd quotation appearing under the 13th topic, which is 'Philosophy'.

The numbers and titles of the topics appear at the tops of the pages.

Index of Topics and Key Words

Barrel Organ: Topic 150, *see also* 34.1, 137.7–8, 161.1, 180.10, 190.8
barytone: 77.7
base: b. barreltone voice 204.43
   Earth made the *b.* 1.4
   let the b. of heav'n's deep organ 15.48
bass: 204.19
Bassoon: Topic 151, *see also* 188.18
   for he heard the loud b. 151.1
beer: embodied spirit of b. 173.1
   Too much b. and beard 48.5
   tub of pork and b. 76.7
Beguine: begin the B. 195.2
bell: merry as a marriage b. 223.10
   sorrows with a tolling b. 15.55
   what passing b. for these 199.9
Bells: Topic 152, *see also* 12.10, 25.2, 170.1, 226.17
   b. on her toes 16.4
Berlin: 216.10, 231.11
billiards: Let's go to b. 230.19
bird: sweet b., that shunn'st the noise 10.19
bird-cage: performance on a b. 163.5
birdsong: 10.18, 25.2, 39.5, 93.1
blancmange: musical equivalent of b. 61.5
blow: B., bugle, b. 153.1
blowing: B. is not playing the flute 158.2
blues: 184.9, 194.2, 194.14–19, 195.1, 200.33, 203.3
bonbon: pink b. stuffed with snow 75.3
bones: tongs and the b. 170.6
bop: 203.5–8
brandy: b. of the damned 180.3
breast: to soothe a savage b. 12.19
Bugle: Topic 153, *see also* 199.3, 199.9
butterflies: 26.17
   like a flight of b. 73.1

C major: C m. of this life 229.7
   good music to be written in C m. 115.10; *see also* 115.11–12
cacophony: 219.5
   His absurd c. 125.5
carols: 190.7, 226.31
   varied c. I hear 204.73
castrati: 204.12, 209.16, 212.3, 214.3
Cello: Topic 154, *see also* 17.4, 180.18
Chamber Music: Topic 187, *see also* 23.20
cherubim: C. in a box 159.2
children: 117.6, 139.31, 140.1
   best understood by c. 126.3

c. will understand it 143.1
Chime: let your silver c. 15.48
Chinese music: 23.5, 27.41
choir: *see also* quire
   full voic'd c. 169.8
   joins the tuneful c. 169.10
   sweet singing in the c. 226.26
Choirs: Topic 207
chorale: 19.1
chord: I feel for the common c. 229.7
   one lost c. divine 7.4
   struck one c. of music 7.3
   you just pick a c. 197.34
chords: 7.17
choristers: well-fed earthy c. 76.13
Christianity: 37.11, 61.6, 200.23
   C. arranged for Wagnerians 139.22
Church Music: Topic 226, *see also* 53.1, 65.7, 66.2, 169.1, 194.16, 199.6, 200.28, 207.6–7
Clarinet: Topic 155, *see also* 161.1
classicism: 20.2–4, 171.5
Clavichord: Topic 156
codfish: my music has a taste of c. 27.30
colour and music: 2.8, 17.1, 22.5, 26.14, 27.5, 36.2, 45.3
comedy: c. is over 40.15
compass: all the c. of the notes 7.4
compose: c. only for my own pleasure 64.2
   doesn't c., he makes music 78.1
   Only when I experience do I c. 89.2
   we do not c.— we are composed 27.46
composed: I have c. too much 64.3
composer: bad c. is slowly found out 26.18
   c. for the right hand 56.8
   c. in search of oblivion 46.2
   Gibbons is my favourite c. 70.3
   good c. does not initiate 27.72
   good c. is slowly discovered 26.18
   greatest c. known to me 97.15
   greatest c. that ever lived 76.5
   I am a first-class second rate c. 125.2
   most God-gifted c. 64.6
   the c. of childhood 117.6
   try and become a good c. 49.2
composers: 2.33, 3.8, 6.3
   Let our c. grow wings 83.2
   not many c. have ideas 27.24
Composers on Music: Topic 27
composing: c. is . . . making love to the future 27.23
   C. mortals with immortal fire 225.2

see also 197.3
Politics, Musicians on Life and: Topic 218, *see also* 39.40, 139.26, 200.1–2
polonaise: p. for polar bears 121.7
pomp: Pride, p. and circumstance 199.13
pop: 194.32, 197.7, 197.15, 197.30, 219.2, 234.11
Popular Music: Topics 190–9
Popular Song: Topic 193
power: P. is my moral principle 40.3
prima donna: *see* **Divas and Heroes: Topic 212**
Profession of Music: Topic 221, *see also* 26.8, 27.35, 27.40, 180.5, 180.13, 180.16, 187.1
Programme Music: Topic 21, *see also* 13.2, 13.8, 13.14, 13.24, 13.26, 117.5
proportion: p. that beautifies everything 27.25
psalm: voice of a p. 180.1
psaltery: 199.14, 220.2, 226.30
publishing: 26.8, 40.12, 132.1
punk rock: 194.4–6
pure music: *see* abstract music
Purpose of Music, The: Topic 3

quail: q. Whistle about us 10.26
quarter-tones: 25.2
quire: full voic'd Q. below 169.8
  Priest of Phoebus Q. 84.3
  with the q. of Saints 229.12
quires: Cherubic host, in thousand q. 205.31
  q. and places where they sing 226.18

radio: 104.2, 230.7, 234.7, 234.9, 234.11–12
raga: 54.2
ragtime: 194.9–13, 195.4, 200.10, 203.1–2
rapture: only cheap and unpunished r. 2.51
rebec: 182.15
Recorder: Topic 172, *see also* 53.3, 158.4
records and recording: 197.9, 197.20, 234.2–10
reel: 188.21
reggae: 194.30–31
rehearsal: 186.2, 209.17
rehearse: r. your song by rote 204.61
religion: 19.10, 65.7, 76.22, 77.9–10, 102.2–4; *see also* **Topics 226–228**
repertory: r. is hardly even a lake 2.31

requiem: 48.12, 48.17, 64.8, 66.2
  high r. become a sod 10.14
rests: 4.6–7, 4.9
revolution in music: 45.2, 47.1, 104.3, 115.5, 119.4, 149.1, 218.12, 220.6
rhapsodies: 17.21
Rhythm: Topic 5, *see also* 2.54, 10.16, 10.28, 13.33, 17.1, 22.8, 22.12, 30.11, 54.2, 63.4, 188.14, 188.25, 202.8
  All God's Chillun Got R. 5.6
  Fascinating r. 5.4
  I got r. 5.3
  In the beginning there was r. 5.1
  Simple melody—clear r.! 27.63
rhythm and blues: 194.2, 194.20–21, 197.21
rock: 188.10, 194.2–3, 194.22–29, 195.3, 197.18, 197.29, 219.2
  r. against racism 220.8
roll: r. over Beethoven 195.1
romanticism: 17.3, 20.2, 20.4, 20.6, 61.7, 116.8
Royal Academy of Music: 30.8
rubato: 184.4, 184.9
Russian music: 22.6, 22.11, 38.1, 71.2, 98.2, 107.3, 119.5, 126.1, 126.16, 130.1–2, 219.6

sackbut: 199.14, 220.2
sacred music: *see* **Church Music: Topic 226**
salt-box: 111.4, 170.8
Saul: 162.7
Saxophone: Topic 173, *see also* 200.20, 200.28
scales: 1.5
scents: 26.24
Scottish music: 23.5, 23.10, 23.17, 149.1–2, 180.18, 188.21, 205.14, 205.43
Scrabble: 203.5
scream: make the ladies s. 77.10
sensual: only s. pleasure 2.38
Serialism: Topic 24, *see also* 15.58, 115.16–17
sharps: discords and unpleasing s. 10.22
  little s. and trebles 31.16
  sourest s. and uncouth flats 11.1
shawns: 15.9
Silence: Topic 4, *see also* 13.22, 27.1
  Elected S., sing to me 4.5
  ever widening slowly s. all 4.10
  Into our deep, dear s. 204.14

INDEX OF NAMES AND MUSICAL WORKS

In this index the entries refer to individual quotations rather than pages. Each entry has two numbers, the first indicates the number of the topic and the second gives the number of the quotation within that topic. For example, under 'Abbott', the reference is 196.1. This refers to the 1st quotation appearing under the 196th topic, which is 'Musicals'. The numbers and titles of the topics appear at the tops of the pages.

Musical works are indexed under the composers' names.

Books of the Bible are included in this index, but for biblical and mythological characters (Jubal, Orpheus, etc) see the Index of Topics and Key Words.

Index of Names and Musical Works